THE GUN CLUB

U.S.S. Duncan at Cape Esperance

by

Robert Fowler

Published by Winthrop & Fish

Trade Paperback ISBN: 978-0-9990753-0-2
eBook ISBN: 978-0-9990753-1-9

Cover Art by Barry Markowitz
Maps by Chris Robinson
Ship Drawing by Steve Karp
Art Direction/Layout by Jesse Dena

**for
Suzie**

A legend may be true, but it's different from a fact. You learn a fact, but the legend is something you seem to have known all your life.

- Clifton Fadiman

CONTENTS

ENSIGN ROBERT FOWLER AT HOME
KATONAH, NEW YORK
EASTER 1942

Preface

The human heart is the starting point of all matters pertaining to war.
- Marechal de Saxe

My father died at the age of twenty-three in World War II
before I was born. He was torpedo officer on a U.S. destroyer,
and died from wounds sustained in the Battle of the Solomon
Islands. He was credited with torpedoing the second Japanese
cruiser of the war. He was posthumously awarded the
Navy Cross, and a destroyer escort was named for him. My
grandparents' home was haunted by his memory.

My mother received official word of his death in a letter from
the Secretary of the Navy:

> Dear Mrs. Fowler:
> It was with deep regret that I learned that your husband,
> Lieutenant (junior grade) Robert Ludlow Fowler, III, United States
> Naval Reserve, died about October 12, 1942, as a result of wounds
> received in action with the enemy during the Battle of the Solomon
> Islands.
>
> I desire to express to you my deepest sympathy in the loss of
> your husband, and it is hoped that you may be comforted by the
> thought that he was upholding the highest traditions of the Navy
> and in the defense of the principles for which we are now fighting.
>
> Very Sincerely Yours,
> Frank Knox

My father seemed to have done everything right. He was
on the Harvard crew that won the Grand Challenge Cup at the
Henley Royal Regatta in 1939. He graduated *cum laude*, joined
the Navy and became an officer. He married well, too. My
mother was a great-granddaughter of Hamilton Fish, Secretary of
State in the Grant Administration. The Fishes were an important
family in New York State Republican circles. My father may
have been thinking about a career in politics.

On November 12, 1942, *The New York Times* published his obituary under the headline: LIEUT. R.L. FOWLER KILLED IN ACTION; EX-MEMBER OF HARVARD CREW PERISHES IN SOUTH PACIFIC.

Lieutenant Robert Ludlow Fowler, 3rd, United States Naval Reserve, who was a grandson of the late Surrogate Robert L. Fowler of New York County, was killed in action in the South Pacific last month, according to word received by his parents, Mr. and Mrs. Robert L. Fowler, Jr., of Katonah, N.Y. He was 23.

The Lieutenant, who was born in New York and was a member of a family which came to this country from England in 1637, was graduated in 1937 from St. Paul's School, Concord, N.H., and in 1941 from Harvard. He rowed on the freshman crew at the university and on the varsity crew in 1939 and 1940. In 1939, he was one of the Harvard crew which won the Grand Challenge Cup at Henley in England. At Harvard, he joined the Hasty Pudding Institute of 1770 and the Porcellian Club.

Besides a widow and parents, he leaves two sisters, Mrs. Craig Wylie of Washington and Miss Charlotte Pamela Fowler of Katonah, and a brother, H.S. Winthrop Fowler of the Sixtieth Rifles, British Army.

A memorial service will be held at St. Matthew's Church, Bedford Center, N.Y., at 4:30 P.M. tomorrow.

His prep school alumni magazine summed up his life with more texture:

Robert Fowler, who was killed at the age of 23, was a man of the finest character and great promise. The facts of his tragically short life fail to produce anything like a picture of him. Well as he had done at everything that it had fallen on him to do, he was valued for what he so evidently was, even more than anything he had as yet had an opportunity to achieve. To a remarkable degree for one of his age, he inspired confidence. His superb physique, his keen intelligence, his sense of humor, his warm interest in all about him, combined to give an impression of latent strength. He was wonderfully balanced; neither enthusiastic nor cynical, proud without a trace of arrogance, unambitious without being indifferent ... Fowler was at once recognized as a person of unusual soundness and charm.

My mother was so convinced he was predestined for greatness she never seriously considered that he might die. The captain of his ship wrote to her that my father was largely responsible for sinking a Japanese cruiser. He said my father was "a hero" who "died bravely." My mother tore up that letter.

Both my mother and my grandparents received many notes of sympathy. Lt.(jg) Hunty Thom, my father's roommate at Torpedo School, wrote from the cruiser *Juneau* at Espíritu Santo that "Bob's death has left me with a permanent hollowness." He said he had heard from "a reliable authority that [Bob] and his weapons were directly responsible for the sinking of a Jap heavy cruiser."

> I assume that the effectiveness of Bob's final sacrifice will receive official recognition. Few ever have an opportunity to make such a major contribution towards winning the war and I know Bob would consider himself fortunate.

My grandfather wrote to the captain that he had a few questions. He asked him to let him know when he was going to be in New York City.

My grandfather cut a story out of the newspaper that he thought might be about "Bobby's battle:"

> Aboard a United States Cruiser in the Solomons Sea, Oct. 27 (Delayed)--This is the story of the United States Navy's first surface victory in a battle between heavy ships since the Spanish-American War.
> Led by this ship, with a rear admiral in command, a force of cruisers and destroyers surprised and wiped out a similar Japanese force in the pitch darkness of night October 11 near the tiny island of Savo, off Guadalcanal...

Two weeks before Christmas 1942, my grandfather received a note from the captain saying that he would meet with him on December 21 at 11:45 A.M. in the lobby of the Hotel Biltmore.

So, two months after his eldest son died, my grandfather went to meet with the captain. My grandfather knew him by sight because he had attended *Duncan*'s commissioning, but was surprised to see that he was now a full commander.

Edmund "Whitey" Taylor had been a Naval Academy football great. He had picked up the nickname "Whitey" at the Academy when his hair turned white while he was still a midshipman. He was more than 6 feet tall and now weighed more than 220 pounds. With his white hair and pronounced paunch, he looked much older than his forty years.

He took my grandfather's hand and held it too long. "I'm so very, very sorry," he said. "Bob was a wonderful guy. A great loss. I can tell you he died a hero. You can be very proud. How's his wife holding up?"

"She hardly ever comes out of her room," my grandfather said.

"We have to make this quick. I'm headed up to Boston to take command of a new destroyer."

"I hoped you could give me an overview of the battle. And my wife has a few questions." My grandfather was jotting down everything Taylor said.

"We were a cruiser-destroyer force," Taylor began. "Our orders were to stop Japanese from landing on Guadalcanal. We met them at night. There was no moon. It was hard to know what you were seeing. The only light was from flares. We caught them at five miles." He described with his hands the two forces converging. "We made out the outline of a battle cruiser and opened up with everything. They ran right into us but didn't even start firing. At about 2,500 yards, Lieutenant Fowler directed the firing of the first torpedo, which scored a hit. That was the first Jap warship sunk by a torpedo I'm told. Shellfire from a second Jap cruiser destroyed *Duncan*'s bridge and killed a lot of officers and men. Lieutenant Fowler was mortally wounded. They say we got three cruisers and three destroyers. The *Duncan* was the only U.S. ship lost."

My grandfather was silent.

"I'm so sorry about Bob. Is there anything else can I tell you?"

Glancing at his wife's list of questions, he asked, "Did Bob suffer?"

"No. He was unconscious. They gave him plenty of morphine."

"He received adequate medical attention?"

"Oh, absolutely the best. There was a wound at the base of his skull and shrapnel all over. There was nothing they could do."

"Was he buried?"

Taylor nodded. "At the U.S. Army post on Espíritu Santo Island."

"A Christian burial?"

"Full military service," Taylor said. "Christian chaplain. I was there."

He was unfolding a piece of paper. "I want to show you this," he said, "I'm sending it to Adm. Nimitz through Adm. Halsey. I'm recommending Bob for the Navy Cross."

My grandfather put on his glasses to read.

> Lieutenant (j.g.) Robert L. Fowler, III, D-V (G), USNR, (deceased) - He accurately set up his torpedo director and in firing the first torpedo secured the first torpedo hit in an enemy cruiser. Before he could fire remaining torpedoes he was mortally wounded by a shell bursting in the vicinity of the torpedo director.

Six months after my grandfather's meeting at the Biltmore, his youngest son Harry, who was in the British Army, was in Algiers prior to the Taranto landings when he unexpectedly stumbled onto a piece of the puzzle. Old Algiers Harbor was full of warships, and Harry was out on a pier studying the lines of the *USS Boise,* one of the new U.S. cruisers, when an officer on deck waved him aboard. Harry noticed as he was walking up the gangplank that the officer was suppressing a smile. Then he recognized he was Sidney Biddle, a Harvard classmate of Bobby's. They laughed about what a small world the military was becoming. Biddle had left Harvard to join the Navy at the end of sophomore year. When he asked about Bobby, Harry told him Bobby was dead. Biddle was shocked speechless for a moment, then he wanted details. Harry did not know anything, except that Bobby's ship was in the Pacific. Biddle asked the name of his ship. When Harry said, "The *Duncan,*" Biddle said,

"Oh my god. We sank the *Duncan*!"

Growing up without a father, I was aware there was a mystery surrounding his death. Both of my grandfathers and assorted uncles had dug into it after the war, but their questions never got answered to anybody's satisfaction. My mother was convinced that the Navy was covering something up. Shortly after the battle, some survivors from his ship, including the executive officer, stopped by to pay their respects. My mother was too undone by her loss to comprehend much of what they told her, but she was left with the impression that "the captain went off on his own trying to be a hero and got them sunk."

In 1959, when I was sixteen, I had a summer job as a runner on Wall Street. On weekends, I would escape to Fishers Island and stay with my Uncle Harry. He was already president of a small Wall Street investment bank called Fiduciary Trust Company. One weekend, he said to me, "How would you like to meet Admiral Halsey? He's a new client of the bank. He's staying at the Big Club."

I thought I was finally going to learn what happened to my father. The next day at the beach club, I followed my uncle across the sand, my heart pounding.

Adm. Halsey was sitting alone on a beach towel wearing only a bathing suit.

"Admiral," my uncle said as we walked up. "Harry Fowler."

Halsey squinted up at us blindly. "Oh, Harry, yes. Hello."

I was shocked when I saw him close up. He was so different from the hero of my imagination. He was small and very old and pale.

"Admiral, meet my nephew. This is Robin Fowler. His father was on the *Duncan*."

"The *Duncan*, the *Duncan*," Halsey repeated slowly. "Oh, yes." He looked up at me for a moment and then his gaze drifted out to sea. "Yes, I think I remember the *Duncan*."

My uncle looked to me to say something, but I was speechless. I could not think of a single question. It was obvious Halsey knew nothing at all about my father. He barely even remembered his ship. That was when I realized how big the war really was and how small my father's role in it had been. Halsey died that summer.

In 1991, my mother, long since remarried, received an invitation to attend a reunion of the *Duncan* crew in Ft. Lauderdale, Florida. I accompanied her. Warship reunions are attended mostly by old enlisted men. Few of the former *Duncan* men even remembered my father nor any of the junior officers. They remembered the captain only slightly. There was one officer they all vividly remembered -- the much-despised executive officer, who they remembered looked like the country singer Eddy Arnold. I picked up some other tidbits at that reunion: *Duncan*'s log had survived, except for the last twelve days (because logs were turned in at the end of every month); the Battle of Cape Esperance was the U.S. Navy's first actual *planned* battle of the war; and *Duncan* was the first Allied ship to penetrate a Japanese battle line. Also, quite a few of the men told me that when they read Herman Wouk's novel The Caine Mutiny they thought it was about the *Duncan*.

I attended half a dozen of these semi-annual *Duncan* events. A lot of ex-*Duncan* men had put a great deal of thought into trying to comprehend what befell them. Most of them had a piece of the puzzle and their own pet theory. Many of them tolerated me year after year as I refined my questions.

Before the Battle of Cape Esperance, it had been forty-four years since the U.S. Navy was last engaged in a planned battle. Not a single man was left in the U.S. Navy who had ever been in a naval battle. When tested in the early battles of the Pacific War, U.S. ships, commanders, and tactics were all found wanting.

U.S.S. *Duncan* was every pre-war warship in microcosm.

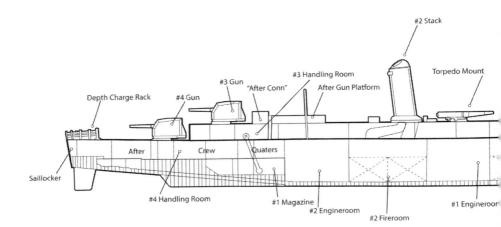

Depth Charge Rack

#4 Gun

#3 Gun

"After Conn"

#3 Handling Room

After Gun Platform

#2 Stack

Torpedo Mount

After

Crew

Quaters

Saillocker

#4 Handling Room

#1 Magazine

#2 Engineroom

#2 Fireroom

#1 Engineroom

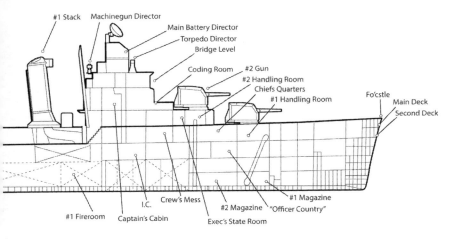

#1 Stack

Machinegun Director

Main Battery Director

Torpedo Director

Bridge Level

Coding Room

#2 Gun

#2 Handling Room

Chiefs Quarters

#1 Handling Room

Fo'cstle

Main Deck

Second Deck

#1 Magazine

"Officer Country"

#2 Magazine

Exec's State Room

Crew's Mess

I.C.

Captain's Cabin

#1 Fireroom

Part I

THE WARRIOR CLASS
January-August 1942

Who built the Seven Gates of Thebes ...?
When the Chinese Wall was built, where did the masons go to lunch?
When Caesar conquered Gaul, was there not even a cook in the army?
When the Armada sank, we read that King Philip wept. Were there no
other tears?

- Bertold Brecht

LIEUTENANT COMMANDER EDMUND
"WHITEY" TAYLOR
CAPTAIN, U.S.S. DUNCAN

Chapter 1

THE OFFICERS' HANDBOOK
January 5-May 20

The thoughts of others were light and fleeting, of lovers meeting or luck or fame; mine brought trouble, and I was readying when trouble came.
- A.E. Housman

Twenty-three days after Pearl Harbor, on the first Monday in January, 1942, Ensign Robert Fowler reported to the precommissioning detail of the *U.S.S. Duncan* at Federal Shipbuilding & Dry Dock Company in Kearny, New Jersey. Three senior officers, six junior officers, and forty-four enlisted men were present when Lieutenant Commander Taylor addressed them that first morning.

Taylor's white hair made him seem impossibly old to the

junior officers. He said he was a "tin can sailor." That meant he was a destroyerman at heart. Older men in the crew applauded; there was a sloppy *esprit* among destroyermen. *Duncan* was the fifth destroyer Taylor had served on and his first command. He said he was proud to serve with them and that he was depending on them to be the backbone of the crew. "Our job is to get this ship ready for battle," he said. "We have inexperienced officers and green sailors to whip into a battle-ready crew. It's a daunting challenge. We have a long way to go."

LCdr. Taylor was just completing a two-year tour at the Navy Department when the war came. He was a staff officer in the Bureau of Navigation, which handled personnel, training, and the staffing of ships. He had flourished in Washington because he had a political streak and his name opened doors. In the institutional memory of the U.S. Navy, "Whitey" Taylor would forever be the captain of the Naval Academy's 1924 varsity football team.

Knowing that he was going to have a crew made up largely of green officers and raw recruits, Taylor had felt he needed a really tough executive officer to run day-to-day operations. The toughest officer he knew was Lieutenant Louis Bryan.

Lt. Lou Bryan was a youthful thirty-three-year-old from Kentucky. He was practically a caricature of the idealized U.S. Navy officer -- aggressive, handsome, smart, athletic. At the Academy, Bryan played football and made All-American, and he was Gate Commander, the "five-striper" who commanded the entire midshipman brigade. Taylor had met him at the Academy in the fall of 1934 when Taylor was teaching Ordnance and Gunnery and Bryan had returned as an assistant football coach. Since then, Bryan had followed the legendary Whitey Taylor's career path into the surface fleet and ordnance.

The battleship limitation treaties of the early-1920s had encouraged navies into a technological arms race. Throughout the 1930s, U.S. Navy officers with certain specialties moved up in grade faster than others. Moving up fastest was a corps of surface fleet officers that came to be known as "the Gun Club."

All Gun Club members were exceptionally bright and

LIEUTENANT LOUIS BRYAN
EXECUTIVE OFFICER, U.S.S. DUNCAN

competitive. Most played football at the Academy. Supposedly, the Academy does not have secret societies, but these men all belonged to a very secret and select midshipman society called the Green Bowlers (who were mostly athletes, mainly football players). Gun Club members all went on to study explosives at the advanced ordnance school. Between the wars, they had rotated between the fleet and either the Bureau of Ordnance, which developed armaments, or the Bureau of Navigation, which handled personnel and training. At a time when the Navy was emphasizing gunnery more and more, this cadre continued returning to sea in increasingly important commands -- as captains of destroyers, then captains of cruisers, then captains of battleships. When war finally came, these were the men who were in command positions throughout the fleet.

As junior members of the Gun Club, LCdr. Taylor and Lt. Bryan approached *Duncan* as a career opportunity. Bryan joined Taylor in Washington two weeks before Christmas. They quickly settled on their respective roles. "You take care of the ship," Taylor told Bryan. "I'll take care of the Navy."

Putting their heads together, they came up with the bones of a crew. Their main concern was a gunnery officer. With the inception of all the new electronics, gunnery was evolving faster than most officers could keep up. Both Taylor and Bryan had officers in mind for the job, but all were unavailable. They settled for a man they did not know who BuNav pushed on them.

LIEUTENANT PHILIP HAUCK
GUNNERY OFFICER, U.S.S. DUNCAN

Lt. Philip Hauck was a twenty-eight-year-old from Brooklyn, New York. He was married to the daughter of Capt. Olaf Hustvedt, chief of staff of the U.S. Atlantic Fleet. He had been attending a course in advanced gunnery aboard the old battleship *Utah* at Pearl Harbor when the Japanese attacked. *Utah* was bombed and torpedoed. Hauck was one of the last three men out of the ship. He squeezed out through a porthole in the captain's cabin and walked over the side in his skivvies as the ship rolled over.

The main order of business for a precommissioning detail is developing a ship's organization. The organization of U.S. Navy ships normally involved six "departments," but in smaller ships, like destroyers, there was a lot of doubling up. On *Duncan*, there would be only three departments (not counting medical): gunnery, engineering, and communications.

Ultimately, the ship's organization would be depicted on a large wall chart known as the "Watch, Quarter, and Station Bill." This would graphically detail where every enlisted man was to be under every conceivable circumstance -- billet number, bunk number, locker number, division, battle station, and watch stations under five different watches.

Lt. Bryan met continually with officers and senior petty officers to coordinate the development of the organization. Bryan always gave the impression that he knew exactly what he wanted and how he wanted it done, which was always "the Navy way."

Lt. Hauck met constantly with the gunnery officers to rough out the organization of the gunnery department. Gunnery was anything that shoots -- main battery guns, anti-aircraft machineguns, torpedoes, depth charges.

A dozen more petty officers were transferred to *Duncan* from the precommissioning details of the battleship *Washington* and the cruiser *Juneau*. Lt. Hauck had brought with him five fire controlmen from the *Utah*. With competent petty officers at a premium, captains were promoting men and training them on the job. Advancements were occurring in all departments.

A huge number of new ships were coming on line fast, so there was a desperate shortage of Academy officers. Each new destroyer required fourteen officers. Half would be reserves. All the new captains were worried about this because to Academy men reserve officers were barely even officers.

Six reserve junior officers were assigned to *Duncan*, and they were a decidedly mixed bunch. Three were Ivy League, and three were dyed-in-the-wool southerners. All of them, except Lt.(jg) Richard Wharton, were in their early twenties.

Wharton was ten years older. He had attended Harvard, where he took Naval Science, but, when he graduated in 1932, the Navy did not need him. His father got him a job on Wall Street. When he was finally called up eight years later in 1940, he was a partner in a brokerage firm. Newspapers reported that he was the first member of the Big Board to "enlist," but in fact he went in under protest, peeved at having to abandon a lucrative career.

The three Ivy League junior officers were Lt.(jg) Wharton, Ensign Fowler, and Ensign Clifford Beebe. Cliff Beebe was a lanky, soft-spoken New Englander and a graduate of Yale, class of 1941.

The three junior officers who were southerners were all ensigns -- Jack Smyth, Wade Coley, and Theodore Rhodes. Smyth was born in Queens, New York, but grew up in Wilmington, Delaware. He had served one tour in the merchant marine. Coley was a coal-miner's son from Charleston, West Virginia. Rhodes was a redhead who liked to be called "Dusty." All were products of their states' college systems and were very unmilitary.

The crew all spent a lot of time climbing through the ship memorizing the layout. *Duncan* (DD-485) and her sister *Lansdowne* (DD-486) were parallel on inclined building ways. The two ships were 1939-vintage *Benson-Livermore*-class, which was the culmination of pre-war "1,500-ton" destroyer development. The 1941 destroyer construction program called for the new, more powerful *Fletcher*-design, but *Livermore*s were still being constructed. *Duncan* and *Lansdowne* had been under construction for five months.

Destroyers were relatively small warships, but up on keel blocks they looked enormous. *Duncan*'s bow rose 22 feet to a high forecastle (fo'csle) deck forward that dropped down to the main deck, which dropped further as it swept aft, giving her a sleek look. The hull displaced 1,620 tons. She was 348 feet long, longer than a football field, yet just 36 feet wide -- destroyers were ten times longer than they were wide, which made them susceptible to rolling.

Divided into watertight compartments, destroyers were constructed like deep ice trays stacked. On "second deck," the deck below the main deck, chief's quarters was at the bow and crew quarters at the stern. Aft of crew quarters were the after steering engine room, with the hydraulic pumps that moved the rudder, and the saillocker, which contained a sewing machine, the carpentry shop, and the small arms locker. Forward of crew quarters was the machinery space -- two enginerooms and two firerooms arranged in line: engineroom-fireroom-fireroom-engineroom. The machinery space occupied a third of the length and half the volume of the hull. Forward of the machinery space were the ship's office and the internal communications room ("the I.C."). Then came the mess hall, galley, and sick bay. A narrow passageway led forward to the officers' staterooms ("officer country"). At the bow was chiefs' quarters, where bunks were already installed. Some chiefs had already moved in; somehow chiefs always got themselves squared away first.

Cranes were lowering beams, plates, castings, piping. The two destroyers were getting their bridge superstructures and two after deckhouses. The after deckhouses would contain the machine shop, tool locker, engineering office, ammo lockers, and the clipping rooms where machinegun shells were prepared. On the roofs of the two after deckhouses would be the after gun platform (containing two machineguns), the after conning station ("after conn"), and the torpedo mount.

Between the two deckhouses and also between the forward deckhouse and the bridge superstructure were exterior passageways from port to starboard. Off the forward passageway were hatches that led down to officer country and the mess hall. In the bridge superstructure on main deck level were the wardroom and wardroom galley.

Junior officers were always sneaking off to re-inspect their battle stations. As "Prospective Torpedo Officer," Ens. Fowler's battle station was at the torpedo director, which would be located on the bridge roof. He and Ens. Rhodes, "Prospective Machinegun Officer," whose battle station would also be on the bridge roof, were continually scaling the bridge superstructure. It was a tough climb because no ladders were installed yet.

On 0-1 level was the radio room, the commodore's cabin (which Lt. Bryan had claimed), and the forward clipping room (where shells for the two forward 20mms would be prepared).

On O-2 level was the captain's stateroom and the coding room with the safes and all the classified documents. There was a hole in the deck on O-2 level where a 20mm gun platform would go. 0-3 level was bridge deck. It was a tangle of pipes and wiring. From there, it was 35 feet to the water, and the horizon was almost 50 miles. The space inside the bridgehouse seemed impossibly small, considering that more than twenty men had battle stations in there. The forward section was the pilothouse. A few steps aft was the navigation bridge. A few more steps aft was space for the captain's sea cabin (which was barely the size of a bunk).

Up on the roof of the bridge, there was no protection. Fowler and Rhodes could not help noticing how exposed they were.

* * *

At the end of the third week, all the junior officers were temporarily detached to advanced instruction courses at various service schools. Ens. Fowler was ordered to Advanced Fire Control School. He was to report to the Washington Navy Yard the following Monday. As he was getting married on Saturday, LCdr. Taylor went to bat for him with the Navy and got him an extra day for his honeymoon.

Ens. Fowler married Patricia Cutler on Saturday, January 18, 1942, in St. Mark's-in-the-Bouwerie, New York City's oldest church. The groom, best man, and the few ushers who were able to make it were all in uniform. Bobby's brother Harry, the best man, was wearing his new British Army uniform.

The reception was in the Hamilton Fish house at 55 East 77th Street, where my mother's mother grew up. Unable to sell the place, the family had been renting it to the German government. It was the German Consulate until just recently when it was hastily evacuated.

The reception was a happy, oddly carefree affair. Alistair Horne, the Cutlers' fourteen-year-old "bundle from Britain," remembered "something of the atmosphere of the ball on the eve of Waterloo about it."

BOBBY AND PAT CUT THEIR WEDDING CAKE,
AS BOBBY'S BROTHER HARRY, THE BEST MAN, LOOKS ON,
JANUARY 18, 1942

The newlyweds honeymooned on an estate in Virginia horse country for twenty-four hours. Then they drove to Washington, where they moved into a gloomy old mansion at 1205 Thomas Circle. The house belonged to the family of Craig Wylie, who had been a French teacher at St. Paul's School. My father had introduced him to his sister and now they were brothers-in-law.

On Wednesday, January 22, Ens. Fowler reported to Advanced Fire Control School at the Navy Yard. He was taking the six-week main battery course, which focused mainly on electrical ordnance but included instruction in the mechanical fire-control "computer."

*　*　*

One month later, on February 20, *Duncan* and *Lansdowne* were launched.

It was a cold, overcast morning, yet hundreds of yard workers looked on. Launchings were a spectacle, especially twin launchings. The mood was bittersweet because the Japanese had just invaded Bali and bombed Port Darwin, one of the last links in the Java lifeline.

The ceremonies, which would transform the two hulls to ships, were short and simple. *Duncan*'s began with the ranking officer present, Cdr. George Holderness, Assistant Supervisor of Shipbuilding at Federal, reading a letter from Rear Admiral Adolphus Andrews, newly-appointed Commander Eastern Sea Frontier. Addressing the destroyer shortage, R/Adm. Andrews hailed the twin launchings as "a powerful symbol of the day of reckoning for the enemies of this free country." After a short prayer, Mrs. Dorothy Thayer stepped up, champagne bottle in hand. The ship was being named for Silas Duncan (1788-1834), a hero of the Battle of Plattsburgh on Lake Champlain on September 11, 1814. Mrs. Thayer was Silas Duncan's closest living relative, first cousin three times removed.

Duncan shuddered as men below on the ways knocked out blocks with sledgehammers. Wooden timbers groaned and creaked. "I christen thee *U.S.S. Duncan*," Mrs. Thayer shouted as she smashed the bottle against the bow. *Duncan* looked naked without guns, but flags were flying, and men on the fo'csle were waving. The band struck up as *Duncan* started sliding slowly toward the Hackensack River. Onlookers cheered as she gained momentum rushing toward the river. There was a tremendous cascade of water. And then she was floating. Everyone applauded. A tug moved alongside her to take her to drydock.

The Navy officials, the band, and many of the guests wandered over to the adjoining way, where the ceremony was repeated. *Lansdowne* was named for LCdr. Zachary Lansdowne, who was killed when his dirigible crashed in Ohio in 1925, and was christened by his daughter. *Duncan* and *Lansdowne* were launched eleven minutes apart. After the ceremonies, guests walked to the Officers' Club for lunch.

U.S.S DUNCAN LAUNCHED AT FEDERAL
SHIPBUILDING & DRYDOCK COMPANY,
KEARNY, NEW JERSEY, FEBRUARY 20, 1942

* * *

Six weeks later, all the *Duncan* junior officers had reported back. *Duncan* was still in dry dock, but now she looked like a warship. The three-story bridge superstructure was completed, and the two low afterdeck superstructures were in place. The two stacks and two masts were in.

Title A equipment was aboard. These were the big add-ons that needed to be bolted down, like the fire-control director and the main battery guns. The fire-control director was a steel cocoon just big enough to hold half a dozen men. It was installed one level above the bridge roof. There were four main battery guns that were 5-inch (127mm)/38 cal. dual purpose (surface and anti-aircraft). Each gun, which arrived as part of an assembly that included handling room and powder room, weighed 25 tons. Two were installed forward of the bridge and two at the stern.

Returning junior officers all made beelines to check out the new equipment in their divisions. The torpedo division now had a torpedo director, a torpedo mount, six K-guns, and depth charge tracks. Ens. Fowler first climbed up the newly-installed ladders to the roof of the bridge. The torpedo director and the machinegun control director were both installed on the centerline, torpedo director forward and machinegun director aft.

The MK-27 torpedo director was a massive piece of optical engineering that stood almost five feet on an iron pedestal. The working part was a big ungainly-looking brass box sprouted with dials, handwheels, and cranks. A telescope was bolted to the top. The firing key was part of the telescope assembly.

Next, Fowler went down to look at the torpedo mount. It was bolted to the roof of the forward deckhouse between the two stacks. The MK-15 torpedo tube mount supported five 21-inch tubes and was trainable in all directions.

Down on the main deck, the six K-guns (depth charge projectors) were bolted to the sides of the after deckhouse. The depth charge tracks were bolted in at the stern.

Fowler and Cliff Beebe elected to share a stateroom. Beebe

had put in four years in the Naval Reserve Training Corps while at Yale, so he outranked Fowler by six months. Their stateroom was an airless little space the size of a sleeping car roomette. It was jammed with two bunks, a desk, a chair, and personal items -- clothing, helmets, life jackets, gas masks, books, manuals, paperwork marked "Pending," .45-calibre pistols, inventory lists, custody chits, foul weather gear, photos of wives. There was barely room to turn around.

Two more Academy officers had reported: Lt. Herbert Kabat as engineering officer, and Lt.(jg) Robert Weatherup as communications officer. Both were small, slight men by Academy standards. Kabat was Jewish, which was unusual for an Academy officer. Weatherup was from a family of upstate New York dairy farmers.

Lt. Bryan was especially relieved to have Kabat aboard because the engine and boiler rooms, the heart of the ship, were alien to most topside men, and Kabat had just completed the Navy's Advanced Steam Engineering course.

Lt. Bryan ran the officers. He was the boss they had to deal with every day. Every Navy regulation and every word in every training manual was of equal importance to him. Bryan was a perfectionist in everything, including himself. Proud of his physique, he was obsessive in maintaining it, endlessly doing push-ups and chin-ups and challenging others to do more than him. He never let up. He had a deflated lung from pneumonia but passed his physical every time. Bryan could do everybody's job better than they could. "Bryan was a star," Fire Controlman Jack Sobelman remembered. "He could do everything. He was a shiphandler, gunner -- a real gunner, he knew his shit. If he asked you a question, you knew he knew the answer. The man was smart." The dress sword he had carried as a midshipman brigade commander was mounted on the bulkhead in his stateroom. "Bryan thought he was god almighty," Lt.(jg) Wharton remembered bitterly.

Executive officer was a 24-hour-a-day job. The exec was responsible for practically everything -- the proficiency of the crew, the efficiency of the departments, battle readiness. The position almost demands that the officer be disliked, but Bryan was disliked more for his personality. He was authoritarian and a hard man. His leadership style involved instilling fear. He thought nothing of berating junior officers in front of enlisted men. "That's one of the worst things an officer can do," Seaman Quentin Edwards remembered. "Bryan did it all the time."

Bryan's meanness was revealed in his relish for issuing unpopular orders. One day at Federal he ordered all the metal doors on junior officers' staterooms removed and replaced with sliding curtains. The junior officers assumed he ordered it so he could more easily catch them sacked out. In fact, it was a Navy-wide weight-reduction measure, but Bryan encouraged them think it was an idle whim of his, probably because it increased their fear of his power over them.

A tough taskmaster was what *Duncan* needed. Inspections were continual, one leading to the next. The weekly "field day" on Fridays involved cleaning the ship in preparation for the regular weekly inspections (Friday afternoons for lower decks, Saturday mornings for upper decks and crew). The ship too stood regular inspections by Navy technicians or staff officers from the Inspector General or the Chief of Naval Operations or the Board of Inspection and Survey. These covered technical, operational, administrative, and material readiness. Ships were graded "unsatisfactory" to "outstanding." *Duncan* was always "outstanding."

Duncan's complement had grown to four senior officers, seven junior officers, twelve chiefs, and about 120 enlisted men. She was still drastically under-manned. Both LCdr. Taylor and LCdr. Smedberg of *Lansdowne* made concerted efforts to fill out their crews. Every morning, an officer from each ship drove into Manhattan in his captain's gray Navy sedan to scour Pier 92, the Navy Receiving Barracks. They were looking for men with needed specialties, but they would take almost anybody.

Duncan's torpedo division gained a crusty old chief named David Boyd and some trained torpedomen, including a champion swimmer from Hawaii named Frank Watson.

The senior members of the crew fell into three groups:

Naval Academy graduates, Old Navy (career enlisted men), and upper-class East Coast boys who, as either Anglophiles or Francophiles, had joined up early for their own (mostly political) reasons.

Most of the enlisted men were high school graduates who had the bad fortune to graduate in the middle of the Depression. Almost to a man, they had struggled economically. When military enlistments finally opened up in 1939, these men flooded in, grateful for almost any employment. The Navy was suddenly getting a better class of sailor. Unlike Old Navy types, these new men were fired with resolve to make something of themselves.

Chiefs, desperate for bodies to fill out their divisions, lay in wait for recruits on the dock. Even before a new man set foot on his ship, he found himself buttonholed by a chief pitching for his rating.

For men on the bottom rung, advancement was open in all directions. A man was pointed toward a specialty by a series of tests that led to a "rating" that denoted the occupation that would become his daily job. Once the seaman first or fireman first tests were passed, a man would "strike" for (apprentice in) the specialty of his choosing.

Most enlisted men lived in barracks in the yard. Most officers lived off the yard and commuted home when the workday ended at 1600. LCdr. Taylor and the *Lansdowne*'s captain, LCdr. William Smedberg, were best friends, and they and their families were sharing a house in nearby Montclair.

Ens. Fowler and his bride had found a little month-to-month sublet in Manhattan in a grand old building with a uniformed doorman at 160 East 72nd Street. The apartment was small but sunny. Bobby enjoyed the commute because it gave him time to read the newspapers and keep up with the war news. The war in the Pacific, the Navy's war, was being fought halfway around the world, but it felt awfully close to Navy men.

The *Duncan* men were overwhelmed by the amount of equipment that was arriving every day. Every piece had to be checked out and signed for by an officer. Additional Title A equipment arrived -- searchlights, navigational gear, radar, sonar, radio, communication gear. Title B equipment was pilferable items, like electric drills. Last aboard was Title C equipment, the easily-expendable items -- hammers, chisels, spare parts.

Bobby and Pat spent Easter weekend at his parents' place in the country. The whole family was there. Younger brother Harry was departing for England within the week to join the 60th Rifles (The King's Rifles). Eldest sister Angie was up from Washington with her husband Craig Wylie, who was on leave from the Navy, and their two children. Youngest sister Pam was home from Smith College. This was the last time they were all together.

They attended Easter service at St. Matthew's Church in Bedford. As the Reverend Arthur Ketchum was reading a list of the local boys in the service, he pointed out Bobby and Harry and others in the congregation, and afterward everybody came up and shook their hands and wished them luck.

That week, officers from the Navy Board of Inspection and Survey boarded *Duncan* to hold "Dock Trials and Inspection." They noted work that still needed to be done: painting, laying linoleum, "ratproofing." The captain's chair was missing from the bridge. Their conclusion: "DUNCAN is recommended for acceptance under the terms of Contract NOd-1500."

U.S.S. DUNCAN BEING TOWED ACROSS NEW YORK HARBOR
TO THE NEW YORK NAVY YARD IN BROOKLYN, APRIL 14, 1942

Two days before *Duncan* was commissioned, the maze of lines that had kept her tied to land for almost two months was untangled, and she was released. Two tugs towed her across the harbor to the New York Navy Yard in Brooklyn.

That day, there was a rush of excitement among U.S. destroyermen at news of the first German submarine sunk by U.S. forces. *U.S.S. Roper*, an old flush-decker from the Great War, sank the sub off Cape Hatteras. At the officers' club at the New York Navy Yard that evening, an endless round of toasts celebrated *Roper*.

Duncan was commissioned on April 16, thirteen months after her keel-laying and eight weeks after her launching. As commissionings were now occurring about every two weeks, they were no longer such big events. Only small contingents from the Navy and Federal Shipbuilding were present. There was still a sizable crowd, mostly wives, girlfriends, and families of the crew.

The ceremony was held on the fantail. A band set up on top of the after deckhouse forward of gun #4 and played two tunes.

U.S.S. DUNCAN COMMISSIONING CEREMONY,
NEW YORK NAVY YARD, APRIL 16, 1942

U.S.S. DUNCAN OFFICERS AND CHIEFS AT COMMISSIONING:
FRONT ROW: LCDR. TAYLOR (left) and LT. BRYAN (right)
SECOND ROW: LT.(jg) WHARTON, LT. KABAT, and LT. HAUCK
THIRD ROW: ENS. FOWLER, ENS. SMYTH, ENS. COLEY, and ENS. RHODES

Then the crew filed topside. Officers wore Service Dress Blue with Blue caps and gloves. Enlisted ranks were in blue hat and overcoat. Newer enlisted men wore watchmarks around their shoulders (white for seamen, red for firemen). They were a young crew. More than half were non-rated seamen and firemen. Few petty officers had even one hash mark (four years service). The officers stood between the depth charge racks with the chiefs behind them. A Marine Guard was at the stern. The rest of the crew formed up tight in ranks outboard the depth charge racks, both facing inboard. The ceremony took place in the few feet of open deck in the middle.

A bosun's pipe trilled "Attention" as R/Adm. Edward Marquart, Commandant, Third Naval District, came aboard, trailed by a Navy chaplain and the commander of the Navy Yard. Marquart spoke first, addressing his remarks to the officers and crew. "In sight of the men who build and repair our ships, you men who do the fighting are taking over the helm," he said. "Our success in this war depends on both." He read the Navy Department orders directing that *Duncan* be placed in commission. Turning to LCdr. Taylor, he said, "You may now assume command." Taylor saluted. Bryan ordered the officers to turn and face the colors. The band struck up the National Anthem, during which the American flag and R/Adm. Marquart's flag were hauled up the mast. When the anthem concluded, Taylor read his orders aloud. Then in a booming

voice he said, "I assume command of the *U.S.S. Duncan*."
Applause and cheers erupted. The new captain ordered his exec
to set the watch. A bosun's pipe trilled "All hands." The PA
clicked, and Bryan's voice came on: "NOW HEAR THIS. SET
THE WATCH ON DECK. FIRST SECTION." Taylor waited
until the first section watch had proceeded off before he nodded
to the chaplain. The officers, crew, guests, and spectators all
bowed their heads. The chaplain's invocation was, as always, for
"those in peril on the deep." Taylor delivered some welcoming
remarks. He concluded by inviting all the guests aboard for
lunch. As the crew hurried below, the band struck up "Anchors
Aweigh." Chief Boatswain's Mate John Shanahan piped R/Adm.
Marquart and his party ashore as signalmen hauled the Admiral's
flag down and the commission pennant up.

The ship's log officially began: "U.S.S. DUNCAN
commissioned by the Commandant, Third Naval District at
berth 13, U.S. Navy Yard, New York, pursuant to Bureau of
Navigation orders No. 17017, Nav-31-as of January 14, 1942,
Lieutenant Commander Edmund B. Taylor, U.S. Navy, assumed
command. The flag of Commandant, Third Naval District, was
broken."

For about an hour, guests trooped through the ship,
except for the parts that were strictly off-limits -- the internal
communications room, the radio room, the coding room, and the
two boiler rooms. A buffet luncheon was served on board.

*   *   *

Duncan was settled into a daily routine. Practically
everything that happened on board was dictated by either the
captain's Night Order Book or the exec's Plan of the Day. The
Night Order Book covered everything between taps and reveille,
and the Plan of the Day covered everything between reveille
and taps. Otherwise, shipboard routine was commanded by the
watch schedule. A brass clock on the bridge bulkhead and the
ship's bell on the foremast struck every thirty minutes.

After morning muster, men reported to their section petty

officers who put them to work. Whether the job was cleaning guns, repairing phones, chipping rust or repainting, nothing on U.S. Navy ships needed doing only once.

LCdr. Taylor was of the school that believed in letting the executive officer run the ship. Lt. Bryan made almost all decisions on day-to-day operations, while Taylor spent most days in his cabin. Being naturally sociable, Taylor was desperately bored most of the time. Emerging from his cabin, he often headed straight for the nearest man to have a chat. He never had much to say, but enlisted men liked him because he seemed so inoffensive compared to Bryan. He had a chuckle that rumbled up from deep inside him, which everyone found endearing. In late afternoons, Taylor would aimlessly wander the ship or stand on the bridge, staring off, sucking on his pipe or relighting it; he was never able to keep it lit even in the slightest breeze. When the captain's chair was finally installed in the pilothouse, he would sit in it for hours on end, sucking on his pipe and staring off wistfully at the far horizon. To anyone who expressed concern, Chief Lennon Paige, his yeoman, explained that the captain yearned to be at sea.

April 19 was Ens. Fowler's twenty-third birthday. He and Pat celebrated with a quiet dinner at a favorite little restaurant around the corner from their apartment. They were feeling especially celebratory because all the news that day was about an air raid on Japan by sixteen U.S. Army B-25s. It was the biggest morale boost in the war so far. Pat gave Bobby a silver ID bracelet from Tiffany's.

Departments on *Duncan* were scrambling to get organized. Lt. Kabat, the engineering officer, had his hands full with all the new machinery below deck: two Westinghouse geared steam turbines; two pressure-fired Babcock & Wilcox radiant-superheater-control diesel boilers; hydraulic pumps to move the fourteen-ton rudder.

Lt. Hauck was having the usual gunnery problem. Shipyards were never able to aligned gun roller paths exactly horizontal, so fire controlmen had to deal with five different roller path inclinations (four guns and the "computer"). The gunnery division was constantly practicing. Main battery practice was held a few times a day. It always started with Lt. Bryan ordering Lt. Hauck to aim at a particular smokestack or church steeple.

Naval gunnery was so complex as to be all but incomprehensible. The key factor was pre-determining the time-of-flight of the projectile. Every piece of equipment in the I.C. was there to aid in solving the time-of-flight problem: the mechanical fire-control computer (built by Ford Instrument Company) actually calculated time of flight; the "stable element" (built by Arma & Company) maintained perfect level; the main gyro (built by Sperry) established heading information; and the massive switchboard (built by General Electric) carried information electrically throughout the ship.

The solution to the time-of-flight problem was a geometric function of the angles and relative speeds of the two ships. In theory, it was a simple equation in spherical trigonometry, except there were so many variables -- ranges, bearings, courses, speeds, air temperature, barometric pressure, powder temperature.

All the officers were rushing to fill out their libraries of equipment manuals. Publications and changes were being issued so fast every publication was already partially out of date when it was issued. Communications had it worst because they depended on codes and call signs that were changed daily, and District Headquarters was never sure they had issued a "full bag."

Everyone sensed a gathering momentum. The ship's complement was growing faster. Fire controlmen loaded the first ammunition, small arms ammo -- 10,000 rounds of .22-caliber, 7,200 rounds of .30-caliber, and 6,000 of .45-caliber. Each officer was issued a pistol that he kept in his stateroom and wore to general quarters. All other small arms were kept in the saillocker: a Thompson submachine gun, four .30-caliber Springfield rifles, and four .45-caliber pistols.

There was already grousing about the chow. Charged with feeding the enlisted men on 75¢ per man per day, Chief Commissary Steward William Mitchell, whose prior duty station was the Portsmouth [N.H.] Naval Prison, had brought his book of prison recipes to *Duncan*. Potatoes were the mainstay of their diet; each man on average ate ten pounds of potatoes per month. Lt. Bryan dismissed all complaints about the chow as healthy enlisted-man grousing. Navy men *always* complain about the chow.

On April 26, *Duncan* received her first official duty order: ready-duty for 24 hours. A Socony barge pulled alongside and pumped 85,476 gallons of Navy Special Grade fuel oil aboard. (A destroyer carried up to 90,000 gallons of fuel, which was 503 tons.) Men loaded groceries until the spud locker on deck was filled with 1,700 pounds of potatoes, which was a month's supply.

On April 29, Lt.(jg) Frank Broccolo reported for duty as medical officer. The doctor's arrival caused a stir because when the medical officer reported a warship was ready to go. That afternoon, orders came down: *Duncan* would depart in the morning.

Early the next morning, the air filled with the high whine of blowers building up speed. The PA crackled, "NOW HEAR THIS. GO TO YOUR STATIONS ALL SPECIAL SEA DETAIL."

The special sea detail mustered the most experienced and reliable deck force sailors at key stations during docking, undocking, and other delicate maneuvers. Bosun's mates manned the hawsers.

Up in the pilothouse, the captain turned to Chief Paige, his phone talker, and said, "Take one to the capstan and heave around. Tell the engineroom to stand by to answer all bells."

A yard pilot conned the ship out of yard waters. "She'll fall free. Let her drift," he shouted.

Bryan tugged the whistle cord, and *Duncan* let out her first official cry, a long, resonant, steam-powered bellow.

"All ahead two-thirds," the yard pilot called. "Indicate turns for 10 knots."

"All ahead two-thirds," Paige echoed.

Chief Quartermaster William Lehman repeated the order for

his pilothouse crew. Grabbing the brass spring-grip handles on the engineroom telegraph with both hands, Lehman pushed them forward until the locking lugs fell into the notches that arrested the indicator at "Two Thirds." He then twisted a knob beneath the annunciator until the numerals "9-8" appeared in the tiny glass windows of the panel. 98 was the number of shaft revolutions per minute that delivered 10 knots.

In the on-line engineroom, bells clanged. Machinist's mates spun throttle wheels counter-clockwise backing valves open until the numerals "9-8" registered on their revolution indicators. Astern, a great dome of churning water erupted as the twin bronze screws bit in.

Duncan steamed across the harbor to New Jersey, where she tied up to the deperming pier at Bayonne Terminal. Deperming demagnetized the hull to reduce its attraction for underwater mines. The process involved wrapping the entire ship in cable. The men had to remove their watches when electricity was passed through the cable. It took all day.

The next day, May 1, *Duncan* went up the Hudson River to the Naval Ammunition Depot on Iona Island 4 miles south of West Point. It took them six tries to get moored there because the river current is so strong. "Nobody knew how to run that ship," Seaman Louis DeLucca remembered.

Lighters loaded with main battery ammunition pulled alongside. Enlisted men loaded the ammo -- 1,400 5-inch cartridges, 1,400 projectiles, and 15,000 20mm cartridges. It took most of the day. It was after dusk when they started back downriver. It was dark when they anchored in New York Harbor.

The next morning, as soon as a harbor pilot was aboard, *Duncan* steamed up the East River. At Hart Island, the pilot was let off. Taylor took the conn. After steaming through Flushing Bay, they entered Long Island Sound. Early that evening, they moored in the harbor at Newport, Rhode Island.

The next day was Sunday. Men received permission to go ashore to church. During the service at Trinity Episcopal, the minister announced news of a carrier battle in the Coral Sea.

It rained that afternoon. A range tender lighter with five

torpedoes and five warheads tied up alongside. The torpedo crew loaded the torpedoes and warheads in the rain.

The Mk15 destroyer torpedo was a huge ungainly object 20 feet 6 inches long and 21 inches wide. It weighed 3,209 pounds. To wrestle one aboard, they put a strap around the centerline and, using the whale-boat davit, hoisted it onto the deck. Then they hoisted it into the mount using the torpedo-loading crane. A warhead weighed only 730 pounds, so they were much easier to manage.

The torpedo was a destroyer's most potent weapon supposedly, but there was little respect for them anymore. All the pre-war gaming at Newport predicted the primacy of rapid, long-range shellfire. The Mk15 torpedo had not been redesigned in any major way in 27 years, since introduced into the fleet in 1915. Nobody even knew for sure that they worked because they were so expensive ($7,500) that they were never test-fired in a live exercise. According to recent submariner and pilot scuttlebutt, they were missing targets or failing to explode. It was suspected that they were running about 4 feet deeper than they were set. [In fact, they were running at least 10 feet deeper than set, and the firing pins were frequently being crushed before they could fire.]

In the morning, *Duncan* went five miles up Narragansett Bay to the fuel depot at Melville, Rhode Island. Melville was also home to the Motor Torpedo Boat Training Center, so MTBs were everywhere zipping about. Before *Duncan* had finished tying up at the fuel depot, a motor torpedo boat tied up to her.

When the MTB captain came aboard, there was a stir on deck because everybody quickly recognized Lt.(jg) Douglas Fairbanks, Jr., the stage and screen star. He was swarmed for autographs. Lt. Bryan sent his yeoman, Frank Coninx, down to invite Fairbanks and his officers to lunch in the wardroom, "with the Captain's compliments."

There were only eight seats at the wardroom table, so the junior officers all missed it. Reportedly, the talk at lunch was mostly Navy scuttlebutt. Taylor and Fairbanks got in an argument about whose craft was faster. It got heated. The tension was still in the air when the junior officers joined them on deck afterward for cigarettes and coffee. When *Duncan* completed fueling, Fairbanks and his exec excused themselves. Taylor was watching from the bridge as their boat sped away. "He was off at 40 miles an hour," Machinist's Mate Malcolm Bethune remembered. "Zip-zip-gone." Taylor took this as a slap in the face. "He thinks he's fast? Let's show him what a destroyer can do," he said to Chief Paige. "Reverse standard speed."

The crew in the forward engineroom, hearing the order, all looked at one another. "You're supposed to ease out, y'know, but Taylor puts it down," Bethune remembered. "Reverse Standard Speed. We spun that engine over." In backing away too fast from the dock, the anchor scraped along the dock and snagged on a piling, snapping the anchor chain. "All of sudden," Bethune remembered, "everybody's shouting, 'Stop!' and 'Forward!'"

Duncan was 200 yards out in the river, and her anchor was back at the dock on top of a piling. Lt.(jg) Weatherup, the OOD, noted laconically in the log: "Port anchor chain parted due to strain caused when anchor was caught between dock and ship, leaving port anchor on the dock. 1314 - Moored portside to Melville Fuel Depot to recover anchor."

Leaving the anchor behind was never considered. *Duncan* would have been the laughingstock of the fleet. Bryan rallied Ens. Smyth's deck force to the task of retrieving the anchor, which weighed more than a ton. A bosun's mate climbed up onto the piling and re-attached the chain. Using the torpedo-loading crane, they lowered the anchor into the water, and then hauled it back up into the hawespipe with the capstan. The entire operation took less than half an hour.

Duncan quickly got underway back to Newport. Speed restrictions in the bay kept them to a slow speed so they failed to make it back before dusk when the submarine nets closed. They had to anchor off the channel entrance for the night. Bryan was livid. He was sure that the anchor had been hanging out of the hawespipe at a sloppy angle because how else could it have gotten hung up like that? He blamed Ens. Smyth, who ran deck force. He was so mad he would have banished Smyth to the machinery rooms if he had an officer to replace him.

That evening, *Duncan* received orders: she was to be in Portland, Maine, in two days to begin shakedown.

Eager to get in a day of practice before they faced the Destroyers Atlantic specialists, Taylor took the ship out to the drill grounds in the morning. On the way out, he ran a speed test to see how fast his ship really was. 340 rpm was flank speed -- 36 knots (41.4 mph), officially -- but these destroyers were (secretly) designed to exceed their official top speed by another 3-4 knots. *Duncan* may have topped out at just under 40 knots for a few seconds before he backed her down.

Sixty miles offshore at the drill grounds, they fired the 5-inch guns for the first time. Just powder charges, no projectiles ahead of them -- "firing a bale of hay" it was called. There was little concussion but a lot of fire and smoke.

The strong odor of smokeless powder still permeated the ship in the morning when they got underway to Portland. Steaming up the coast, *Duncan* transited the Cape Cod Ship Canal, then steamed into Cape Cod Bay, headed due north.

Casco Bay off Portland, Maine, is a vast protected anchorage big enough for a fleet. Much of the U.S. Atlantic Fleet was moored there when *Duncan* steamed in. Casco was "BASE SAIL," the port of departure for Atlantic-bound escorts. It was also the inner base for the U.S. Navy's Support Force. In addition, Casco was headquarters of Destroyers Atlantic (DesLant).

Duncan went out to the drill grounds the first morning. The sea was so rough everybody was seasick. Above 40° north, sea state 3 (4-foot waves lasting 5 seconds) is the condition about half the time.

It was early May so the nights were very cold. That evening, Seaman DeLucca discovered just how cold the water was. *Duncan* was moored when destroyer *O'Brien* pulled alongside. "I was throwing them this hawser," DeLucca remembered. "I got my foot tangled, and over the side I go. I'd been in the Navy two months, what'd I know? I don't know how we ever won that war."

That evening was their first liberty in Portland. Most of them headed for the bars or the skating rink. Some of the more fastidious went shopping for clothes.

The dress code on destroyers was far more relaxed than on cruisers or battleships. Destroyermen often wore "tailor-mades" because the pant legs in the issue dungarees were so straight you looked like you were wearing boxes on your legs. Tailor-made dungarees had a rakish silhouette.

When liberty ended at 0100, quite a few men had not made it back. When *Duncan* got underway at 0649, half a dozen were still missing. They all eventually straggled back, and were put to work in punishment details around DesLant Headquarters for the day.

That afternoon at the drill grounds, *Duncan* test fired the 5-inch guns with live ammo for the first time. The PA warned that they were going to test fire the main battery -- one round from each of the four guns. The men all set themselves as if awaiting the report from a giant firecracker. As the projectile hurtled out at 800 mph, the ship exploded in a shattering blast. The concussion was in the *whoomph* hitting your ears. The ship shook with the shock of the gun recoiling. Even being ready for it, everybody jumped out of their skins. No matter how many times you heard the PA warning and set yourself, no nervous system could withstand that level of sound without cringing.

The wind howled continually at Casco. The captain gave up trying to keep his pipe lit and switched to cigars. Bryan told Wharton to keep the ship's store stocked with cheap cigars. Bryan was always fawningly respectful of the captain. "All those Naval Academy boys," Wharton remembered, "anybody ahead of you, you ass-kiss."

During shakedown, destroyers normally fired torpedoes with dummy heads, but aiming a torpedo director from a violently pitching deck was all but impossible and a torpedo fired in such heavy seas was as good as lost. So *Duncan* never fired any.

Another Academy officer reported aboard for duty: Ens.

Frank Andrews had graduated number six (out of 654) in his Academy class of 1942. He was assigned to Hauck as another assistant gunnery officer, but everybody knew Bryan was measuring the new man for deck force.

One day the wind suddenly stopped howling. It became very still. Fog set in. By morning, the fog was so thick that all the ships in shakedown remained at anchor. The next day was the same.

On the third day, even though it was still foggy as ever, *Duncan* got underway as a unit in battleship *North Carolina*'s screen. Posted at the bow, Seaman Arthur Fischer was supposed to shout out if he saw anything. "You couldn't see 10 yards," Fischer remembered. "I couldn't see the sides of the channel going out or the channel buoys. Then in the afternoon the fog lifts, and there's *North Carolina* off the port bow. That's when I realized how good radar was."

Radar had been in wide use in the fleet for less than a year. It was so new that old hands dismissed it as a gimmick. Both radar and sonar were so secret nobody but radarmen and sonarmen and fire controlmen knew anything about them. Everybody else was continually amazed by what the new equipment could do.

Duncan passed all her DesLant tests. On May 24, she was officially accepted into the fleet. Cdr. Thomas Ryan, "Prospective Commander Destroyer Division 24," moved aboard, so Bryan had to move out of the commodore's stateroom.

Cdr. Ryan was forty years old. In 1923, when he was a twenty-one-year- old ensign, he was studying Japanese in Yokohama when the great earthquake hit. He was awarded the Medal of Honor for rescuing an American woman from the burning wreckage of the Grand Hotel.

Destroyer squadrons and divisions were being assembled at Casco.[1] A squadron was nine ships in two unequal divisions -- a lead division of four ships and an "off" division of five. But none of this applied in the real world because the Navy was struggling to get enough destroyers in one place to make up even a single division, much less a squadron.

When Cdr. Ryan got underway, his new "division" consisted

of only two ships -- *Duncan* and *Lansdowne*, which had arrived the day before. *Duncan* was underway for the first time that day as a fleet unit *and* division flagship. At the drill grounds, the two destroyers fired main battery anti-aircraft practice, firing at a "sleeve" (a fabric tube) towed by a plane. They test-fired the 20mms and the 1.1 gun.

20mm Oerlikons were replacing .50-caliber Brownings in the fleet. *Duncan* had four of the new 20mms, which were called machine cannons because they fired explosive shells. One 20mm could lay up 450 rounds a minute, but it made so much smoke (even firing smokeless powder) that after about twenty rounds the gunner could not see a thing. "You could fire bursts, but that's all," Sobelman remembered.

The best 20mm gunner on *Duncan* was a divinity student from Boston named David Fowler. [No relation.] He had an uncanny knack for leading the target and was almost always able to shoot down a sleeve with just a few bursts. Hauck took him off the gun to give others a try.

There was one 1.1-inch (75mm) machine cannon on board that was only there because of a shortfall in the production of 20mms. The 1.1 was a water-cooled, medium-range anti-aircraft weapon dubbed the "Chicago Piano" for the way it fired four barrels together in rapid sequence at a rate of 150 rounds a minute, one-third the rate of a single-barrel 20mm. The 1.1 had other drawbacks. "You couldn't keep it going," Sobelman remembered. "It vibrated so badly it tended to jam." And the shells had a triggering mechanism in the nose that was so sensitive that if you fired through a rainsquall you had a string of explosions out to the target. Also, the shells had no self-destruct mechanism so, if a round did not hit something in the air, it might well land on shore where it would explode like a hand grenade, pissing off Marines.

On May 28, with Destroyer Division 24 up to its full complement of five ships, Cdr. Ryan transferred his flag to *Lansdowne*, because *Lansdowne* still had weeks to go in shakedown. On *Duncan*, Lt. Bryan moved back into the commodore's stateroom.

DesLant specialists and builder's reps were on board when DesDiv 24 set course for the drill grounds that morning. The scratch division maneuvered in "line-ahead formation" (single file) with Cdr. Ryan calling turn and execute orders over the very-high-frequency TBS (Talk Between Ships radio).

At the drill grounds, the destroyers took turns firing main battery practice at each other with gun sights offset so shells landed safely astern their targets. They fired 20mm anti-aircraft practice at a towed sleeve, but, without Seaman Fowler on a 20mm, *Duncan* failed to hit the sleeve even once. LCdr. Taylor was humiliated, so Lt. Bryan was infuriated. Lt. Hauck quickly returned Seaman Fowler to a machinegun. After dark, they fired night spotting practice. They remained at the drill grounds overnight.

In the morning, the five destroyers took position 15 miles off Cape Elizabeth Lighthouse for engine tests. The full-power crash backing test -- full ahead into reverse -- was sure to make the guts of a ship tear out if they were ever going to. Approaching 40 knots, the captain shouted, "All engines, back emergency full." Chief Lehman echoed the order and clicked his stopwatch. The blades of the backing turbine, acting as a brake, emitted a high-pitched whine as the full volume of steam poured in. The propeller shaft speed dropped fast to zero. As the propeller began picking up reverse speed, the ship bumped and shimmied as if she was grounding. When they were dead in the water, Chief Lehman clicked his stopwatch. The goal was full ahead to full reverse in 90 seconds. They also went full astern to full ahead, which they were supposed to be able to do in three minutes.

Then they performed a series of full-power steering tests. With the ship at full power, the captain ordered, "Right standard rudder." (Standard rudder is the degree of rudder that causes a ship to turn in a circle of a 1,000-yard diameter.) "Hard right rudder." The helmsman put the wheel around clockwise until it stopped at 20°. *Duncan* heeled over more than 45°, and seawater sloshed over her deck as she turned in a diameter of less than 900 yards. One turning test required the two propellers to turn in opposite directions. With the ship at full speed in reverse, the captain ordered, "Left full rudder. Starboard ahead full. Port back one-third." The helmsman spun the wheel counterclockwise. The ship twisted, and overhead piping vibrated. "Rudder amidships. Port back full," the captain shouted. The ship seemed to spin in place, turning in a diameter of less than 450 yards.

With engine and steering tests completed, shakedown was completed. It had been an exhausting twenty-four days. *Duncan* now awaited duty orders.

On the following afternoon, a group of Destroyer Flotilla officers boarded *Duncan* to check her "last request" list. This was a list of the captain's priorities before his ship was dispatched to a war zone. At the top of Taylor's list was a request for an ice cream machine for the wardroom mess. Due to lack of refrigeration space on destroyers, not even officers rated ice cream. But preparing a last request list was the art of knowing how much to ask for and how far to push it. Late that evening, a 5-quart, hand-cranked ice cream machine was delivered aboard.

Duncan received orders that evening: she was to depart for New London, Connecticut, in the morning.

Duncan departed Casco the next morning, and, by late that afternoon, she was steaming up the Thames River at New London. "It was a Saturday, so we all just wanted to get up to Boston for liberty," Seaman Fischer remembered. "Approaching State Pier, *Duncan* came in head on, but that river has unexpectedly strong currents." The bosun who threw the line to the dock did not heave it far enough, and it fell in the water. "Next thing I knew -- *bang*," Wharton remembered. "We'd stove in the bow, a big gash. Naval Academy men missing a dock landing was bad enough, but they gashed the bow." *Duncan* backed out and tried again. Nobody ever noticed the damage because so many of the new ships had dings and dents.

Lt.(jg) Wharton and Ens. Fowler were officers of the deck that evening. It was Bobby's first time back in New London since the Yale-Harvard Boat Race in June 1939 when he was on the Harvard crew, and he reminisced about it that night. He remembered on the morning of the race all the crew being taken out in a launch to look at all the yachts. Mrs. William Harkness's *Cythera* was the biggest. They saw their stroke's fiancée aboard her father George Whitney's yacht *Wanderer*. The Coast Guard reported a thousand boats in the harbor. The crowd along the riverbanks was estimated at 50,000. Now, the only ships in the dark harbor were a couple of fishing boats and a car ferry. Bobby's memories from a lifetime long ago gave Wharton "chills."

The next day, Sunday, *Duncan* held open house for families of crew from the area. Sailors escorted parents, girlfriends, wives, and children through the unrestricted parts of the ship. Yeoman Coninx, demonstrating for his parents how a depth-charge throwing K-gun was fired, grabbed the T-lever and popped it, and a 300-pound charge flew off across the harbor. Everybody froze or hit the deck. The depth charge hit the water with a huge splash. Fischer remembered, "I'm laying on the deck waiting for it to go, but the charge wasn't set so nothing happened. It sank." The incident was covered up because Coninx was regular navy and one of the captain's favorites. The log mentions only: "1150 -- Lost one gasoline drum [and] one kerosene drum ... 1159 -- Recovered kerosene drum." That evening, diving operations were undertaken to recover the "gasoline drum," but without success.

Duncan began the month of June with 175 men. The manpower shortage was a real worry for the captain. Shakedown was his last chance to get up to a full complement of 240 men. The rule for captains was to try to get more men than needed during shakedown, then keep the best and dump the rest.

The chow in the mess got worse as supplies ran low. The spud locker was empty. Cooks were substituting the dreaded canned mashed, which was like glue.

For the next six days, *Duncan* went out every day to the drill grounds and steamed back and forth as a target for submarines. At the end of the third day, she went upriver to the Submarine Base to fuel, and, while backing and filling trying to get tied up, the cruiser *Juneau* came in. "Whenever we wanted to dock somewhere, it was always in and out, in and out," Fischer remembered. "*Juneau* came up around us, *pfft, pfft*, forward, backward -- liberty. They're on liberty already before we're even organized. Everybody was saying how we ought to ask for a transfer and get on that ship."

Quite a few *Duncan* men had transferred from *Juneau*, and many others had friends on *Juneau*, including Ens. Fowler. Fowler looked up Hunty Thom, his roommate from Torpedo School, and Ens. Thom escorted a group of envious *Duncan* men on a tour of the new light anti-aircraft cruiser. *Juneau* was spacious and luxurious compared to *Duncan*. Their only consolation was they returned to *Duncan* loaded down with cartons of ice cream, their first groceries in a month.

On June 6, *Duncan* got underway to New York. She was enroute when she received the long-awaited message: "DEPTH CHARGE RETRIEVED."

Docking at the New York Navy Yard, *Duncan* went through her usual tortured maneuverings. They had all seen skippers go in close to a dock and back down, and the ship would just ease up to the pier. "Neither Taylor nor Bryan were great ship-handlers," Shipfitter Clarence Wickstrom remembered. "Most of the other officers were a bunch of college kids. What'd they know? We were all getting experience."

"Back in New York, everybody's surprised to see us," Fisher remembered. "Guys are all saying, 'We heard you were sunk in the North Atlantic.' They were happy to see us but surprised. The word was we'd been sunk!"

They were told that June 16 would be their departure date. That gave them nine days in New York. The junior officers arranged their own schedules, doubling up watches to give themselves more time away from the ship.

Bobby had two days of unofficial leave. He called Pat from the pier. They had not seen each other for forty-one days. They met for lunch at Hamburger Heaven.

Bobby spent the next morning sprawled on the bed in their sunny apartment poring over newspapers. There had been a lot of news while he was away. Just three days earlier was a big naval battle off Midway Island. The Navy had not announced it yet, but the Japanese lost four carriers in the battle while the U.S. lost one. Adm. Nimitz was quoted in the papers that morning saying that the remaining Japanese warships around Midway were withdrawing.

Duncan was all but deserted. Both LCdr. Taylor and Lt. Bryan were home on six-day leaves. Bryan left a residue of bad feelings in his wake, as usual. A sailor whose wife was about to have a baby had asked him for an extended leave, and, in denying the man, Bryan told him, "You only need to be there for the keel-laying, not the launching."

Lt. Hauck was acting exec. Lt. Kabat was sharing the OOD rotation with the junior officers. Since the news of Midway, everybody was in an upbeat mood. Suddenly, there was a feeling that the Japanese might be stoppable after all.

When Bobby left for Brooklyn on the morning of the 16th, Pat was sure she was never going to see him again. But he came home that evening. She felt the same despair the next morning. And the next. He would wake up before dawn each day and catch the subway to Brooklyn, then be home again by 6. It was as if life was almost normal. Except they never fought, never had a single fight, hardly even a disagreement. They both so wanted the days left them to be perfect that they walked on egg shells around one another and did a lot of pretending -- everything was fine, they were never happier -- when what they were really feeling was terror and exhilaration and bewilderment. They were acutely aware of the unreality of their situation. They found the key to living like that was not to dwell on the inevitable but to live in the present.

On May 18, Ens. Fowler stood the two dog watches. The word now was they would be departing on the 20th. On the 19th, Bobby and Pat went to Jones Beach. It was a lovely sunny day. Pat had moments when she was almost able to forget the loneliness that lay ahead for her.

At 4:30 on the morning of the 20th, Bobby got up quietly, trying not to wake her. But she was awake. She had hardly

PAT TOOK THIS PHOTOGRAPH OF BOBBY AT JONES BEACH ON
MAY 19, 1942, THE DAY BEFORE U.S.S. DUNCAN DEPARTED NEW YORK.

slept. When he was dressed, he sat beside her on the bed, and
he kissed her and tried to say things to stop her tears. He kept
talking, and she kept nodding but not hearing a word he said.
She was unable to speak because her feelings were beyond
words. He held her until the last minute when he had to go. He
kissed her wet cheeks and kissed her softly on the lips. Then he
stood up and turned and walked out. Lying in the dark, sobbing,
Pat listened for the sound of the apartment door closing. She
heard the elevator coming up and stopping and the doors opening
and closing, and she listened as it went down until she could not
hear it any more. In her mind's eye, she saw him step out onto
72nd Street and stride up the dark empty street. Turning at the
corner, he left her alone forever, and she cried until dawn and for
years and years after.

Chapter 2

THE TRADE SCHOOL BOYS
June 20-August 21

Nearly all men can stand adversity, but if you want to test a man's character, give him power.

- Abraham Lincoln

Only a handful of relatives and some yard workers were waving from the pier when *Duncan* backed into the East River. Two things taught in the Navy are never say goodbye and don't look back.

Crossing the harbor to Bayonne, *Duncan* slipped under the Brooklyn Bridge. As she passed between Governors and Bedloe's Islands, men crowded the decks for a last look at the Statue of Liberty.

The mood on board was uncharacteristically up-beat because two days earlier a truck had carted away all their cold weather gear, so now they all thought they were headed for the Pacific. They had heard grim stories at Casco about North Atlantic convoy -- the terrible seas, the freezing, drenching cold. The Pacific promised warm, palm-fringed islands and unimaginable, exotic adventures.

Lt. Bryan had reshuffled the ship's organization again. The inevitable befell Ens. Smyth, banished below (much to his relief). Normally on destroyers the lowest-ranked ensign ran deck force, but on *Duncan* the lowest-ranked ensign was Ens. Fowler, who was the only junior officer who had attended Torpedo School. So he was kept on as torpedo officer and Ens. Andrews was assigned deck force.

Ens. Andrews knew he was going to have his hands full because deck force had no chief. Chief Boatswain's Mate John Shanahan had a seizure while they were in New York and was taken to the U.S. Naval Hospital, and he never returned. Lt. Bryan was not concerned because he was so impressed by Boatswain's Mate First Class Howard Dernehl that he did not think deck force needed a chief. Dernehl was only twenty-one years old, but he was mature for his age and was smart and responsible and tough. But lead petty officer on deck force was an especially challenging job because deck force sailors were all bosun's mates and non-rated seamen, and bosun's mates were hard-drinking, pugnacious types and the non-rated seamen were all raw recruits. "Bryan thought Dernehl could handle it," Andrews remembered.

Duncan anchored in the Narrows off Ft. Lafayette. An ammunition barge pulled alongside. The men loaded main battery ammo until all the magazines were full.

Then they got underway to Norfolk.

It was the 20th of June, which was payday. (The 5th and the 20th of the month were paydays.) Lt.(jg) Wharton was paymaster because of his Wall Street background. He paid the crew while the ship was steaming out of New York Harbor. After thirteen days in New York, most of them were broke. Wharton's paybook was already a mess of jottings that only he could decipher. He would fuss over his paybook like a dotty old accountant, always double-checking his figures before he doled out the "invasion money" (which looked like dollars, except the seal was gold).

There was little use for cash money on the ship. The little store carried only essentials -- toothpaste, razors, candy, cigarettes, and cheap cigars. Men ran out of things to buy before they ran out of money. You could pay to have your clothes washed. Seaman Clovis Wood ran the laundry as a for-profit operation. It was rumored that he was the wealthiest man on board. Most men washed their own clothes, either to save money or because they were finicky about their appearance; navy laundry always came back a wrinkled, matted mass of skivvies, socks, and dungarees. The only way to go broke on board was to join in the on-going crap game in the after crew compartment. Action in the game always peaked on paydays. It was not unusual for a man to lose his two-week's pay before the day was over.

The ship went to general quarters as they cleared Ambrose Channel, the southern entrance to New York Harbor.

The next morning at dawn they were idling off Hampton Roads, Virginia, awaiting a harbor pilot. When he was aboard, they passed through the submarine nets. Once they had entered the James River, Ens. Fowler took over as OOD. (Junior officers could only serve as OOD in harbors.)

Duncan steamed across Chesapeake Bay. She tied up to the fuel pier at the Naval Operating Base at Norfolk.

That evening, another Academy man reported aboard for duty. With the arrival of each new Academy officer, LCdr. Taylor was able to relax a bit.

The new officer was Ens. Arthur Lane. He arrived straight out of the Academy, an early graduate from the class of 1943. Lane was married to a daughter of R/Adm. Leigh Noyes, former Director, Naval Communications.

That night, Watertender John Puzines, who was the Navy's heavyweight wrestling champion, was arrested while he was on shore patrol. During mid watch, Puzines was returned to the ship under guard by two shore patrol. He was charged with "drinking liquor while on Shore Patrol, interfering with civilians on the street, threatening other Shore Patrol, attempting to strike Shore Patrol, disobeying patrol orders, using obscene and threatening language, and [s]etting police station on fire while being confined awaiting delivery to ship." Puzines stood summary courts-martial before the captain the next morning. His pay ($72 per month) was docked $48 per month for two months.

LCdr. Taylor was counting on picking up at least fifty men at Norfolk. Lt. Bryan was first in line outside Personnel when it opened, but they did not have even one man to give him. Desperate, Taylor directed Bryan to the brig and told him to grab whoever he could.

Duncan received orders: to depart in the morning with a convoy to Cuba.

That afternoon, Ens. Fowler found time to write his parents:

Dear Mum and Dad:

The chief point of this letter is to tell you not to expect any more as conditions and the life here on board is not conducive to letter-writing. I'm writing this one standing up. Also the only time we have to sit and laugh and talk is the only time we have to write letters. From 5:30 to seven at night we are kept busy with only a few intermittent minutes out for drinks of water and a smoke. It's actually damned good fun, and interesting but the comforts of life and the leisure necessary for correspondence do not exist. It's been hot as the hinges of hell to-day. I worked from 5:30 to seven then had breakfast; at seven thirty back again until eleven in the plotting room … It's where the gun directors can plot the course of fire long after all the turrets and plotters in the conning tower are shot away. It is heavily protected by yards of steel plate - so well protected that no air as far as I could see gets in. It was 99° at 5:30 this morning 105° at about 8 o'clock and over 115° at eleven when we finally finished polishing and shining all the instruments, waxing all the woodwork and sand-papering all the steel. I've sweated in four-mile races etc. but I never knew what it was to sweat ... It was good, however, and we all agreed that physical labor to people who know nothing of it is or can be quite gratifying no matter how exhausting …

LCdr. Taylor went ashore that evening to attend the convoy meeting. Three freighters bound for Cuba would be screened by four escorts. As senior officer among the escort captains, Taylor was escort commander. One of the freighter captains, usually an old Navy man dragged out of retirement, was named "convoy commodore," and he was in charge of the internal discipline of the freighters.

Late that evening, Lt. Bryan returned to the ship with twenty-five men from the brig. Most were seamen firsts and seconds. All had been awaiting court-martial. Bryan promised them that if they volunteered for war-zone duty their misdeeds would be forgotten. Twenty-three went to deck force. "They were some pretty rough characters, a lot of them," Andrews remembered. "Man, we had some sailors on that ship."

Duncan got underway from Norfolk early on June 24. Taylor formed up the convoy outside the harbor. The three freighters were refrigerated stores ship *Merak*, general stores issue ship *Pollux*, and ammunition ship *Nitro*. The other escorts were destroyers -- *Palmer*, *Hamilton*, and *Charles F. Hughes*. Once Taylor had the freighters formed up, *Duncan* took the vanguard and began her new life on "South Atlantic" convoy.

*   *   *

The sea in the Caribbean was much rougher than in Maine. Towering waves dwarfed the ships. Just going down into the hot stuffy mess hall and seeing spare ribs sloshing back and forth in a steam tray was enough to whip the appetite out of even the hardiest sailors. The cooks stopped serving sit-down meals and instead served sandwiches three times a day. Half the crew was severely seasick. Navy bread was the best cure. Everybody was nibbling bread.

After four days of battering seas, lookouts sighted Castle Island Light. Soon, the four escorts were entering Guantánamo Bay. *Duncan* transferred two men to the U.S. Naval Hospital. One had amputated his "left index, middle, and ring fingers at the proximal joint" with a hatchet.

Almost everybody went ashore that evening. Officers went to the officers' club, and enlisted men to the enlisted men's club. There was nowhere else to go at Guantánamo.

The next morning, they were ordered to repaint *Duncan* in the two-color gray and bluish-gray pattern that were North Atlantic colors. Everyone stopped talking as a silent despair came over them.

Late in the afternoon, *Duncan* received orders: depart for the Canal Zone. It always took a couple of hours to get up steam so they were finished painting by the time they got underway.

Guantánamo to Colon, Panama, is 794 nautical miles. Enroute, between Cuba and Haiti, is the Windward Passage, which was infested with German submarines.

On June 30, officers gathered in the wardroom in the afternoon to celebrate Ens. Andrews's twenty-first birthday. There was ice cream and a cake baked by Tomas Marzan, the officers' Filipino cook. Festivities were cut short by surprise firing practice, and that was followed by steering engine drill, after which they exercised for forty-five minutes at a battle problem, followed by anti-aircraft gunnery drill.

The captain instituted a rigorous underway-training program in the Caribbean. They went to general quarters a dozen times a day, always timed by stopwatch. The speed at which they got to battle stations was singularly important to the captain, who told them he had a specific time in mind. Other drills were on-going, often four or five a day: fire and rescue drill and boarding and salvage drill were daily; man-overboard drills were a couple of times a week; abandon ship drills were weekly. In addition, each department held its own drills: communications men rigged up emergency sound-powered phones; "the black gang" (engineering department personnel) switched over steam lines and cross-connected engines.

Underway training was a captain's last chance to shape his men into a battle-ready crew. They seldom drilled while at sea because the sea was so rough, but, while in port, they drilled and drilled. Fire controlmen and gunner's mates almost never stop drilling, and every gun drill completely disrupted the ship's work routine because gun crews were mostly made up of men from other divisions. More than half the crew, about 130 men, had battle stations in guns. So when the PA blared -- "NOW HEAR THIS. ALL GUN CREW MEMBERS NOT ON WATCH REPORT FOR LOADING DRILL." -- half the crew left their jobs running.

Lt.(jg) Wharton was already convinced that becoming an officer was the worst mistake he had ever made. Enlisted men were under a lot less pressure, and it was obvious that they had a lot more fun. The only advantages Wharton could see in being an officer were the semi-private staterooms, the stewards, and the wardroom.

Except on *Duncan*, the wardroom was no sanctuary for junior officers. Whenever Bryan caught one of them in there, he would grill the man mercilessly. He did not care who was present. The wardroom steward, Mess Attendant William Shurney, was always hovering nearby. The result was that junior officers avoided the wardroom.

Lt. Bryan was personally affronted by the very presence of reserve junior officers on his ship. He especially resented that they were making grade so fast. Throughout the 1930s, advancements for regular officers had come painfully slowly. Professional officers put in years honing their craft. Taylor was a full lieutenant for seven years before he made lieutenant-commander. Bryan had already been a lieutenant for six years. These new reserve officers were ensigns for six months, jgs six months, then full lieutenants. It was hardly surprising they knew so little. Academy officers regarded reserve junior officers as something less than officers -- semi-officers, officer-trainees. Bryan saw them all as useless or, worse, an embarrassment to his ship. They did not even look like real officers. They did not stand right, did not salute right, did not look sharp in uniform. They barely knew anything about the Navy -- ships, guns, radar, engines, the sea, the stars, nothing. Bryan called them "officer-passengers."

The reserve junior officers all nursed feelings of superiority toward the U.S. Navy. They called the Academy officers "the trade school boys."

Meals in the wardroom were the worst part of the day for the junior officers. "Taylor and Bryan would be talking and the rest of us were silent," Andrews remembered. "Nobody wanted to be noticed by Bryan or they were sure to get chewed out for something." The moment the captain left, Bryan would pound on the table, "What're you talking about down there?" ("He never bothered to call us 'men' or 'gentlemen'," Wharton remembered.) "We were talking about the Harvard-Yale game," one would answer. Or, "The stock market took a tumble." One day during lunch, Bryan decreed, "From now on you will talk nothing but Naval Regulations at this table." Junior officers who were late to meals were made to stand out on deck until the next seating. Preferring to stand outside rather than be trapped at the table with Bryan, they all began arranging to be late; tardiness to meals among junior officers became epidemic.

Duncan gained sixty-one men in June, and the manpower crisis was over. The end-of-month "Recapitulation Sheet" reported thirteen officers and 240 enlisted men. Full complement.

The passage from Guantánamo Bay to Colon, Panama, took 41 hours, at an average speed of 19 knots. Colon Harbor is the port for the city of Cristóbal and also the Atlantic terminus of the Panama Canal.

Sailors on liberty in Cristóbal all headed for a fabled square full of prostitutes. "They had this big, beautiful nightclub called Kelly's Ritz where you could eat dinner and they had a stage show," DeLucca remembered. "They even had a couple of American girls working there." Curfew in the Zone was midnight.

Duncan received orders in the morning: to escort three merchants to Guantánamo. The 15th Naval District was finally receiving enough additional forces that even the Panama Sea Frontier was organizing escorts. Among the five escorts assigned to the convoy, *Duncan* was the only destroyer. Two were large yachts, and two were harbor patrol craft. Taylor was escort commander.

"The Caribbean is the roughest place I ever saw," Seaman Arthur Ehrenberg remembered. Convoying doctrine dictated that merchant ships, the solid core of a convoy, be in column 600 yards apart, but, in the towering seas, communication was hopeless. Basic convoy doctrine went out the window. Faster ships ranged ahead while slower ships labored. Inevitably, the convoy was soon hopelessly spread out. "We'd go up one wave," Ehrenberg remembered, "and, when we came down the other side, the screws would come out of the water and the whole ship would shake."

The towering seas made life aboard utterly miserable. During one moment of violent pitching, Fireman August Mardos fell from the gig 20 feet to the deck, cracking his head and cutting his thigh. During supper in the wardroom one evening, Taylor turned green, stood up, and stumbled out, croaking, "I left my cigars on the bridge." He did not return for dessert, which was very unlike him. Wharton noticed that "a lot of the Naval Academy boys get seasick."

The C.Z.-Gitmo run that had taken 41 hours independently took 99 hours in convoy.

Duncan was fueling in Guantánamo Bay when they received orders: to steam independently 270 nautical miles to Jamaica. They just managed to make it out of the harbor before the sub nets closed.

At dawn, they were off the channel to Kingston Harbor waiting for the sub nets to open when a fight broke out in #2 gun, which was directly below the bridge so the captain could hardly ignore it. He sent Lt. Hauck down to break it up. Hauck found Gunner's Mate Howard Dunn and Fireman Andrew Slovenec screaming at one another. Slovenec said Dunn was "picking on the new kid on the rangefinder." Dunn was an officious, overbearing boozer who was widely disliked, but he was regular navy so Hauck was practically obliged to take his side in any argument with a reserve like Slovenec who was not even rated. "Look, you men have a good gun here," Hauck said, launching into his "for-the-good-of-the-ship" speech. He told Slovenec to apologize to Dunn and all would be forgiven. Slovenec would not do it. "I ain't never apologizing to that bum," he said. So Hauck summoned Chief Boyd, the master-at-arms. Boyd placed Slovenec under arrest for disobeying a direct order.

Slovenec was put in the makeshift brig, which was the saillocker. It was just an open space screened off from after crew quarters by wire mesh. It was the brig because it had one of the few doors on board that actually locked, and it had a big padlock. But, as soon as Slovenec was inside, he kicked the door so hard he broke the padlock. So door had to remain open. But Slovenec agreed to stay inside. He felt he had made his point. In a quick mast (a sort of court) held while *Duncan* was entering Kingston Harbor, the captain gave Slovenec three days in the brig on bread and water. "The guys [from #2 gun] were happy I'd told Dunn off," Slovenec remembered, "and they're bringing me food."

Lt.(jg) Wharton had let it slip that he knew the senior naval officer at Kingston, so Bryan ordered him to go ashore and invite the man for dinner. In fact, Commander Robert Huntington was a Newport acquaintance of his parents and Wharton had never actually met him. He went ashore with Lt. Weatherup in the first boat, feeling very uneasy about his mission but knowing that if he could "deliver a senior officer like that [it] would be a real coup." Cdr. Huntington welcomed him immediately as if they were old friends and seemed genuinely pleased to see him. He agreed to come for dinner on *Duncan* the following evening. "He was a real gentleman," Wharton remembered. "He knew me getting him would be a feather in my cap."

Kingston was full of life, which made it a great liberty port. "These little kids," Sobelman remembered, "they'd take beer can tops and put them in their toes and tap-dance on the concrete."

Most of the enlisted men were unmarried, and they all headed first to the open-air bars, where rum was 10¢ and Coke 25¢, and then to the whorehouses, which were also open-air. "The walls was 6 foot high and open to the sky," Machinist's Mate Bethune remembered. "Like I'd be banging away and here'd be [Motor Machinist's Mate Helmar] Berquist looking over the top yelling down at me, 'Come on, Shorty. Go, go, go.'"

All the *Duncan* officers, except for Wharton, were married or engaged. They mostly stayed out of the bars and whorehouses and socialized with one another. In the social hierarchy of the U.S. Navy, officers only socialize with other officers of more-or-less equal rank. Ashore, LCdr. Taylor socialized with Lt. Bryan, Lt. Hauck, Lt. Kabat, and sometimes with Lt.(jg) Broccolo (because he was a doctor). A captain never invited an ensign to dine, unless the junior officer was a movie star or a relative. The only junior officer Taylor socialized with was his brother, Ens. Tom Taylor of *Lansdowne*.

That night, Ensigns Fowler and Beebe went out on the town together. They started with cocktails at the Myrtle Beach Hotel. Then they hired a horse and driver and went on a carriage tour of Kingston by night.

Wharton was on shore patrol that evening. When he returned to the ship at 0045, he could see that a storm was brewing. A light wind riffled the harbor. "A little tropical storm there can come up in a hurry," Wharton remembered.

Early that morning, a tremendous wind blew down from the green hills. It whipped furiously across the harbor. *Duncan* began swinging at anchor. Within half an hour, she had swung completely around. Kingston Harbor is deep and has a sandy bottom, and, if a ship does not have enough chain out, an anchor will drag. *Duncan* was anchored in 42 feet of water with 180 feet of chain to the port anchor. She began dragging anchor. She was bearing down on a merchant when general quarters sounded. "Stationed all special sea details for preservation of ship's safety," Beebe noted in the log. Men rushed aft with fenders. "Just in time they gave it some juice," Fischer remembered. The fantail missed the merchant by inches. *Duncan* re-anchored, again with only one anchor but with twice as much chain.

Cdr. Huntington came aboard for dinner that evening. Wharton was invited to join them. "I was even allowed to sit next to Cdr. Huntington at the table," Wharton remembered. During dinner, Taylor and Bryan treated Wharton as if he were an admired fellow officer and valued friend. "That didn't last long," Wharton remembered. "The next morning I was back in the doghouse again for something."

Every liberty in Kingston was an adventure. On the first night, a gang of men after their money chased Seamen Arthur Fischer and John Cormack back to the dock. On the second night, Seaman Joseph Manna had every stitch of his clothing stolen, and he returned aboard stark naked. The third day was a Saturday so liberty started early and ended at dusk. While waiting on the dock for the liberty boat, Seaman Aaron Derr, one of the men from the brig, was receiving oral sex from a local girl when he saw Taylor and Bryan approaching. Panicking, he socked the girl to get her off him, and she became so enraged she bit down and ripped off his foreskin. Derr was yowling in pain and hopping around with his bleeding penis hanging out when Taylor and Bryan walked up. He was transferred to the British Naval Hospital with what the log described as "acute appendicitis."

Ens. Fowler wrote his parents from Kingston:

Dear Mum + Dad:

A line to let you know that I and the Navy are still alive + active in one way or another. We have not yet reached our final destination, having been detained for some special work in a most unattractive part of the world for a few weeks. The heat is unbelievable + we are on the go all the time which is lucky since at sea the temperature is 10 or 20 degrees cooler than in port.

I've become resigned to Navy life - days + weeks slip by it seems without anybody noticing them - every day is just the same as the last and every hour the same as the preceding one. By the time you get this letter July will be well on its way - half done perhaps or more I don't know. It seems like only yesterday that I left home - which is a good sign. There's never a minute of boredom since morning, noon or night - whenever one can sneak off for even fifteen minutes lying down is the irresistible urge and sleep then becomes inevitable.

Everything is fine on board and the ship's in good shape as am I. I don't [hate the Navy], I like it really. I only wish I was more certain that we were accomplishing something, that we were damaging the enemy definitely and absolutely. All this effort + expensive equipment and the results are so debatable and without visible proof as yet. We can only hope + try + keep on trying …

The men were broke and anxious to get moving. After four nights in Kingston, *Duncan* received orders: to get underway with a convoy to the Canal Zone. A new Guantánamo-Canal Zone convoy route had been officially instituted just two days earlier.

This convoy consisted of four merchants and three escorts. The other escorts were an old 1919 flush-deck destroyer assigned to the Panama Sea Frontier and a Brazilian subchaser. The four merchants were all foreign. Taylor formed them up outside the channel.

Communication was a problem in convoys because most merchants had the longer-wave radios which were forbidden in convoys because submarines could home in on them. Communication during daylight was by megaphone, semaphore, or blinker, and, during nighttime (when blinkers were forbidden), by megaphone or steam whistle. But there was always confusion. Escorts inevitably spent a lot of time running messages among the merchants. When merchants were foreign, it was even more difficult because foreign merchants seldom had blinkers and, due to the language problem, were slow to read flag hoists. It took Taylor almost two hours to get just four merchants formed up.

During the past nine days, a German submarine had been tormenting the Panama coast. As escort commander, Taylor wanted to see every message that related to the sub. The most junior communications officer was the coding officer, but, as there were so many messages about this one sub, all three communications officers -- Weatherup, Beebe, and Lane -- worked in rotation decoding.

On July 2, the sub had steamed into the harbor at Puerto Limon, Costa Rica, where it sank a steamer at the dock with two torpedoes. Four days later, an Army patrol plane spotted it and tried to bomb it, but missed. Five days after that, off Colon, the sub fired five torpedoes at a U.S. net tender that all missed. The next day, a Navy PBY search plane spotted the submerged sub on radar and dropped flares and straddled it with four depth charges. By daybreak the next day, the search had been joined by a B-18, three P-39s, and a second PBY. That was the situation when *Duncan* departed Kingston. A subchaser that arrived on the scene that day reported that the sub was trailing an oil slick. The subchaser dropped all six of her depth charges just ahead of the rising oil bubbles. Over the next ten hours, the sub covered 25-30 miles while three Army attack planes dropped twenty-four depth bombs and eight depth charges on it. The next day the sub sank two merchants in Colon Harbor right off the entrance to the Panama Canal. Colon Harbor was closed to outbound traffic. That evening, *Lansdowne*, *Duncan*'s sister, joined the chase. *Lansdowne* made a sound contact and dropped an eleven-depth-charge pattern after which a great quantity of fresh oil was seen rising to the surface.

At noon the next day, *Duncan* was approaching the channel to Colon when she was diverted to the chase. Three hours later, she arrived on the scene to find that all the ships and planes were gone. Slowing to 15 knots, *Duncan* began a sonar search that continued through the night.

At first light, they could see Courttown Cays Light 19 miles distant. A couple of hours after dawn, Taylor called off the search. They raced to Colon at full speed.

Completing her first Canal Zone-Guantánamo-Canal Zone roundtrip, Duncan tied up to a pier in Colon Harbor. Awaiting them on the pier were Cdr. Tommy Ryan, ComDesDiv 24, and LCdr. Bill Smedberg and other *Lansdowne* officers. Smedberg, who was a little bantam rooster, was practically dancing for joy. All of them were extremely full of themselves because *Lansdowne* was being credited with sinking the sub, which was the Panama Sea Frontier's first sub kill (and only the seventh by U.S. forces). And it was *Lansdown's* second sub kill. She was being credited with another German sub sunk off Norfolk two weeks before (July 3). *Lansdowne* officers -- especially Smedberg and Whitey's brother, Ens. Tom Taylor -- were not above gloating.

Duncan and *Lansdowne* remained docked in Colon Harbor for two days. On the third day, both ships received orders to get underway with ten freighters bound for Guantánamo. One of the freighters had been converted to a troop transport and was carrying South African soldiers. Cdr. Ryan was escort commander.

COMMANDER THOMAS RYAN
COMMANDER, DESTROYER DIVISION 24

The passage was uneventful, except for the towering seas. It took them four days at an average speed of 8.4 knots.

Duncan and *Lansdowne* tied up to the fuel dock at Guantánamo, topped off, and then anchored together in a nest in the harbor. There was no mail again. Another day without mail. *Duncan* had yet to receive any mail. This was seriously impacting morale. That night, most of the enlisted men went to the club on the base where there were only three things to do -- get drunk, fight, or get drunk and fight. Brawls were the norm at Guantánamo.

Duncan's other sister, *Lardner,* arrived the next morning with a convoy from Norfolk. This was the first time since Kearny that the three DesDiv 24 destroyers were in the same place at the same time. *Meade* and *Mervine,* two more *Livermore*-class destroyers, arrived that afternoon.

Late that afternoon, the five *Livermore* destroyers held a round-robin baseball marathon. The heat was blistering. The players stood around in the field with a glove on one hand and a beer can in the other. Afterward, they all returned to their ships for a mass swimming party. The five destroyers were anchored close together in two nests. A couple of men went out in a whaleboat with 30-06 Springfields to watch for sharks. As it was past dusk, few *Duncan* men went in.

Ocean swimming had been ruined for them by a recent novel, Delilah by Marcus Goodrich, which is set aboard a U.S. destroyer in the Philippines in 1915. In one graphic scene, a sailor swimming off the ship one evening is attacked by a shark while men on deck watch helplessly. It was the third most in-demand book in the wardroom library after Modern Gunnery and Tobacco Road, and everyone who read it thought twice about going in the ocean at dusk.

There was a huge brawl outside the service club that night. Some officers on shore patrol tried to break it up but were dragged into it. "Jeez, it was a real battle royal," DeLucca remembered. Liberty ended early at Guantánamo -- 2100 -- for good reason. Some *Duncan* men returning to the ship were so drunk they jumped off the liberty boat and swam to the ladder.

Ens. Fowler was OOD that night on mid watch when a call came from #1 fireroom. Machinist's Mate Frank Quinn, the fireroom talker was shouting hysterically, "#1 fireroom's on fire! The fireroom's on fire! Light the ship! Call out the fire party!" Lighting a ship inside the nets of a foreign harbor was strictly forbidden under almost any circumstance short of the most extreme emergency. But Ens. Fowler ordered Chief Lehman to light the ship. It turned out there was no fire. Fireman Paul Duffy, who was on watch in #1 fireroom, had been drinking gilly (torpedo alcohol mixed with pineapple juice), and he mistook live steam escaping through an open turbine blower drain for fire and sounded the alarm. "Duffy was half in the bag," Quinn remembered. But Duffy never owned up to being drunk, and, as he and Lehman were regular navy, they got off clean while Fowler and Quinn, the reserves, were in the doghouse for unnecessarily risking the ship.

Morale was very low. The unrelenting heat made tempers short. Below deck, it was unbearably hot. It was always hotter in ports where the air was still. The wardroom was using most of the ice on board to make ice cream so the mess was always short of ice. There was never enough even for iced tea. Enlisted men had begun to view the ice cream freezer as emblematic of officer arrogance.

Duncan, *Lansdowne*, and *Lardner* got underway to escort another convoy to the Canal Zone. Late that day, *Duncan* escorted two merchants to Jamaica. She escorted them to the channel to Kingston Harbor, then raced to regain the convoy. In less than half an hour, they could smell the odor of soft coal from 20 miles ahead.

The next afternoon, *Duncan* made a sound contact. She dropped two depth charges, and promptly lost the contact. The sea was very rough. Men moving about had to hold onto something or go flying. The next afternoon, a listing vessel was sighted on the horizon. Cdr. Ryan ordered *Duncan* to investigate. After steaming for two hours, they came upon a schooner wallowing in the heavy sea, all but dismasted. She was out of St. Andrews Island, Colombia. They got no response when they hailed her, and no signs of life could be seen on board. Lt. Bryan took half a dozen men over in the whaleboat and boarded her. They found several Panamanian families huddled below. They all insisted they were fine. They said were headed for Cuba to work in the cane fields.

Duncan completed her second Canal Zone-Guantánamo-Canal Zone roundtrip in the morning. With *Duncan*, *Lansdowne*, and *Lardner* in the harbor, DesDiv 24 was almost complete. Only *McCalla* was still missing.

Two days later, the three DesDiv 24 destroyers got underway to escort twelve merchants to Guantánamo. The sea was heavy as ever. One exceptionally large wave took overboard "[o]ne reel with three lengths of fire hose and one telephone box with two sets of headphones."

Seasickness was chronic. Many men were noticeably wasting away. When *Duncan* tied up in Guantánamo Bay, Lt. Kabat ordered Machinist's Mate Quinn to Gorges Hospital. Quinn was diagnosed with prolonged seasickness and was pumped full of fluids. A doctor hinted that he could probably get shore duty if he requested it.

That evening, the three DesDiv 24 destroyers received mail for the first time. *Duncan* received bags and bags of letters and packages. LCdr. Taylor got several boxes from his wife, each containing a pecan pie and a dozen expensive cigars. Most men received a dozen letters or more. Almost all of Ens. Fowler's were from his wife. She had been writing to him every day, always on blue Merrimade stationery. Opening one and reading that she was pregnant, he let out a whoop. That evening, he wrote a stern note of instructions to his mother:

> Dear Mum:
> The day if not the hour if not the minute you get this letter find out what doctor Pat is going to + have him write me by air mail how she is + how everything is going and will go. If you ever urge him to lie to me I'll never forgive you. In great haste. Sorry - no time for more now. Best to all.

Duncan, *Lansdowne*, and *Lardner* remained at Guantánamo

for two days. There was a lot of activity suddenly. Men in ordnance and deck force went to the 20mm range in relays. Supply officer Ens. Rhodes and his chief, Whitney Chamberlain, led parties of junior officers and petty officers ashore to scour warehouses and storerooms for machine and ordnance parts and whatever else they could scrounge. Something was brewing.

On August 6, halfway around the world in the Solomon Islands, where it was August 7, U.S. Marines were landing on Tulagi and Guadalcanal in the first U.S. amphibious action of the war.

Lansdowne, *Duncan*, and *Lardner* got underway from Guantánamo Bay that morning with another Colon-bound convoy.

Duncan's spud locker was empty. "They served dehydrated potatoes and raisins in a salad," Fischer remembered. Talk in the after crew compartment, which was usually about women and memorable liberties and food, was now only about food. After a week of canned mashed potatoes, men were refusing to eat it. Then one night somebody heaved every can of dehydrated mashed potatoes overboard. The next morning, lower-rated enlisted men were made to run laps around the ship until somebody confessed. Nobody ever did. They were kept running until it was time for lunch. The case was never solved. Everybody assumed it was one of the mess stewards.

Duncan completed her third Panama-Cuba roundtrip. That evening, Cdr. Ryan received orders: DesDiv 24 would transit the canal in the morning.

That evening, Ens. Fowler wrote to his sister:

> Dear Ange:
> ... We are leaving this unnamed area where we have spent a few uneventful and horrible weeks and going many thousands of miles farther away without a stop at "civilization" as sailors on board call these big Navy Yard towns ... It's hard to keep one's sense of humor sometimes. Too god damned much happens in a short time. How I would like to get this war over with + run + hide on a forgotten farm in some secure + fertile part of the country + be able to say to hell with adventure + queer places + the so-called romance of excitement. I'd like to have a year in which nothing

happened to me or Pat which would interest either of us. God I'd like to be bored with life again for a brief interlude.

This war is a damned nuisance, and the sooner America decides to throw in men, ships + everything necessary to win at whatever the cost, the better we'll all be. Our revered country is too cautious. The men that make this war + all our professional war-makers (officers, that is) are taught that the worst disgrace is to lose one's ship. Or one's men. That in wartime to my mind is a great drawback. Waiting for an easy + overwhelming victory that would entail smaller losses will take forever. The Germans + Japs know that + are without doubt of my school of thought. To attack is the important thing for us now ... Well, criticism is one method of blowing off steam in this life – a much needed catharsis.

Must stop this now. I wish you'd try to persuade Pat to give up that apartment of ours + come + live with Mummy + Daddy. They'd like it, wouldn't they + I'd feel a hell of a lot better.

*　　*　　*

On August 11, just before 0500, harbor pilots boarded the three destroyers and conned them out of Cristóbal Mole. The three ships took turns making runs over the degaussing range. Then the pilots left the ships, and the captains took the conns. Men crowded the decks as they steamed across Limón Bay. They all knew this was it -- the start of the long-awaited great adventure. After they passed canal buoy #3, canal pilots came aboard and conned them in column to the entrance to the canal.

The three destroyers entered the first chamber of Gatun Locks, squeezing in side by side. Each ship was 36 feet wide and the lock was 110 feet wide, which allowed about one foot of clearance on either side. After the gates closed, the chamber flooded for twenty-two minutes, lifting the three ships 50 feet. They were thirty-eight minutes in the second chamber and twenty-one minutes in the third. Then they steamed together across Lake Gatun.

On the other side of the lake, they entered Pedro Miguel Locks to start down the other side. Where Mira Flores Locks empties out, fresh water mixing with salt water created a lot of turbulence. *Duncan* lost control and was coming broadside to a motor torpedo boat squadron tied up nearby. The boat crews were sunning on the decks. "We're all shouting," Fischer remembered. "They're looking up and, seeing us coming, they're jumping up. We butted some boats, but they all had fenders on. We just pushed them back, but, oh man, those boys were screaming."

Within minutes, the three destroyers were steaming into Balboa Harbor, the port for Panama City. They tied up at a fuel dock. LCdr. Taylor got on the PA. He said they were going to escort a convoy to the Pacific, adding, "but we might be here for a while."

On sailors' favorite street in Panama City, the bars were all on one side and the whorehouses were on the other. Shore patrol's job was to keep U.S. Navy men from crossing that street. Wharton and Seaman Edwards were shore patrol that evening. "Everything was fine until they'd had a few drinks," Wharton remembered. Wharton's Army opposite number was an MP who had a jeep. "We must've visited forty whorehouses at least," Wharton remembered. "All of them one room and double bunks and all. A *Duncan* man was in every damn one. Most had a girl in one hand and a beer in the other. 'Hiya, Mr. Wharton.' 'How ya doin', Mr. Wharton?' 'They got some good looking dames here, huh, Mr. Wharton?' 'Lemme buy you a beer, Mr. Wharton.'" Wharton never resented enlisted men more.

In the morning, 15,060 rounds of 20mm ammo were delivered on board.

The heat and humidity are unrelenting in Panama in August, and Balboa Harbor, which is an artificial harbor, is so sheltered there is hardly ever a breeze. Ships' deckplates bake in sun, then steam off in the rain. Sometimes it rained two inches in two hours, then dried up in two minutes. It never cooled off below deck because portholes had to be kept closed at night. The unrelenting heat and humidity were draining on men already drained to exhaustion by a month of too little sleep and perpetual queasiness in high seas. Tempers were on edge. To make matters worse, on the third day, *Duncan*'s air conditioning conked out.

That day, harbor pilots shifted the three destroyers out to a nest in the anchorage. As soon as *Duncan* was tied up, the PA squawked, "FIRST DIVISION, TURN TO AND PAINT THE SHIP." They had painted the ship seven or eight times over by then. DeLucca remembered, "I tell the skipper, 'Captain, if we ever get hit, this ship's going up like a firecracker.' He says, 'I just run this ship. I don't run the Navy.'"

The three destroyers were repainted in a bluish-gray camouflage pattern, Pacific colors. Just as they were completing the job, a migration of butterflies fluttered in. "The whole sky is full of these white butterflies," Fischer remembered. "Splat! Right onto the paint. 'FIRST DIVISION, LAY UP TO THE PAINT LOCKER AND GET YOUR BRUSHES.'"

Every day, they went to GQ again and again. They had long since achieved the captain's desired time, but they were kept at it until every man could go from a deep sleep in his bunk to his battle station dressed in full battle gear in less than three minutes, less than two minutes, less than one minute. They went to GQ so often that every man could arrive at his station without even opening his eyes. That was the whole idea -- drill until every man reacted so automatically that he was sure to react automatically when the time came.

There was no letup in complaints about the chow. So many men complained about it so often to so many officers that Bryan instructed officers to stop telling him about each and every complaint. Resentments increased. "Men inadequately fed over an extended period of time grow to feel somewhat nasty about the affair," Seaman Earle Ham remembered. There had once been a time, after boot camp and A-schools, when they had accepted the discipline and the inane, arbitrary orders, but any positive feelings they might have once felt for the Navy had been poisoned by their experience on *Duncan*. Most were now just looking for somebody to blame for their misery. The officers always wore .45s at battle stations supposedly to repel boarders, but junior officers suspected it was more likely they would be called upon to shoot one of their own men. Morale was so low that ashore *Duncan* men would not even defend their ship's honor. For sailors, silence often speaks louder than words.

Wallowing in the nest day after day, the three destroyers stewed in a miasma of odors from enginerooms and firerooms and galleys and crew quarters. Nobody was able to repair the air conditioning, though everybody tried.

The enlisted men's frustrations were focused on the officers. Enlisted men instinctively dislike officers as a class, though individually some are less disliked than others. The three least disliked were Broccolo, Fowler, and Lane, who each had an easy, relaxed manner and a sense of humor about himself and their mutual situation. Part of what endeared them to the crew was that each had a quirk that annoyed Bryan: Broccolo was always obsessively combing his thick wavy black hair; Fowler was always taking off his shoes and rubbing his feet; and Lane was constantly removing his big, clunky Academy ring. The three most disliked officers were Bryan, Andrews, and Wharton, who were all tightly wound and self-important. Bryan was a mean bully. Andrews was overeager and pushed too hard, a common trait among Academy ensigns. Wharton was an upper-class snob who was completely lacking in the common touch. Wharton would walk on deck for a last cigarette in the evening wearing a monogrammed bathrobe from Brooks Brothers and holding his cigarette like Noël Coward.

In the unrelenting heat and humidity, minor resentments grew into major episodes. Boatswain's Mate Milek, one of the men from the Norfolk brig, got so fed up with Bryan that he challenged him to a fight, and Bryan, who thought he could beat any man in a fair fight, was so frustrated that he accepted. It was strictly against Regs for an officer to fight an enlisted man, but, having accepted, Bryan did not feel he could honorably back down. The two men met on the dock in what was a private affair. No witnesses were present. Bryan reportedly removed his uniform beforehand. Apparently, there was no clear winner because afterward each exhibited a new-found respect for the other.

With too much time and too little to do, some men got tattooed. Others blew their pay in the bars and whorehouses.

After four days of liberties, most of them were broke. Even daily liberty became a bore. Men stopped going ashore. The endless, oppressive days ate at them. Everyone had to find his own escape from the boredom. The principal recreation was cards. Among officers in the wardroom, it was cribbage and bridge. Enlisted men played poker. When their money was gone, they played for cigarettes, and, when their cigarettes were gone, they played for matches. Whatever their escape, they tended to become obsessive about it. Some men read endlessly. Others slept continually. A lot of men repeatedly shined their shoes. Machinist's Mate Quinn mostly sat on his bunk weaving square-knot belts out of Belfast cord.

Every day without mail added to the frustration level. Their first and last mail was two weeks earlier at Guantánamo. They all wrote a lot of letters because they knew this was their last chance to get them mailed reliably.

As enlisted men's frustrations grew, their anger focused on the officers' ice cream freezer. The chow line that they stood in three times a day wound past the wardroom, where they could see the table set with a white tablecloth and silverware. They usually had to step around Mess Attendant Shurney who was often sitting on the deck outside the wardroom cranking the ice cream freezer. The chow line then continued down the ladder to the mess hall, where it was normally about 110° and the iced tea was warm because the officers had taken all the ice. The ice cream freezer had become a symbol of the officers' abuse of power or flaunting of power.

The second week in Balboa the pace picked up. One day, *Duncan* received five men from Advanced Base Depot. Taylor could even afford to prune a few men. Five were dispatched ashore that day. The first to go were men who were perpetually seasick and the next were the continual disciplinary problems.

Ordnance started coming aboard. Also, tons of groceries, including 5,000 pounds of potatoes.

On the eighth day in Balboa, word came that they were waiting for a fancy new warship. Seven men were received aboard for duty that day, and seven were dispatched ashore.

Ens. Fowler wrote to his parents on the 18th with his new address - "c/o Postmaster San Francisco California" - and a short note expressing his growing frustration with Academy officers and the management of the war:

> Dear Mum + Dad:
> We are headed for places as yet unexplored by the average man as far from home as one can get. So this will be my last letter-writing effort for some time ... I wrote a long letter to Angie ... filled with invective against the whole military tradition of these Professionals who run the war. Too bad us people who just joined up for the fight can't run the war. We're the only ones who are really in a hurry to win it. For the others it's a means to greater influence + faster promotion + not bad fun; the damned fools. Well, I hope public opinion at home will force us into using some of this great power we are undoubtedly building + have built instead of keeping it all to tie up in Brooklyn + Philadelphia after the war or bury in junk heaps around the countryside. We really must begin to attack at any cost soon if we want to get this damned thing over with in any kind of time at all.

There was a rush of excitement when two old submarines, *Bonita* and *Barracuda*, stood in. Late that night, cruiser *Juneau* moored. So many *Duncan* men had friends on *Juneau* that Signalman Francis Benson spent most of the next morning semaphoring personal messages to the cruiser, including one from Ens. Fowler to his former Torpedo School roommate: "ENS. FOWLER SENDS COMPLIMENTS TO ENS. THOM."

June 20 was payday so everyone who went ashore that evening had money. All the DesDiv 24 officers not on duty went to the officer's club. A large contingent of *Juneau* officers was there.

As of August 21, the three DesDiv 24 destroyers had been in Balboa Harbor for ten days. Taylor addressed the crew on the fantail at 0800 muster. "Men, the *Duncan* has received orders," he said. "We have a job to do. We leave port within the day." That day, the three destroyers came under the joint command of ComDesFlot (Commander Destroyers Flotilla) and ComDesPac (Commander Destroyers Pacific).

Seaman Darrell Lake, one of the men from the Norfolk brig, purposely chopped off his finger that morning rather than depart for the war zone. He was delivered ashore "for treatment and disposition."

Over the past seventeen days, fourteen men had been let go, five because of seasickness. Of the twenty-five liberated from the Norfolk brig, twenty remained.

Cdr. Ryan and the DesDiv 24 captains and execs reported to *Juneau* that morning for the convoy briefing. The big surprise at the briefing was the presence of R/Adm. Willis Lee.

Willis "Ching Chong China" Lee was a celebrated surface fleet officer. He had been the Director of Fleet Training Division at OpNav earlier in the year when it was renamed the Readiness Division. Most recently, he was Assistant Chief of Staff (Readiness) to Adm. Ernest King, Commander in Chief U.S. Fleet.

R/Adm. Lee was a fifty-four-year-old Kentuckian who was cerebral and looked it. He wore glasses and chain-smoked. He was the new Commander Battleship Division 6. When he told them he was flying his flag in *South Dakota*, there were audible gasps. The new battleship would be one of Pacific Fleet's most closely-held secrets.

The task group, which was designated TG.2.9, consisted of battleship *South Dakota*, cruiser *Juneau*, and destroyers *Lansdowne*, *Duncan*, and *Lardner*. Cdr. Ryan was commanding the escort. Two destroyers would depart before dusk to sweep the channel, and one would depart with *South Dakota* after dark. *Juneau* needed to undergo repairs so she would be departing during the night and would steam independently and rendezvous with the task group in four days at "the line" (the equator).

When Taylor and Bryan returned aboard *Duncan*, word spread quickly that their destination was Tonga. This was it -- the war zone. Most of them did not care where they were going so long as they got moving.

Late in the afternoon, *Duncan*'s PA boomed, "ALL DEPARTMENT HEADS LAY UP TO THE BRIDGE AND MAKE THEIR READINESS-FOR-SEA REPORTS TO THE

EXECUTIVE OFFICER." Bryan called away the special sea detail. The order came to stand by lines. A harbor pilot came aboard.

"Engineroom requests permission to test main engines, sir," Chief Paige reported.

Taylor nodded.

In backing out of a nest, the wash of the propellers frees the vessel in the middle by pushing away those on either side. *Lardner* in the middle went first.

"Tell the fo'csle and the fantail to take in all lines," Taylor said.

Men on sea detail hauled in lines as *Duncan* drifted free.

As *Lardner* was pulling away, her international call letters were run up her mast.

Out on *Duncan*'s port bridgewing, LCdr. Taylor shouted over to Cdr. Ryan who was out on *Lansdowne*'s starboard wing, "Permission to get underway, Commodore?"

Ryan saluted. "Rendezvous off the sea buoy and form up there," he shouted.

Turning to Chief Paige, Taylor said, "Tell the engineroom to stand by."

"Stand by," Paige echoed into his phone.

"Stand by," Chief Lehman echoed for the navigation crew.

Bryan took a long, careful look around the harbor before finally reporting, "All clear, Cap'n."

"Starboard engine back one-third," Taylor called.

"Starboard engine back one-third," Paige echoed.

Duncan issued the customary three toots on her siren and a long whistle blast as she backed into the stream.

When the men went down to supper at 1700, *Duncan* and *Lardner* were off the channel entrance in Balboa Bight. "We hadn't gone out of the breakwater yet," Fischer remembered. "Shurney was there on deck with the ice cream freezer. One of the other boys [mess stewards] there had this beautiful chocolate layer cake" that Officers' Cook Marzan had baked for Lt. Hauck's birthday in two days.

After supper, Seaman Fischer's ritual was to walk aft to get some air. As he was headed aft, he saw a cluster of men on the fantail. When he was closer, he recognized that they were all from the black gang. They had the officers' ice cream freezer, and they were frantically scooping out ice cream with their hands and devouring it. By the time Fischer got there, the freezer was completely cleaned out. He watched as Watertender Puzines lifted the freezer over his head and "just depth charge it into the sea."

When word came that *Lansdowne* was starting out of the harbor, *Duncan* and *Lardner* went to GQ and came around and patrolled closer to the channel.

Lansdowne emerged first. Looming behind her was "the biggest damn ship," as Wharton remembered it. *South Dakota* emerged from the channel at 2000. "Oh, man, what a sleek beautiful-looking ship," DeLucca remembered. "Like a New York skyscraper on its side." *Duncan* had operated with *North Carolina* and *South Dakota* at Casco, but everybody was still awed whenever they saw one of the new battleships. "Seeing her again was like seeing her for the first time," Wharton remembered. The officers took turns on binoculars.

When the new battleship passed the sea buoy, a course change flag ran up her mast -- 180°T., due south. As they swung onto the new course, *Lansdowne* remained in the van. *Duncan* and *Lardner* fell in at screening stations 800 yards to starboard and to port of the battleship. Task Group 2.9 increased speed to 18 knots.

At 2245, R/Adm. Lee ordered a westerly base course. They were underway to Tonga by the Great Circle Route [250°].

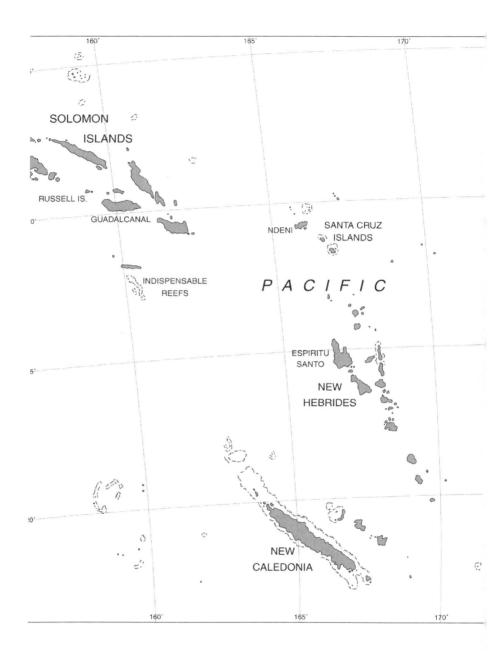

SOUTH PACIFIC AREA

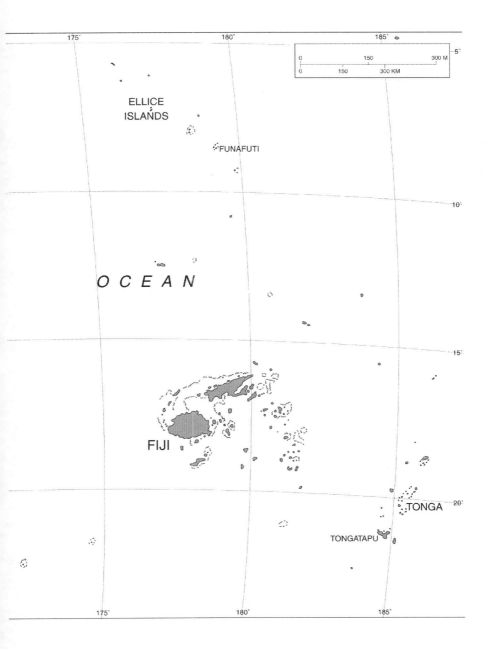

Part II

OLD NAVY
August 22-October 11

The Navy is a master plan designed by geniuses for execution by idiots.
- Herman Wouk

Chapter 3

FIRST BLOOD
August 22-September 16

Dogs and sailors probably get along better together than any other people in the world. They all have troubles too deep to talk about.
- Arnold S. Lott

Underway at sea a ship makes her own wind. An invisible river of air carries away the smells of paint and diesel and gunpowder. When the last seagull, swooping and screaming in the sunset wake, turns back, there is silence finally. That first quiet moment is an epiphany for a lot of men.

When land is left astern and the last colors fade from the sky, the horizon disappears and night creeps up until your eyes give up trying to see. Sometimes you can hold your hand in front of your face and see *nothing*. For the first time, you *feel* the night. Stars glimmer like jewels in an ink-black overhead sea. There is absolute rightness in the idea that navigators always steered by the light of Vega, because wherever one hails from Vega is always in the same place: right ascension 18° and 34 minutes, declination 38° and 44 minutes north. The night is never more impressive than when you first go to sea.

* * *

When Lt.(jg) Wharton walked into the wardroom that first morning at sea, Lt. Bryan pounded the table and snarled at him, "You had the 4 to 8 watch?"

Wharton nodded uneasily.

"Are you aware there was a mutiny on my ship last night?"

"No, sir."

"Did you inspect the officers' pantry?"

"No, sir."

"Why didn't you?"

"Well, sir," Wharton began haltingly. Then he quoted the part in Regs where it said the OOD was supposed to stay on the bridge.

"Well, somebody stole our ice cream maker!" Bryan screamed.

Out of the corner of his eye, Wharton could see junior officers trying not to smile.

"I've already begun an investigation," Bryan continued. "I spoke to Shurney. He says he cleaned the freezer and returned it to the rack on deck."

Mess Attendant Shurney, the wardroom steward, was serving breakfast while pretending to be deaf.

Shurney's routine was to transfer the ice cream to a container and give the container to the officers' cook, then return on deck and clean the freezer. Changing his story, Shurney now claimed that when he returned on deck it was gone.

Bryan summoned the chiefs and all the firsts up to the bridge. He addressed them in such a funereal tone some of them thought the captain had died. When he finally got to, "Somebody stole our ice cream freezer," men had to bite their tongues to keep from laughing.

The next morning at 0800 muster, Bryan stepped out to speak but words failed him. He stood silent for a few moments. Then he began speaking so softly men leaned forward to hear. "I know you hid it," he hissed under his breath like a curse. "We'll find it. You'll suffer for this." Most of them did not know what he was talking about and thought he had "gone off his rocker." Fischer thought Bryan "felt betrayed."

In the afternoon, Bryan summoned the junior officers to the wardroom and ordered a top-to-bottom search of the ship. Late in the afternoon, the search was interrupted by formation anti-aircraft practice.

At supper, Bryan summed up his thoughts on the investigation. He said he did not believe any regular navy man would ever mutiny. That neatly eliminated half the crew from suspicion -- the guilty party was a reserve. Bryan's faith in regular navy men went only so far. He did think it was possible, likely even, that one of them might have heard something. But if the guilty party was in the black gang, no on-deck man was going to say anything, certainly not publicly, because on-deck men did not mess with below-deck men. But Bryan thought they might talk to him privately, if he approached it right. He planned to personally interview every regular navy sailor individually. He thought he could appeal to their pride and patriotism.

The next day, during Bryan's inquest, every regular navy enlisted man reported to the bridge and stood alone in front of Bryan, who warned each man not to let this unfortunate incident ruin his career. Then he asked for the man's help in putting this shameful episode to rest. Questioning 133 men, one by one, took all day. In the end, not one of them admitted knowing anything about the ice cream freezer. Bryan pushed each man to guess who might have done it, and virtually every one of them said it was probably a mess steward.

August 23 was Lt. Hauck's twenty-ninth birthday. In the afternoon, the officers gathered in the wardroom for the party. Shurney served them cake and coffee. The festivities were muted somewhat by the obvious lack of ice cream, but everybody was pretending they did not notice. Unable to continue the pretense any longer, Bryan's anger suddenly flared, and he ordered another search of the ship.

The next day, the junior officers searched the ship again, and the following day, too, for the fourth time. On the fifth day, after yet another fruitless search, word came down: return the freezer, no questions asked. When this failed to get a response, Bryan knew he was defeated. A few days later, he appeared in the machine shop and told Shipfitter Wickstrom to make an ice cream freezer. But then word got around that Wickstrom was making the officers an ice cream freezer, and Taylor called it off. He must have thought the officers already looked foolish enough.

As Bryan saw it, the crew was mutinous. As punishment, he ordered the ice ration to the mess hall cut off completely. Most of the crew thought it was worth it. An injustice was righted. Quinn remembered, "We weren't getting any ice cream and neither were they." Most of the enlisted men harbored a new-found grudging respect for Mess Attendant Shurney, despite his vehement protestations of innocence.

The formation passed through fog banks, and it was uncomfortably chilly. That night, the three destroyers held torpedo attack practice, closing on *South Dakota* and simulating launching torpedoes.

Every morning after muster, there was a long line outside sick bay. After eleven days in Panama, shanker warts and the clap were epidemic. Sick bay was a little partitioned-off cubicle in a corner of the mess hall. One part was Doc Broccolo's office-examining room, and the other part was the dispensary where Chief Pharmacist's Mate Isaac King and Pharmacist's Mate First Class Brunner Flowers dispensed pills. There were no beds. Anybody too sick to work reported to his bunk.

Days went by when they saw nothing but the occasional sea turtle. Every morning, the deck was littered with flying fish, which were thought to be inedible and were swept overboard.

The task group ships crossed the equator on August 25, and they all held "crossing-the line" ceremonies. These always involved Neptunus Rex, Sovereign Ruler of All the Seas, administering personalized punishments on individual officers and enlisted men. The worst cruelties were always inflicted on snitches, suck-ups, and cooks. On *Duncan*, Edward Bowers, the short order cook (who many believed was largely responsible for the poor quality of the cuisine) was hurting for days.

The next day, the three DesDiv 24 destroyers fueled for the first time while underway. Destroyers were fuel hogs. At 15 knots, their range was 4,700 nautical miles, but, at 25 knots, it was half that. At 30 knots, they burned twice what they burned at 25 knots and five times what they burned at 10 knots.

Duncan pulled up along *South Dakota*'s starboard side while *Lardner* pulled up to the cruiser's port side. Sailors on the cruiser tossed each ship a monkey fist. On *Duncan*, a bosun caught it and pulled over the heaving line that pulled over the towing line that pulled over the 10-inch hawser. When the ships were fully alongside, the bosun threw the hawser's eye over a pair of short steel posts (bitts), but without putting a manila line and block and tackle on it. "He should've had a 21-thread on it and put it through a jigger," Andrews remembered.

The start of fueling began a string of foul-ups. First, one of *South Dakota*'s little Kingfisher scout planes came in low between the battleship and *Duncan* as if looking for calm water to land, and the plane hit the water and flipped over. All you could see was a pontoon sticking up. *Lansdowne*, trailing 500 yards astern, rescued the pilot and radioman and, on instructions from R/Adm. Lee, sank the plane. The next excitement came when *South Dakota* dropped one end of a whaleboat they were lowering and dumped six men into the sea. *Lansdowne* rescued them all.

The third incident began when *South Dakota* unexpectedly started pulling away. "We were being towed by the hawser," Andrews remembered. The hawser was under so much tension that bosuns could not muscle the eye off the bitts, and they could not put a come-along on the hawser and get slack in the line because there was not a 21-thread and jigger on it. There was so much tension on the fuel lines Bryan was screaming over the PA: "SECURE FUELING! SECURE FUELING! CAST OFF! FO'CSLE, CAST OFF!" Andrews shouted, "Cut it! Cut it!" A bosun grabbed an ax and chopped at the hawser. All along the deck, men were chopping lines. Chopped free, the big fuel line aft snaked across the deck, spewing oil.

Watertender Romney Boyle, the "oil king," was below in the mess taking soundings on the fuel tank that vented up there. Everybody had been looking forward to lunch because *South Dakota* had sent over spaghetti and the cooks had made meatballs. But the fuel tank started gurgling, and somebody shouted, "They're overfilling the tank! Bail out!" Everybody dropped their trays and ran, but oil was already spewing out of the vent, and most of them were already covered in black oil. Weatherup wrote in the log in his usual laconic manner: "1445 - Completed fueling having received 85,398 gallons of fuel oil."

LCdr. Taylor was humiliated that *Duncan* sent *South Dakota*'s hawser back with the eye chopped off. Now, a *South Dakota* bosun was going to have to retie the giant eye. It reflected poorly on *Duncan* and on Taylor. "He was as angry as I ever saw him," Ens. Andrews remembered. "I caught hell for cutting those lines from Captain Taylor himself, who I seldom caught hell from. Whitey was mad for about five minutes. Then it was over. That's how Whitey was. The truth was none of us knew what the hell we were doing. We were all green. Those guys [on *South Dakota*] were as green as we were."

Fuel oil was everywhere topside on *Duncan*, and oil was draining down into the lower deck and puddling on bunks in after crew quarters. Cleanup was the black gang's responsibility. It was a huge, horrible undertaking. #5 bunker is the next thing to tar when it cools. "Oh, that heavy, thick bunker fuel, there's nothing like it," Bethune remembered. "You have to keep it hot or you're screwed. Man, the black gang worked all night. They had nowhere near enough rags."

The moon was full that night. The sea was like glass. It had been like that since they hit the Pacific.

On August 27, chronometers were set back 1 hour to +8 zone time. August 28 ended their first week at sea.

Nobody knew much about the strategic situation that brought them here. In the U.S. Navy, information on the war was dispensed on a strictly need-to-know basis. The captain was as much in the dark as anybody; his operation orders covered only their immediate assignment. Personal radios were forbidden; supposedly, the enemy could triangulate a position from the signals. The only news they got was whatever radiomen copied down from short-wave broadcasts. Radiomen would mimeograph major news reports and tack them up on bulletin boards. Men following particular sports teams or stocks could usually get a radioman to listen up for a score or quote. Officers always knew who won the Navy game. The New York stock market was going up finally. It was up 20 points since bottoming out at 95.35 in April. Stock quotes were a hot topic in the wardroom.

Each day was like every other day. Men only knew the date because the Plan of the Day said so. To pessimists, it was one more day since they left and, to optimists, one day closer to home.

Standard wartime routine called for general quarters half an hour before sunrise and half an hour before sunset. The uncertain half-lights of dawn and dusk were thought to be the most likely times for enemy strikes.

Maintaining Condition Baker (guns one-third manned) imposed a constant strain because another third of the gun crews had to sleep on the deck near their stations. You considered yourself lucky if you got six hours sleep a night. Even that was interrupted. "You go four on, four off, you're always tired," Bethune remembered. "You never catch up." They lived on coffee. Every gang had its own pot of Navy jamoke. A man could go almost anywhere and get a cup. Ship's Cook Edward Beavers, the baker, always had some of his fabulous bread to go with it. But lack of sleep is cumulative. It brings on a deep, total exhaustion. Trying to sleep at different hours leaves you fogged and disoriented. Men were frequently caught sleeping on watch. As hard as it was to stay awake on deck, it was even more difficult in the magazines and handling rooms where shells leaked ether fumes into enclosed spaces. Bryan caught Seaman Frank Carroll sleeping on watch in a handling room one night, and he pulled his pistol and pointed it at Carroll and said, "I could shoot you." Carroll was so tired he was beyond caring. "Go ahead and shoot," he said.

After a week at sea, *Juneau* was sighted forward of the task force. She had reduced speed and was falling back on the convoy. "She looked like a greyhound that wants to run," Wharton remembered, "and she went out ahead and was gone again."

The next morning, the sea increased to force 4 from the southeast. *Juneau* and the three destroyers fueled from *South Dakota*. Beforehand, *Duncan* received a snide message: "DUE TO THE LIMITED NUMBER OF FUEL LINES, DUNCAN WILL FUEL LAST."

Day after day, men on watch went through the same routines. Days were the same, nights the same. Chow was the same bad chow. Banter was the same lame banter from the same boring faces. Emerging topside after a meal, men would blink, sniff, and walk over to the lifeline, where they would look out at the empty sea and spit and think, "Here we are. I can't say where."

Since those first few hours after leaving land, the ship seemed to have stood still. It was as if the horizon was a giant painted backdrop against which nothing moved. Water rushed by, yet the ocean stood still, and the ship was always in the center of the ever-encircling sea. If you stared hard enough, your eyes played tricks, and the sea became a great flat wheel, turning slowly, pivoting on the horizon.

As of noon on September 2, they were twelve days and 5,779 miles from Panama. By dawn the next day, they were in the Tonga Islands. At 0630, they crossed the 180th meridian, the International Dateline. Clocks were set *ahead* 23 hours to -12 zone time (and also the reckoning of the Greenwich Hour Angle shifted from westward to eastward of the prime meridian). Dropping one calendar day, the date jumped ahead to September 4.

In Lahi Passage, on approach to the channel to Nuku'alofa Harbor, Tongatapu, sightseers hung on lifelines, straining for a glimpse of green palms and white surf pounding a coral atoll. What they saw were fighting tops and radar antennae. Warships filled the lagoon, tankers and transports and cargo ships, reefers, beef boats, ammunition ships, hospital ships, repair ships, tenders.

*　*　*

As *Duncan* was anchoring in Nuku'alofa Harbor, Bryan came on the PA and announced that there would be no liberty. Everyone was confined to the ship, except for the communications officers and the garbage party.

Lt.(jg) Beebe returned from the island with tales of a royal palace, which he said looked like a big Victorian house. Others claimed they saw Queen Salote herself. The big news was that the natives were buying and supposedly would buy anything.

South Dakota sent over a lighter with a crate of apples because *Duncan* had been out of fruit for days. By the time the crate got down to the refrigeration room, every single apple was gone. Taylor got on the PA and said if the apples were returned he would not order punishment, and every apple came back, except one.

The three DesDiv 24 ships held a swimming party. "Oh, Bryan was a great one for the sea," Bethune remembered. It had been two weeks since anybody was in the water. "EVERYBODY OVER THE SIDE," Bryan called over the PA. "Almost everybody just dived over," Bethune remembered. "Anyway, there's safety in numbers, and men are out in a whaleboat watching for sharks."

Later that afternoon, locals came rowing out to the anchorage in *bumboats* with bananas and coconuts and bully beef to sell or trade. Fischer traded some of his clothes for beef. The natives had rolls of money. They were paying high prices for navy sweaters. Men were trading whatever they had. "There was a lot of stuff in those sea bags of ours," Fischer remembered. "We were taking advantage of them, and they were taking advantage of us. Queen Salote put a stop to that in a hurry."

September 5 began their third week in the Pacific. That day, R/Adm. Lee received departure orders from ComSoPac (V/Adm. Robert Ghormley): "TASK GROUP 2.9 DEPART TONGATAPU DURING DAYLIGHT L [local] 6 SEPTEMBER ARRANGING HOUR OF SORTIE TO AVOID INTERFERENCES WITH ENTERING UNITS."

Officers visiting aboard *Atlanta* the next morning heard hair-raising first-person accounts of a naval battle that had taken place in the Solomon Islands thirty days earlier. Less than forty-one hours after the U.S. 1st Marine Division had started landing on Guadalcanal and Tulagi, seven Japanese cruisers and a destroyer plowed into a screening group of U.S. and Australian cruisers and destroyers off Savo Island. Three *New Orleans*-class cruisers were sunk in ten minutes, and, within thirty-two minutes, four of five Allied heavy cruisers were sunk. Twenty-two Allied warships were damaged, with no notable damage to any Japanese ship. It was the worst defeat of the U.S. Navy in a fair fight ever. The only good news was that the Japanese had failed in their mission, which was to sink the Allied transports off-loading at Guadalcanal. And the next day U.S. submarine S-44 sank heavy cruiser *Kako*, the first Japanese cruiser sunk by U.S. forces in the war.

Spontaneous discussion groups on board *Atlanta* second-guessed the battle. Most thought R/Adm. Turner's distribution of his force was faulty. He had split his force into three groups to try to defend all three entrances to the bay.

The meetings on *Atlanta* were in progress when torpedo-damaged carrier *Saratoga* limped into Nuku'alofa Harbor. She was aided by a tug and was escorted by cruisers *New Orleans* and *Minneapolis* and seven destroyers, including *Laffey* from DesRon 12.

Lansdowne, *Duncan*, and *Lardner* got underway before noon. *South Dakota* emerged from the channel at full speed. About an hour out, in an uncharted area in Cape Lahi Passage, *South Dakota* struck an uncharted pinnacle. Suddenly, the masts of the U.S. Navy's prized new battleship were thick with signal flags. *South Dakota* slowed as she came around and headed back to Tongatapu, trailing a large oil slick.

It was disheartening to see such a great ship (especially one you were charged with escorting) brought down so stupidly. Morale sank to a new low. To combat the wide-spread despair, Cdr. Ryan authorized liberty.

Tongatapu did not live up to expectations for a Pacific island. It had no facilities, not much of anything really. Men could pay to ride little horses like Shetlands, but there were no saddles. "You just sat there on a ragbag," Quinn remembered, "and got your whites all crapped up from horsehair." U.S. sailors did a lot of trading -- shirts for skirts. "Our guys wanted grass skirts," Slovenec remembered. "The natives wanted regular clothes. Money didn't mean nothing to them guys." Entertainment was watching a kid climb a coconut tree for a quarter. Tongan men seemed nervous when their wives were around U.S. Navy men. That evening, a *Duncan* sailor was chased down a road by an angry man with a spear.

Divers worked all night assessing the damage to *South Dakota*, which had extensive underwater hull damage. Losing the new battleship before she even arrived was a tremendous blow to SoPac.

V/Adm. Ghormley directed R/Adm. Lee to proceed to the war zone with the remaining TG.2.9 warships. R/Adm. Lee transferred his flag to *Juneau*, and got underway with the three DesDiv 24 destroyers, plus *Laffey*.

They set course west-northwest toward the New Hebrides. Lee received a message from Ghormley that evening directing him to rendezvous with the carrier *Wasp* in the New Hebrides in three days. A ComSoPac dispatch noted, "NO KNOWN ENEMY ACTIVITY ALONG ROUTE TO RENDEZVOUS."

The wind was moderate from the southeast. The night was clear. Men sleeping on *Duncan*'s deck awoke to shouts of "Torpedo!" Fischer thought he saw two porpoises. "They said the torpedoes went underneath us," Fischer remembered. "They must've been set for depth. If they'd been set for shallow we'd have gone to kingdom come."

The nautical chart was dotted with islands, but they never saw any. "We were trying to avoid land is what it was," Fischer remembered, "but it was always, 'Keep a sharp lookout.' One day, I'm lookout on watch in the gun tub of one of the forward 20mms and suddenly I'm getting berated by Bryan because I didn't notice a puff of smoke on the horizon. You know, you look into the sun at that ocean long enough you just want to go to sleep. I had the sun lookout my whole time aboard that ship and never saw a submarine, a Japanese plane, even the wake of anything except those two torpedoes that I thought were porpoises."

The next morning, *Juneau* made radar contact on an airplane at 20 miles. The ships all went to GQ before the plane was recognized as friendly.

That afternoon, clocks were set back 1 hour to -11 zone time. Finally, they were in the same time zone as the war. That evening, in the New Hebrides, they set course for the rendezvous point southwest of Efate Island.

Early on September 10, *Juneau* made radar contact on two airplanes that were quickly recognized as friendly. One dropped a message on *Juneau*'s deck. It said *Wasp* was 30 miles ahead.

There were a lot of warships in the area. Task Force 17 with carrier *Hornet* and Task Force 18 with carrier *Wasp* were operating together as combined Task Force 61, SoPac's striking force.

The *Juneau* task group joined up with R/Adm. Leigh Noyes's TF.18. R/Adm. George Murray's TF.17 was just over the horizon.

Juneau joined the cruiser force, which was under the command of R/Adm. Norman Scott (ComCruTaskFor18) in *San Francisco*. Cdr. Ryan's four destroyers joined the destroyer force, which was under the command of Capt. Gilbert Hoover (ComDesRon12) in *Farenholt*.

An intelligence report that day warned of four Japanese carriers that were presumed to be closing on Guadalcanal. They had departed Truk two days before. R/Adm. Noyes, anxious to get in the first strike, ordered TF.61 to the east of the Santa Cruz Islands to flank them.

In the morning, TF.18 rendezvoused with TF.17 well west of the Espíritu Santo-Ndeni (Santa Cruz Islands) line. An intelligence dispatch predicted: "POSSIBILITY EXISTS ENEMY MAY ATTEMPT OFFENSIVE GUADALCANAL OR SANTA CRUZ ISLANDS."

September 12 began *Duncan*'s fourth week in the Pacific. At dawn, they were 100 miles off San Cristobal, the large island at the southeastern end of the Solomons chain. The two carriers took almost two hours to launch nineteen Marine F4Fs to Guadalcanal. An afternoon intelligence dispatch reported a Japanese carrier and a cruiser 500 miles north. B-17s from Espíritu Santo searched but failed to locate them. That evening, TF.61 redeployed eastward to its flanking position east of the Santa Cruz Islands.

TF.61 cruised east of the Santa Cruz Islands on the 13th. *Duncan* was on plane guard. Over the past two days, 1st Marine

Air Wing ("CACTUS Air Force") had received forty-two new F4Fs, and reported a milestone: "FOR THE FIRST TIME TODAY WE OUTNUMBERED TOJO IN THE AIR AND HE TURNED AND FLED." Even V/Adm. Ghormley was sounding optimistic. "SITUATION NOT VIEWED AS TRANSITORY," he messaged Adm. King.

At dawn on the 14th, R/Adm. Turner's TF.62 sortied from Espíritu Santo with six transports carrying the reinforced 7th Marines. R/Adm. Turner planned to land them on Guadalcanal in the morning. They were just north of Espíritu when intelligence reported four Japanese battleships and seven cruisers 325 miles northwest of Guadalcanal. Turner stalled with his transports.

On the morning of the 15th, Japanese planes located TF.61 east of the Santa Cruz Islands. One Japanese plane was shot down. *Duncan* and *Farenholt* raced to where it went down, and found an oil slick, flotsam, and two dead airmen. *Farenholt*'s whaleboat recovered papers from the bodies.

On the 16th (local time), TF.61 was 170 miles southeast of San Cristobal Island. In the morning, two Navy SBDs chased a Japanese bomber into view of the task force. *Duncan's* AA rattled away at it. The sky was so clear visibility was practically unlimited. A 20-knot trade wind from the southeast was blowing up whitecaps. At 1100, a Japanese flying boat scrutinized the task force. At 1220, an F4F in the CAP (combat air patrol) shot down a Kawanishi scout bomber.

At 1223, air ops completed, the formation swung to the southeast. *Wasp* messaged: "NO FURTHER FLIGHT OPERATIONS TODAY. WILL COMMENCE STRIKES AT FIRST LIGHT TOMORROW." (It was understood this did not include the regular CAP changes that took place every four hours during daylight.) The formation changed base course again at 1240. At 1253, they started zigzagging.

They zigzagged for almost an hour and a half. Then, at 1420, the formation executed a simultaneous turn into the wind, in preparation for launching the CAP. *Wasp* launched planes for the CAP and for long-range search, then landed the planes that had been flying in the CAP for the past four hours. Flight operations were completed in twenty minutes. The two destroyers on plane guard had started hauling up their whaleboats.

Duncan was in her regular screening station half a mile to starboard of the carrier. Even at that distance, Lt.(jg) Weatherup, the OOD, remembered the carrier towering over them "like a great block of sea-gray steel." DeLucca was in a forward 20mm. "As usual, I'd put on my dark glasses and closed my eyes," he remembered. "The guy on watch on the other side would cough -- that was our code. That meant it was his turn to close his eyes." Sobelman, on watch in the I.C., "was reading to the guys from a magazine what a Jap admiral said about our fleet, which was that the *Wasp* was a terrible weapon because it could carry seventy-two planes."

The task force began turning to starboard. Weatherup walked out onto the port bridgewing to better keep an eye on *Wasp*. "I was keeping station on her," he remembered.

Standing half-asleep in one of the forward 20mms, DeLucca was awakened by the ship turning. Opening his eyes, he saw a torpedo. It was coming straight at him from starboard. "Torpedo, one o'clock," he croaked. The torpedo almost went directly under the bow. "Torpedo, three o'clock," another lookout shouted. From the bridge, Weatherup could see the wakes of the two torpedoes drilling toward *Wasp*.

At right standard rudder, *Wasp* had completed approximately 90° of the right-hand turn when, at 1447, a torpedo hit her starboard amidships. A geyser went up, and debris flew hundreds of feet into the air. There was a great volume of smoke.

On *Duncan*, Weatherup's voice on the PA was oddly calm: "GENERAL QUARTERS. GENERAL QUARTERS. THE WASP HAS BEEN TORPEDOED."

About eight seconds later, a second torpedo exploded into *Wasp* forward. The carrier shuddered convulsively. Flames blew out of the forward elevator shaft. F4Fs spotted on deck blew over the side.

All the task force ships were still turning to starboard when the carrier signaled that the torpedoes were coming from 080° relative bearing (about 40° off the carrier's starboard beam). Giving the degrees in relative (instead of true) bearing caused more confusion because the carrier was still turning. Escorts were racing off in all directions.

A third torpedo broached the waves and struck the carrier above the waterline sixty feet forward of the bridge.

On *Duncan*, Ens. Andrews was coming up from the after crew compartment when the PA called: "FRANK ANDREWS, GET IN THE WHALEBOAT." A fourth torpedo passed under *Duncan*'s fantail and headed straight at *Lansdowne*, which turned into the torpedo's path. The torpedo scraped along the entire length of *Lansdowne*'s hull before continuing over the horizon toward the *Hornet* formation. *Lansdowne* went to flank speed, retracing the torpedo's wake.

Men on all the ships were scanning the waves for periscopes. "And we're seeing periscopes, too," Sobelman remembered. "They were everywhere! A swab hat in the water -- 'Periscope!' 'Full speed ahead!' And we zoom off after it."

Racing up the torpedo's track, *Lansdowne* arrived 4,000 yards to the south where *Lardner* and other destroyers were conducting sonar searches. *Lansdowne* was slowing when Capt. Hoover on the TBS ordered the destroyers to stand by the carrier. *Lansdowne* came around and headed back toward the carrier at flank speed. *Lardner* dropped one depth charge before starting back.

There was a sudden frenzy of emergency calls from TF.17 ships five miles over the horizon. Now, they were under attack by torpedoes. One missed the destroyer *Mustin* and hit the battleship *North Carolina*. One hit the destroyer *O'Brien*. TBS channels were overloaded with desperate calls.

Steaming at 10 knots, *Wasp* was listing to starboard slightly. Capt. Forrest Sherman ordered the rudder hard to port to compensate. The third torpedo penetrated the void tank and inner fuel tank. An external fuel line was spewing aviation gas. The carrier's entire starboard side was enveloped in smoke. Within a minute of the third torpedo, the hangar deck was in flames. Machinegun shells cooking off were firing across the deck. Men trapped forward began jumping overboard.

Capt. Hoover ordered *Farenholt*, *Duncan*, and *Aaron Ward* to start rescue operations while *Lansdowne*, *Lardner*, and *Laffey* screened them.

Wasp went into reverse with full right rudder trying to back clear of the burning oil on the sea and get the wind to blow the flames and smoke away from undamaged parts of the ship. *Farenholt*, *Duncan*, and *Aaron Ward* steamed after her. The carrier was listing 11° to starboard. The entire forward end of the hangar deck was an inferno and the flight deck above was buckling. Men were now leaping off the forward end in a steady stream.

Wasp had stopped backing and was steaming forward again, hauling away to the southeast like she still had a chance. The wind from the southeast was trailing the heavy smoke cloud toward the northwest. *Farenholt*, *Duncan*, and *Aaron Ward* in column trailed in the carrier's wake. Men on the destroyers were heaving life jackets, wooden crates, anything that would float to survivors in the water.

On *Wasp*, the bridge quickly became untenable. Capt Sherman left for after conn. When he arrived at after conn a few minutes later, the forward hangar deck and forward flight deck were both fully ablaze. Personnel were abandoning en masse. Capt. Sherman had not been at after conn five minutes before he turned to his exec, Cdr. Fred Dickey, and said it was time to abandon.

At 1455, less than ten minutes after the first torpedo struck, *Wasp* sloughed to a halt in a sea of fire. Ruptured fuel lines were gushing bunker C fuel oil and gasoline. Fires on the water were spreading.

Farenholt, *Duncan*, and *Aaron Ward* maneuvered toward the carrier, skirting patches of flame. About a hundred yards off, at the edge of the burning oil, the destroyers lowered their small boats, and they steered through the flames toward the mass of men in the water under the carrier's starboard quarter. Shells cooking off on the carrier splashed around the boats.

Ten minutes after *Wasp* went dead in the water, gasoline

U.S.S. WASP BACKING AWAY FROM SMOKE AND FLAMES AFTER THREE
TORPEDO HITS FROM JAPANESE SUBMARINE 1-19,
SEPTEMBER 16, !942 (local time)

vapors on hangar deck detonated in a tremendous explosion that
ignited torpedoes and bombs and ruptured more fuel lines.

Thirteen minutes after that, R/Adm. Noyes directed R/Adm.
Scott on *San Francisco* to assume tactical command of TF.18.

On *Wasp*, Abandon Ship was ordered. The complement of
2,247 men (200 officers and 2,047 enlisted) were clambering
down the port side all at once.

A dozen small boats were steaming around the carrier. Capt.
Hoover ordered *Farenholt*, *Duncan*, and *Aaron Ward* to drag
cargo nets. The three destroyers came around and, lowering their
nets, maneuvered in as close as fifty yards from the carrier and
slowly steamed through the mass of survivors in the water. The
stronger men were able to swim to the nets and pull themselves
up.

On board *Duncan*, Quinn, Fischer, and others climbed down

onto the propeller guard to try to reach men in the water. "A good sea was running," Quinn remembered. "If you couldn't grab a man when he was close, he'd go right by and you'd lost him." Several *Duncan* men jumped into the ocean to help men who were foundering. Machinist's Mate Roman Olek grabbed a line and dove in. Boatswain's Mate George McIntosh jumped in without a line or a life preserver. Both swam among the survivors, encouraging them, cheering them on.

Many *Duncan* men rescued survivors they knew personally. Wickstrom, who had served on *Wasp*, pulled up several friends. DeLucca rescued his mother's paperboy.

As time went on, fewer and fewer of the men still in the water were strong enough to swim to the nets, much less pull themselves up. Now, most required slings to get them onto the destroyers.

All the survivors were coated in oil and were retching oil and salt water. Some were badly burned. Many were in very bad shape. "We'd pick up some of these guys and the skin would actually be coming off them," Wharton remembered. "You'd reach out and grab them and get just a handful of flesh." One man had a shrapnel hole through his heart. Another laid down on the deck and died from exhaustion. "That was my first taste of death in the service," Fischer remembered. "Funny, I felt so distant from it."

At 1545, there was another tremendous explosion of gasoline tanks on *Wasp*. The carrier was listing so steeply to starboard she looked as if she was about to roll over.

Most of the survivors in the water were too weak to even reach for the nets, even with the three destroyers cruising at their slowest speeds. *Duncan* was trolling through a thick patch of survivors when Taylor ordered the screws shut down. Hundreds of men swam desperately toward the ship. "We just laid to there and these guys were swimming to us," Seaman Arthur Ehrenberg remembered. "We were hauling them up as fast as we could reach for another."

As survivors came aboard, they were instructed to remove their lifevests and go below. Lifevests piled up in huge stacks on the fantail. The dead were stacked in the space aft of #3 gun next to the loading machine.

In the middle of this, sonar made a contact and reported it as a probable sub. Taylor should have immediately ordered full ahead for the safety of the ship, but they were pulling aboard so many men so fast and the sea around them was still thick with survivors. Taylor stalled. He turned to the OOD and said, "Weatherup, you go back there and see if it's a valid contact." Weatherup walked the few yards aft to the sonar shack. He listened to about five *pings* and heard the telltale return echoes. He walked back to the pilothouse and told the captain he heard echoes.

Duncan had rescued so many men she was losing freeboard (the distance from the main deck to the water). Water was sloshing over the deck aft. Survivors were sprawled everywhere topside -- on the main deck, on the roof of the deckhouses, in gun mounts, even on the bridge. Too many survivors on one side or the other were making it difficult to keep the ship leveled off. Repeatedly, survivors were told to go below. Nobody wanted to go. The PA kept repeating, "SURVIVORS, PLEASE DISPERSE."

At 1555, *Juneau* made a sonar contact to the east that was confirmed by *Lardner*. Both ships took off after it. When they reached the point where they calculated the sub was, several destroyers were already there. A large number of survivors were close by in the water. *Juneau* laid down pattern of depth charges and hauled clear, and *Lardner* dropped a pattern of ten depth charges with deep setting. Too late, Capt. Swenson on *Juneau* ordered they not lay depth charges among the survivors, "unless contact is reasonably certain." Men engaged in the rescue were soon finding many more dead in the water. "Suddenly, we're pulling up a lot of guys had their insides coming up through their mouths," DeLucca remembered.

The talker in #3 gun reported, "Torpedo off the starboard quarter (45° off the stern)." Men on the bridge just looked at each other. "We're dead in the water," Quartermaster Johnson remembered. "There's nothing we can do."

When sonar reported a contact 500 yards astern, Taylor reluctantly ordered full ahead. GQ sounded. The engines engaged and poured on full power. Down in the I.C., Seaman Ham looked up at the pit log as the ship leaped ahead. "We went from zero to forty," Ham remembered. As the stern dug in, men on the fantail watched in horror as survivors in the water were sucked under. "I saw men chewed up by the props," Ehrenberg remembered. The ship's wake turned blood red.

There was another big explosion on *Wasp* at 1627. Everybody thought she was about to sink, but, half an hour later, she was still floating.

At about 1700, word came that *Wasp* was to be sunk. Capt. Hoover selected *Lansdowne* for the task because Cdr. Ryan, the destroyer division commander, was aboard *Lansdowne*. Also, *Lansdowne* had aboard two torpedoes with the new magnetic-exploder heads. Ordnance officers were eager to see them in action under controlled conditions like this.

Planes had been taking off from *Wasp* for hours. Most headed for Henderson. After dusk, *Hornet* began landing orphaned units.

At 1719, R/Adm. Scott ordered all ships not engaged in the rescue to clear the area.

Duncan had about three times as many survivors aboard as she had crew. She was dangerously top-heavy and was barely responding to the wheel. With less than fourteen inches of freeboard and half her fantail under water, Taylor decided they could not risk taking on even one more survivor.

At 1745, Capt. Hoover ordered *Duncan* and *Aaron Ward* to the perimeter.

Duncan pulled away without even waiting for her whaleboat. Bryan was shouting over the PA: "GET BELOW OR SIT DOWN AND BE STILL SO WE CAN MANEUVER THE SHIP." Word was passed: no sudden moves.

The medical crew was overwhelmed by the sheer number of injured, especially all the burn victims. The store of medical supplies was already spare. *Wasp*'s senior medical officer, Cdr. Bartholomew Hogan, was aboard. He was quite severely injured

-- he had several fractured ribs and his hands were badly burned – but, as soon as Doc Broccolo patched him up, Hogan was on his feet and taking charge of the medical effort.

Duncan and *Aaron Ward* fell in with the other TF.18 ships at the perimeter. At about 1800, R/Adm. Scott ordered them on a southeasterly course.

They had been steaming southeast for about half an hour when a scout plane with mechanical problems set down on the water nearby. *Duncan* and *Aaron Ward* went to full ahead with GQs sounding and PAs blaring: "CALL AWAY THE PLANE CRASH DETAIL. LOWER THE BOAT TO THE RAIL." *Duncan* won the slow-motion race and rescued the pilot who was severely injured.

Left behind with *Wasp*, Ens. Andrews and the other two men in *Duncan*'s whaleboat continued rescuing survivors for another hour. "We were bringing them over to whoever would have them," Andrews remembered. They rescued R/Adm. Noyes, Capt. Sherman, and Cdr. Dickey and took them all to *Lansdowne*.

Capt. Hoover's order to Cdr. Ryan was to remain with *Wasp* until she sank. The carrier was listing so precipitously part of her forward flight deck was under water. It was assumed she would go down any moment.

At 1855, Capt. Hoover ordered *Juneau* to depart. *Farenholt* trailed away after *Juneau*.

Then only *Lansdowne* was left.

As the task force disappeared over the horizon to the south, LCdr. Smedberg "began to feel very lonely." He knew there was a sub lurking nearby watching their every move.

It stays light late in mid-September. *Lansdowne*'s two small boats and *Duncan*'s whaleboat were still steaming through the debris field. The last man found alive was rescued at 1845. They searched for another half hour.

At about 1915, Cdr. Ryan declared the area swept. Ens. Andrews and his boat crew were taken aboard *Lansdowne*, which took *Duncan*'s whaleboat in tow.

Cdr. Dickey, *Wasp*'s exec, had been watching his old ship for an hour. *Wasp* was even lower in the water and listing even more sharply. One survivor, a young warrant officer who had been on watch in one of the carrier's enginerooms, told LCdr. Smedberg he thought he could get the carrier underway. He said he thought she could probably do 20 knots in reverse, which would keep the fires in the bow area. Cdr. Ryan passed this along to R/Adm. Noyes with the added suggestion that *Lansdowne* could take *Wasp* in tow. Noyes's reply was to carry out his orders.

As Cdr. Ryan understood his orders, he was to wait by the carrier until she sank, unless Japanese forces threatened to capture her. Ryan was feeling a lot of pressure to sink *Wasp* because many of the more than 400 oil-soaked survivors on board *Lansdowne* were dying.

Also, the light was fading. If they were going to fire a torpedo with the new magnetic head, they wanted to be able to see it. Ryan waited until last light before finally ordering up a torpedo with a magnetic head. It was set it to run at 30 feet. *Wasp* was 1,500 yards away.

The torpedo was fired at 1908. It was the first live torpedo *Lansdowne* had fired. It ran hot and straight. "I saw it go straight under the *Wasp*," Andrews remembered. "It was too deep."

Up on the bridgewing, Cdr. Ryan went into conference with Cdr. Dickey and LCdr. Smedberg. They decided not to expend the other magnetic-exploder head. They ordered up a torpedo with the conventional impact head and set it to run 5 feet shallower, at 25 feet. Not taking any chances, Smedberg brought *Lansdowne* in a few hundred yards closer.

The second torpedo ran straight, and it hit the starboard side of *Wasp* just forward of the island. There was an explosion deep inside the carrier but to no apparent effect. They waited for a few minutes for something to happen. Then Ryan went back into conference on *Lansdowne*'s bridge.

Another conventional impact-type head was set to run another 5 feet shallower, at 20 feet. It ran hot and straight, and it appeared to enter the carrier amidships, but there was no explosion, no sound at all.

Darkness was coming on fast. They prepared another torpedo with an impact-type head. Smedberg brought *Lansdowne* in closer still, inside 1,000 yards. The torpedo was set to run 5 feet shallower again, at 15 feet.

The fourth torpedo ran straight. It hit the carrier amidships. There was a big explosion, and the carrier's list increased, but not enough.

Their last remaining torpedo had a magnetic head. Not trusting it to detonate magnetically, they set it to explode on impact. It was set to run at 10 feet. Smedberg brought *Lansdowne* around to the port side of the carrier for luck and another 100 yards closer, inside 900 yards.

At 2011, the fifth torpedo was fired. It hit *Wasp* amidships. It exploded, and the carrier was immediately engulfed in flames. It was dark, but they could see the smoke cloud rising. At 2027, Capt. Hoover's voice came on the TBS ordering them to catch up. Cdr. Ryan stalled a while longer because Cdr. Dickey wanted to see his ship go down. Nervous that they might be silhouetting themselves against the burning carrier, LCdr. Smedberg started zigzagging.

Wasp went down by the bow at about 2100. *Lansdowne* headed southeast at full speed.

When the TF.18 ships secured from general quarters, men were allowed to return to their quarters finally. Many found their bunks occupied by injured survivors. On *Duncan*, Seaman Ham found two men in his bunk. Machinist's Mate Bethune found two in his, both covered in oil. Wharton found three survivors sharing the two bunks in his stateroom, and all three were friends who he did not even know were in the Navy. "It was getting to be a small world out there," Wharton remembered.

Cdr. Hogan, Lt.(jg) Broccolo, and *Duncan*'s medical crew worked through the night and only got to the most seriously injured. The cooks were equally overwhelmed. Supplied to feed 240 men three times a day, they were feeding almost a thousand men twenty-four hours a day. "Beans, bread, and coffee -- they could get that together," Fire Controlman Albert Viering remembered. For the next day and a half that was all they ate.

Duncan's sonar picked up a contact. It was presumed to be a sub, but Taylor did not even try evasive tactics. He was more afraid of capsizing. After that, word came down to dump the bodies that were stacked on deck. Boatswain's Mate John Vandonkelaar remembered burying twenty-seven *Wasp* dead at sea. "We just dumped them over the side," Vandonkelaar remembered. "We were in danger of sinking."

TF.18 arrived off Espíritu Santo the following afternoon. Pallikula Bay was "Base BUTTON," the U.S. Navy's advance supply base for the Guadalcanal campaign. The task force steamed in slowly like a funeral cortège.

The anchorage off the main town, Luganville, was crowded with warships, but no cheers welcomed them. "Usually if a ship was sunk out there we didn't hear about it until a month later," Wharton remembered. On ships in the harbor, bewildered sailors jammed lifelines, staring, silent.

As *Duncan* was pulling alongside *Helena*, excited survivors shifted to the port side. *Duncan* listed precipitously. Bryan screamed a blue streak over the PA until he got the survivors redistributed and the ship righted enough that they could tie up.

For more than an hour and a half, the survivors transferred to *Helena*. The remaining dead (two chiefs) and the severely wounded (two officers and sixteen enlisted men) were transferred to Advanced Base Hospital. Ten officers were transferred to *Salt Lake City* by gig. *Duncan* had rescued so many *Wasp* survivors they had not been able to count them until they filed off. The final tally: 719 survivors and two dead.

Duncan was anchoring in Pallikula Bay when *Lansdowne* steamed in with *Duncan*'s whaleboat bobbing in her wake.

Every *Duncan* man was proud that his ship had rescued so many. They were proud of themselves and of their captain. They knew that the vast majority of survivors had come aboard while they were stopped dead in the water. They all recognized it was a radical move. At the time, Weatherup thought Taylor was courageous for stopping and stalling through a torpedo scare, but, for years after, he would be haunted by dark thoughts of What if ..? "We could easily have wound up with all of us in the water," he remembered. Then stopping would have looked reckless and foolhardy, and Taylor's Navy career would have ended there. That they did not happen to get torpedoed -- did that justify the captain's gamble? Captains of other ships in the harbor seemed to think so. A lot of them sent Taylor messages of congratulations.

But *Duncan* men were acutely aware they had gotten away with something. Men serving in war zones inevitably at some point start quietly calculating their odds. It was from this event that many *Duncan* men began to feel that maybe their time was running out.

Chapter 4

100 FATHOM CURVE
September 16-October 9

But the principal failing occurred in the sailing,
And the Bellman, perplexed and distressed,
Said he had hoped, at least, when the wind blew due East,
That the ship would not travel due West!

- Lewis Carroll

The loss of *Wasp* was a terrible blow to the U.S. Navy,
which was only just getting around to disclosing the sinking of
Yorktown three months earlier. *Hornet* was now the only U.S.
carrier in the SoPac area.

There is never a shortage of opinions in the U.S. Navy,
especially regarding who to blame. Many in the task force
blamed R/Adm. Norman Scott, who had commanded the screen.

Adms. King and Nimitz took three lessons from the string
of disasters: areas of carrier task force operations should be
changed radically and frequently; task force speeds should be
faster in waters known to contain enemy subs; and a carrier
handling aircraft should not maintain a steady course for long
periods. Nimitz added a tactical suggestion: in the event of a
torpedo attack on a carrier, screening destroyers should drop
depth charges and planes should drop bombs to try to make the
torpedoes run erratically.

Within the task group, other ideas were floated: destroyers
should carry more cargo nets; warships should organize teams
of their best swimmers; ships needed more medicine, especially
burn medicine. Everyone suddenly was very aware that they
were just beginning to learn this business of war.

* * *

The *Wasp* survivors left *Duncan* a mess with oil everywhere.
Navy men are meticulous about their bunks and lockers, and
they pride themselves on always being ready to stand inspection.
Some *Duncan* men felt violated. "What really hurt is they
robbed us," DeLucca remembered. "They stole all my money,
my clothes, my shoes."

Duncan was out of food, except for some flour that was full
of weevils. Breakfast was a bowl of lukewarm brown lima beans
and a cup of black coffee. A U.S. cruiser sent over a case of
canned orange juice. An Australian ship sent over mutton. "You
get a piece of that in your mouth and start chewing," Edwards
remembered, "and it has a tendency to swell, and the more you
chew the bigger it gets."

Lt. Bryan sent parties to the beach to scavenge for fruit. They
were told to bring back whatever looked edible.

"Espíritu, oh, jeez," Bethune remembered. "It was hot
and humid. We were warned about cannibals." The cannibal
warning made an impression. Men in scavenging parties were
leery about getting too far from the beach.

Lt.(jg) Weatherup received orders to transfer to *Farenholt* as
the new DesRon 12 staff communications officer. *Farenholt's*
gig came over in the evening and picked him up.

Lt.(jg) Beebe became *Duncan's* communications officer
with Ens. Lane as his assistant. Beebe was the only reserve
officer to head a department on *Duncan*.

In the morning, the TF.18 ships departed in two groups. Half
headed south escorting a convoy to New Caledonia, and half
went southwest to rendezvous with the *Hornet*. The wholesale
juggling of ships was the rule in SoPac.

At breakfast in *Duncan's* wardroom, Ens. Fowler was in the
hot seat. A case of orange juice had been pilfered overnight
while he was OOD. The junior officers searched the ship. Not
one can was ever recovered.

Shortly after noon, lookouts spotted a periscope, and sonar
located a "poor sound contact." Lookouts kept their eyes on the

spot in the ocean where they last saw the periscope whileTaylor maneuvered the ship into position to attack. Fowler ordered up eight depth charges -- five 300-pound charges to be fired from the starboard-side K-guns and three 600-pound charges to be rolled off the stern.

The introduction of sonar had changed anti-submarine warfare tactics -- from random patterns to saturation barrages on small areas. Still, there was a lot of guesswork. Sonar contact broke off 100-150 yards away when the sub passed under the sound beam. They had to guess when they were over it and how deep it was. They would set the cans for a range of depths and often toss over a dozen or more. 600-pounders were believed to be lethal within 35 feet of a sub, 300-pounders within 21 feet. The goal in anti-submarine warfare was cumulative damage. That required repeated attacks. The other approach was to keep the sub under until its batteries ran dry and it was forced to surface. This took time and patience, and destroyer captains had neither. *Duncan* dropped eight depth charges and steamed away, because she was more urgently needed elsewhere.

That evening, southeast of Nouméa, TF.18 rendezvoused with TF.17, and TF.61, SoPac's striking force, was reborn with twenty-three ships: carrier *Hornet*, new battleship *Washington*, oiler *Cimarron*, and twenty ships in the screen. Ens. Lane's father-in-law, R/Adm. Noyes, assumed overall command.

The draining loss of capital ships had V/Adm. Ghormley on the defensive again. His growing concern was for the safety of *Hornet* and *Washington*, SoPac's remaining carrier and battleship. Until *Enterprise*'s return, which was expected to be at least a few weeks, the situation was going to be dicey for *Hornet*. Ghormley finally directed R/Adm. Murray to take the carrier into port at New Caledonia.

On September 23, Capt. Hoover, Commander Destroyer Squadron 12, was named captain of the cruiser *Helena*. He transferred from *Farenholt* to *Helena* while they were underway to Nouméa. His replacement as ComDesRon12 was Capt. Robert Tobin, who was aboard *Farenholt*.

New Caledonia [now Vanuatu] consists of one very large

island and half a dozen very small islands and reefs. The cigar-shaped main island is called Grande Terre, and it is the sixth largest island in the South Pacific. At the western end is the largest town in the islands, Nouméa. Off Nouméa is Great Roads Harbor, which is not much of a harbor, but it is inside a large cove that is protected by the second largest barrier reef in the world. Great Roads Harbor was the U.S. Navy's advance base ("WHITE POPPY").

Once *Hornet* was safely inside the reef, the TF.18 units turned and steamed 250 miles north to the New Hebrides.

The New Hebrides is a chain of volcanic islands five hundred miles west of Fiji. Espíritu Santo is the largest island in the chain.

Lansdowne and *Duncan* moored in Pallikula Bay at Espíritu Santo in the shadow of a towering volcano. *Duncan* was ordered to transfer all but a few thousand gallons of fuel to *Lansdowne*, so they all knew they were going to be here a while.

*   *   *

With the loss of *Wasp*, a stalemate developed around Guadalcanal. To break the stalemate, the Allies were going to have to stop the Japanese supply runs, which meant gaining control of the sea. What this meant was that U.S. ships were going to have to go out and meet Japanese ships at night.

To this end, on September 7, V/Adm. Ghormley created a new cruiser-destroyer force -- Task Group 64.3, "Screening and Attack Force." R/Adm. Norman Scott, who most recently commanded the *Wasp* screen, was named to command.

R/Adm. Scott was Academy, class of 1911. He had mostly served on destroyers. He was decorated for valor in World War I after a German submarine sank his destroyer. Mostly recently, he was on the staff of the Chief of Naval Operations. Adm. King had promoted him to temporary rear admiral and dispatched him to the Pacific to command a task force. Scott was considered a tough commander, and, as an old surface fleet man, he was trusted.

On paper, R/Adm. Scott's command consisted of six cruisers, plus the eight destroyers of Destroyer Squadron 12. But the reality in SoPac was that ships were in such short supply that V/Adm. Ghormley was forever snatching one here to fill a gap there. In the case of Scott's new group, one cruiser and three destroyers were immediately detached, and, within two weeks, all the destroyers were stripped away. Since cruisers were never risked out of harbor without an escort of destroyers, the cruisers could go nowhere.

What occasioned Ghormley's wholesale raid on Scott's destroyers was a September 21 message from Nimitz: "HAVE REASON TO BELIEVE ENEMY MAY MOVE INTO ELICE (sic) ISLANDS ABOUT OCTOBER FIRST WITH WEAKLY ESCORTED FORCES SIMILAR TO HIS GILBERT OPERATIONS. ULTRA. CONSIDER FUNAFUTI SHOULD BE DENIED IMMEDIATELY BY MARINE FORCE FROM SAMOA."

Funafuti Atoll is in the Ellice Islands 900 miles east of Espíritu Santo. Ghormley had been fretting about his right flank so he was quick to respond. His Funafuti landing plan was on Nimitz's desk in twelve hours.

Duncan remained moored in Pallikula Bay. Each of the ship's three watches had distinct duties while in harbor. One was always at GQ. Men on deck watches made fishing poles and hung lines over the side while on watch. The "section watch" performed regular ship cleaning. The third watch, in lieu of liberty, went ashore in scavenging parties in search of food. They would take the whaleboat up the Sarakata River and return with mangos, breadfruit, wild oranges, papaya, red bananas. Fruit was hanging all over the ship. A stream of orange peels floated down the bay.

Lt. Bryan ordered swimming parties a few times a day to keep up morale. The currents are treacherous in Pallikula Bay, but Torpedoman Watson was timed swimming the crawl, and he was only a few seconds off the Olympic record. The gig rescued more than a few men who got caught in the current. A sailor on another destroyer had the first swim fins anybody had seen, and he used them to rescue a man who fell overboard.

The Funafuti landing force units at Espíritu Santo got underway early on September 28. *Lansdowne* (with Cdr. Ryan aboard) and *Duncan* swept the channel entrance. When *Minneapolis* emerged, the three warships zigzagged southeast at 18 knots. In Selwyn Strait, *Lansdowne* sighted a periscope. *Duncan* maneuvered to screen *Minneapolis* while *Lansdowne* dropped depth charges. *Minneapolis* launched a scout plane to Espíritu Santo to report the sub.

At dawn on the 30th, south of Fiji, they were joined by fast transport *USS Crescent City* which was transporting two companies of U.S. Marines from Samoa, screened by *Buchanan* and *Laffey*. Only one unit was missing -- auxiliary sub tender *Ballard*, which was carrying aviation supplies from Pearl.

That evening in the Tonga group near Hoorn Island, they rendezvoused with the Funafuti landing force units from New Caledonia. R/Adm. Wright ordered a northeasterly base course, "thence to occupy Funafuti in accordance with CTF.62 Op.Plan A16-42."[1]

On *Duncan*, Fire Controlman Sobelman started a rumor. He claimed he heard officers talking and that they were on a special mission and it was not certain they would return. That night when the ship went to GQ with the PA calling, "ALL HANDS TO GENERAL QUARTERS," they made it faster than ever. "I come up on deck, and it's raining, moon's out," Fischer remembered, "and I see these two big searchlights on the horizon. I said to myself, Oh boy, this is it. But it was a moonbow. Instead of a rainbow, it's a moonbow. They have them in the South Pacific." Bryan complimented the men on their speed in getting to GQ. Sobelman thought he deserved the credit.

October 1 was "Dog minus 1" for the Funafuti operation. At noon, the landing force was 250 miles south-southwest of Funafuti.

That day, an AlNav dispatch promoted all the VF-5 ensigns to lieutenants (junior grade). On *Duncan*, Fowler, Rhodes, and Smyth were promoted.

The Ellice (Lagoon) Islands -- nine low-lying islands, mostly tiny coral atolls -- are located at the point where the International Date Line crosses the equator.

They approached from the southwest at dawn on October 2. They could see the reef around Funafuti. The island was densely covered in coconut palms and screw pines, but it is so low and narrow they could see through to the other side. It was hard to believe it was worth occupying, much less that it had once been a British colony.

Minneapolis launched two planes to patrol and search. The Transportation Group and Inner Screen destroyers entered the lagoon. They discovered the missing *Ballard* anchored in the lagoon off-loading equipment. *Crescent City*, *Heywood*, and *Libra* started unloading. All day, the three Inner Screen destroyers conducted anti-submarine patrols in the lagoon.

Unloading continued throughout the night and into the next afternoon. On the evening of the 3rd, V/Adm. Ghormley trumpeted the news: "SOPAC OPERATIONS -- FUNAFUTI OCCUPATION COMPLETED."

On the morning of the 4th, R/Adm. Wright dissolved the Funafuti task group. The transports returned to New Caledonia, escorted by *Lansdowne* and *Lardner*. Cruisers *Minneapolis* and *Chester* headed to the New Hebrides, escorted by *Farenholt*, *Duncan*, *Buchanan*, and *Laffey*.

Two days later when *Minneapolis* and *Chester* and their four escorts arrived back in Pallikula Bay, the anchorage was crowded. Thirty-seven U.S. warships and one New Zealand warship were anchored. Everybody knew something was brewing.

*   *   *

In his most recent reconfiguration of SoPac, V/Adm. Ghormley had designated three main units: R/Adm. George Murray's TG.64.1 built around *Hornet*; R/Adm. Willis Lee's TG.64.2 built around *Washington*; and R/Adm. Scott's TG.64.3, the new cruiser-destroyer screening and attack force.

REAR ADMIRAL NORMAN SCOTT
COMMANDER, TASK FORCE 18
and, later, COMMANDER, TASK GROUP 64.3

In the month that he had been in command of the new group, R/Adm. Scott had been riding at anchor aboard *San Francisco* in Pallikula Bay awaiting the return of his destroyers. On the day *Farenholt*, *Laffey*, *Duncan*, and *Buchanan* returned, Scott finally had almost all his task force in one place. Only *McCalla*, the long-missing unit of DesDiv24, was still missing. But then Scott only had them for that brief moment. That same day, V/Adm. Ghormley directed him to designate one cruiser and one destroyer for escort duty. Scott appointed *Helena* and *Duncan*.

That evening, Lt.(jg) Wharton went ashore for a beer. He was waiting for the boat back to the ship when Lt. Bryan joined him on the dock. Wharton had always thought of Bryan as a lonely man, and that night he seemed lonelier than ever. He even struck up a conversation. "We were contemporaries," Wharton remembered. "He was Academy '32, I was Harvard '32. Sometimes when he was low he looked to me as a friend, even though I was reserve. We were looking across the harbor which was full of ships, and he turned to me and said, 'Why do you think I'm so unpopular?' Well, there was an opening, but I didn't know how far to put my neck out. I was always intimidated by him. I didn't want shore duty for the duration. So I didn't tell him the truth. I said something like, 'We had a different education. We don't see eye to eye. Never will.' My proper answer should've been, 'Well, you guys in the Academy aren't taught leadership by being leaders, by setting an example. You're taught leadership by fear of being demoted.' Apparently, the beers in him were making him feel warm toward me because he told me I ought to stay in when the war's over. He said I could probably make captain. At least I didn't laugh. But I always regretted what I said. 'When this goddamn war's over,' I said, 'I'm going back to the stock exchange and make a pile of dough.' He was silent after that."

A flag on *San Francisco*'s signal yard summoning the TG.64.3 skippers and execs delayed *Helena* and *Duncan*'s departure. The officers all made their way across the harbor in their ships' gigs.

R/Adm. Scott met with them on *San Francisco*'s flag bridge. Scott was fifty-three. He was a small, gaunt man. "We're going to raid the Japanese transports" was his opening line. He added, "Our primary mission is to avenge Savo." He introduced Capt. Charles "Soc" McMorris, his second in command. McMorris was the captain of the *San Francisco*. Scott did not say so, but he had selected McMorris as his second because McMorris was the second highest ranked officer in the group. Never mind that they were both on the same ship. Scott was too freshly-minted to challenge protocol.

Scott had four cruisers in his group -- two old heavy cruisers, *San Francisco* and *Salt Lake City*, and two new light cruisers, *Boise* and *Helena*. The determining factor between heavy and light was not displacement but guns. The older heavy cruisers had 8-inch guns, so nominally they were more powerful than the new light cruisers which had 6-inch guns. However, the heavy cruisers' bigger guns needed long intervals between reloads, and the light cruisers' smaller guns could fire more than thirty rounds a minute and were mounted in five triple-turrets.

War-gaming at Newport had proved the concept of "concentration of force" -- the admiral with the most guns wins. Scott's group with only four cruisers was not large enough to engage a Japanese covering force, but with nine warships and nineteen 8-inch guns, thirty 6-inch guns, fifty-two 5-inch guns, and twenty-five torpedoes they had more than enough firepower to damage transports.

There was one other distinction between the heavy and light cruisers in Scott's force. The older heavy cruisers were still outfitted with the older SC (surface-search) radar and "pip-and-grass" scopes, and the new light cruisers had SG, the new centimetric radar, and the new round sweep scopes called Planned Position Indicators (PPIs) that were much easier to read.

SG radar was just being be fitted in ships. *Boise* and *Helena* had SG because both had recently been overhauled -- *Helena* after being bombed in the first two minutes at Pearl Harbor in December, and *Boise* after running aground near Java in February. SG radar was so new -- and so secret -- even admirals had restricted opportunity to develop an appreciation for its effectiveness.

R/Adm. Scott put little stock in electronics; he did not trust radio any more than he trusted radar. Capt. Hoover, who had recently served a tour at BuOrd, tried to inform Scott of the huge breakthrough the new SG radar represented, but Scott showed little interest. Radar would not be a factor in his decision-making.

Determinedly ignorant of the new technology, Scott chose to continue to fly his flag in heavy cruiser *San Francisco*. She had been his flagship when he departed Pearl in July. *San Francisco* had a special allure for task force commanders because she had the most comfortable admiral's stateroom of any warship in the U.S. Navy, having been refurbished for the one night President Roosevelt spent aboard.

So far in night battles, eight Allied cruisers and three Allied destroyers had been lost without a single Japanese warship sunk. The new reality facing the U.S. Navy was that the Imperial Navy excelled in night maneuvers. Scott was painfully aware of this from personal experience. During the battle off Savo on August 9-10, he was 30 miles away on the cruiser *San Juan* covering the eastern approach to the sound.

Scott's main mission as he saw it was to develop a night surface-action doctrine for a cruiser-destroyer force. His biggest worry was being thrown into battle before his ships had time to operate together. He knew he needed a simple battle plan. The less practice they got the more elementary the plan would need to be.

Scott's battle plan may have been intentionally rudimentary, but it was also uninspired. Basically, it was to steam to the western end of Guadalcanal under cover of darkness and trap Japanese transports against the beach and demolish them with superior firepower.

The operation depended on surprise, so it was crucial to Scott that they not to do anything to give themselves away. He had a list of precautions: communications silence would be maintained; TBS radio was to be used only to report enemy contact; blinker tubes were to be dimmed and only blue or red lights used; the two older cruisers, *San Francisco* and *Salt Lake City*, were to turn off their old SC radars during final approach (because intelligence credited the Japanese with having receivers capable of picking up radio transmissions on the SC radar frequency).

Keeping the TBS channels clear was especially important to Scott because, on *San Francisco,* the flag bridge and pilothouse shared a radio circuit and when one was transmitting the other could not hear. This complicated the flow of orders. As a temporary solution, an off-the-shelf, inter-office squawk box had been rigged between flag bridge and pilothouse, and a flag radioman repeated all the Admiral's transmissions for the pilothouse.

As a newly-minted rear admiral commanding his first task group, Scott tried to do everything by the book. Ships were to be in single file when they met the enemy because war games had indicated that the traditional line-ahead formation was still best for bringing the most broadsides to bear. The tactical goal of the line-ahead formation was to flank the enemy's line, or "cross the T." This brought all the broadside guns on one side of the fleet to bear on the enemy while blanking all but his forward guns. Ideally, this was to be achieved at a range of less than one mile because beyond that gunnery effectiveness dropped off precipitously. Crossing the T was the tactical holy grail, but nobody was ever expected to achieve it; in fact, war games had more or less indicated it was an impossibility, that battles would commence at somewhere between 4,000 and 2,000 yards as the two fleets were closing and that shellfire would slow both fleets well before either crossed the other's T.

With advances in communications between ships (assuming electronic equipment did not break down), it was now possible for an admiral to control a fleet. For Scott, who did not trust electronics, having ships in column (where everybody knew where everybody else was) facilitated identification and signaling. Intent on avoiding "friendly fire," he repeatedly stressed maintaining formation and staying closed up. He did not want to risk the inevitable confusion of simultaneous turns at night, so he said he would only be calling for column turns. Column turns could be carried out even if some ships failed to get the word.

The code word to form up for battle was "DOUBLEHEADER." Upon hearing that, they were to fall into column.

The four cruisers, which Scott saw as his strong suit, would be the center core of the column, steaming 600 yards apart. Three destroyers would be in the vanguard and two at the rear, 500 yards apart.

Scott assumed the three van destroyers would run into the enemy first. They were to open fire the moment they spotted a Japanese ship, firing torpedoes at larger targets and guns at smaller targets. Then they were to illuminate the target with starshells and searchlights so the cruisers could neutralize them their bigger guns. Scott warned the van destroyer captains not to get silhouetted against burning ships.

The cruisers were to open fire, also without orders, the

moment they spotted a target. Against smaller ships, the two older heavy cruisers were to use continuous fire rather than full salvos (which were always followed by long intervals during reloads).

Scott was hunting transports, so he was expecting to meet a lot of destroyers. That meant they could expect a lot of torpedoes. Linear gun-line tactics, like line-ahead formation, invited disaster from torpedoes. Scott reminded them (as if they needed reminding) that the Japanese were better trained in night tactics. He warned them about one Japanese tactic -- illuminating and firing. If illuminated, they were to immediately counter-illuminate and open fire.

Scott was most concerned that they not repeat any of the more obvious mistakes of Savo. Mainly, he did not want to get caught by surprise again. He said he would call for general quarters shortly after sundown. He did not want any floatplanes on board the cruisers during the battle. At Savo, planes became infernos on cruiser decks.

While the task group was steaming toward Guadalcanal, cruiser planes were to scout ahead and to the west and then land on Tulagi. The last four planes, which would be launched shortly before the engagement, were tasked with locating and illuminating the Japanese ships.

Any task group ships compelled to fall out of formation were to do so on the disengaged side and not to try to rejoin the formation before giving their approach bearing, voice code, and receiving permission. Ships unable to make 15 knots were to either proceed to Tulagi or rendezvous with the task group the next morning at "Point C" off San Cristobal.

The task group's codename was "SUGAR." Each ship was assigned a code name. *Duncan*'s was "AMERICAN DESTROYER." Also, each ship was assigned a sector their surface-search and fire-control radars were to scan during the approach.

Like almost everything in the Navy, column order for the destroyers was decided by the ranking of their commanders. Two of the captains were Academy class of '24, three were '25, and one was '26. The two ranking captains were LCdr. Wilson of *Buchanan* and LCdr. Seaward of *Farenholt*. *Farenholt* had Capt. Tobin aboard, so she would be in the van. *Buchanan* would take station astern *Helena* at the rear. LCdr. Taylor, 63rd in his class of '25, ranked next, so *Duncan* was to follow *Farenholt*. LCdr. Hank, 301st in the class of '25, ranked next, so *Laffey* was to follow *Duncan*. *McCalla* (due to arrive with a convoy from San Diego next day) would follow *Buchanan* at the rear because *McCalla*'s captain, LCdr. William Cooper, class of '26, was the junior skipper in the group.

After Scott and his staff concluded their briefing, the destroyer captains and execs moved to an adjoining cabin, where they met with Capt. Robert Tobin, ComDesRon 12. As soon as the hatch was closed, they all started bitching about the two-destroyers-astern formation. They considered it defensive. Destroyermen thought of destroyers as offensive weapons. They all thought the five destroyers should all be in the van. Capt. Tobin probably agreed with them, but, twelve days into his new command, he was not about to question Scott's wisdom.

Capt. Robert Tobin, Academy class of 1917, was forty-eight years old. He had a distinguished air about him. He had served on destroyers for years and had taught physics at the Academy. He had a shock of white hair. It had gained him the nickname "The Silver Knight."

Capt. Tobin had his own set of orders for the destroyers. Taylor and Hank, who were commanding the other two van destroyers, were to follow whatever the ship ahead did. Scott warned them to be alert for turn signals by TBS or blinker and to be prepared for surprise maneuvers.

It was almost noon when Taylor and Bryan returned aboard *Duncan*. The ship quickly got underway. *Duncan* was sweeping the channel entrance when *Helena* emerged. The two warships soon steadied on a westerly course.

Their orders were to rendezvous with an auxiliary carrier the next day at 1300 at "E. latitude 1800 South, longitude 162 East," which was twenty miles north of the eastern tip of San Cristobal. They would be escorting the carrier to a designated fly-off point near Guadalcanal and then back to the rendezvous point off San Cristobal. The fly-off, which was designated Task Group 63.8, was under the command of Capt. Hoover.

CAPTAIN GILBERT HOOVER COMMANDER,
DESTROYER SQUADRON 12 and, later,
CAPTAIN, U.S.S. HELENA

The sea so shimmered with moonlight that night that it looked silver. *Duncan* reported a sound contact, and *Helena* executed an emergency 90° right turn and increased speed.

They were approaching the rendezvous point the next afternoon when they sighted auxiliary carrier *Copahee* and two destroyers approaching from the south.

Copahee was a recently-commissioned carrier of the new *Bogue*-class. At 494 feet (barely 100 feet longer than *Duncan*), her flight deck was only 442 feet. Carriers of this class were used as airplane transports.

More exciting for *Helena* and *Duncan* men were the two destroyers, *Fletcher* (DD-445) and *O'Bannon* (DD-450). Both were the new 2100-ton *Fletcher*-class, which were completely different. They were "flush-deckers." They had no raised fo'csle decks forward, and they were longer and heavier than

Livermores and had stronger hulls. They carried five 5-inch guns, two quintuple-tube torpedo mounts, and they bristled with 20mms. Instead of a searchlight on the after deckhouse, they had a twin 40mm. And they had SG, the new surface-search radar.

Fletcher and *O'Bannon* were the first of these new destroyers to reach the Pacific. Until this moment, the U.S. Navy's efforts in the Pacific had been carried out entirely by the three groups of men who were already in the service when Pearl Harbor was attacked -- career enlisted men, Academy graduates, and upper-class, east-coast types motivated by their commitment to the struggle in Europe. Now, warships were joining the fleet with crews that were comprised of men who had enlisted for no other reason than that their country was attacked and was suddenly at war. *Fletcher* and *O'Bannon* had junior officers who were not even commissioned when Pearl Harbor was attacked. The arrival of these ships and men represented a clear ratcheting up of the American war machine. They were a welcome sign to men on *Helena* and *Duncan* that real help was on the way.

The designated fly-off point was only fifty miles to the northwest, and they were not scheduled to arrive there until noon the next day. So they spent much of the next 24 hours steaming in circles. That evening, *Duncan* came alongside *Helena* and picked up guard mail, which included Capt. Hoover's fly-off orders.

Duncan delivered the mail to the other ships. As she was pulling alongside *Fletcher*, an eruption of shouts broke out between the two ships as men spotted old friends. *Fletcher* was under construction at Federal when *Duncan* was there, and many of the men had come to know one another. In the dark in the middle of the ocean, they shouted gossip and scuttlebutt and lies back and forth.

Fowler and Beebe had a mutual friend in *Fletcher*'s communications officer, Lt.(jg) Walter Sullivan, who had been in Beebe's class at Yale and was once a beau of Fowler's wife. [Walter Sullivan will be The New York Times science reporter for most of the next 50 years.] Fowler shouted to him proudly that Pat was pregnant. They were all still shouting when the ships parted.

Fowler went straight down to his stateroom and wrote to Pat. "My Darling Angel," he began.

> Just a hurried line to tell you that I still am OK, alive + kicking - kicking like Hell in fact at the lousy damned life on this crate ... We have just met up with that feller Sullivan's ship - suddenly hove into sight so to speak. It's getting quite sociable around here - no time for society but the atmosphere is correct.

By morning, the little three-ship task group was steaming northwest in Indispensable Strait between the islands of Malaita and San Cristobal. Aboard *Duncan*, there was even more tension than usual because Lt. Bryan and Lt. Hauck were both in foul moods. Hauck was angry because a shell was jammed in the breech block of #2 gun, and he had been up all night with Chief Gunner's Mate Duckworth and the ordnance men, the experts, trying to dislodge it. Bryan was on a roaring tear, screaming at junior officers who had failed to turn in their Title B chits. This was the paperwork that, when filled out, confirmed that the Title B items the officer was responsible for had been audited by him. Junior officers regarded the chits as paper-shuffling and liked to think they had more pressing duties.

Capt. Hoover's orders were to complete the fly-off in time for the planes to arrive at Henderson Field on Guadalcanal before dusk. In the distance to the northwest, they could see the jungle on the eastern tip of Guadalcanal.

They arrived at the fly-off point at about 1230. Just as *Copahee* was ready to fly off the first plane, *Duncan* made a sound contact at 3,000 yards. *Copahee* changed course sharply, while *Duncan* charged at the contact at full speed and promptly lost it. She slowed to try to regain it, then began running a search pattern. Capt. Hoover waited about ten minutes before ordering the fly-off to resume. As soon as *Copahee* swung back into the wind, the first F4Fs of VMF-121 lifted off. [Squadron exec, Capt. Joseph Foss, would soon be the highest-scoring Henderson-based pilot.] It took an hour to fly off nineteen fighters.

The convoy ended officially that evening off the eastern tip of San Cristobal. *Copahee* and the two new *Fletcher* destroyers headed south toward New Caledonia.

Helena and *Duncan* turned back west toward the Solomons.

THE LAST PHOTOGRAPH OF U.S.S DUNCAN TAKEN FROM
U.S.S. COPAHEE, OCTOBER 8, 1942,
FOUR DAYS BEFORE THE BATTLE.

Chapter 5

NO MAN'S LAND
October 10-11

All nature is but art, unknown to thee;
All chance, direction, which thou canst not see;
All discord, harmony, not understood;
All partial evil, universal good;
And spite of pride, in erring reason's spite,
One truth is clear, Whatever is, is right.

—Alexander Pope

Early on October 10, *Helena* and *Duncan* arrived at Point C, which was 65 miles south of the eastern-tip of San Cristobal. The sky was overcast and sporadic rain made visibility impossible, but, on radar, the ocean was full of ships to the south and east. Three U.S. Navy tasks groups were in the area—twenty-seven warships in all.

Late in the morning, the sun burned through, and everywhere around the horizon warships appeared—units of R/Adm. Noyes's TG.64.1 and R/Adm. Lee's TG.64.2. R/Adm. Scott's TG.64.3 was soon steaming in from the west, *Farenholt* in the van.

San Francisco, Scott's flagship, was blinkering to *Hornet* and *Washington.* Scott was proposing to Noyes and Lee a change of plan for the disposition of his cruiser-destroyer group during the landing in three days of the 164th Infantry on Guadalcanal. Ghormley's plan called for three task groups to be covering the beach: *Washington* from 100 miles east; *Hornet* from 180 miles south; and Scott's group from 20 miles west near Savo Island. But Scott saw his group's primary task as sinking Japanese transports, and a key element of his battle plan was to be long gone from the Guadalcanal area before daylight when a Japanese air attack could be expected. They had no indication that the Japanese intended to interfere with the landing, so Scott thought he should not have to interrupt his group's operations.

Semaphores waved, blinkers flashed, flags moved up and down masts as the three admirals debated it. The change was drastic because it meant the west and the north, the two directions from which the Japanese were most likely to come, would be covered only by air. Scott argued that the Japanese would not dare send down warships in daylight. Noyes and Lee agreed, and, in the end, they endorsed Scott's plan. Admirals of equal rank generally endorse one another's plans. For Scott, it meant he would not be supporting the landing at all.

After about fifteen minutes, the discussion wrapped up, and the three task groups steamed off in different directions: *Washington* with two light cruisers and five destroyers headed east; *Hornet* with four light cruisers and five destroyers headed due south; and Scott's four cruisers and five destroyers headed southwest.

Helena and *Duncan* fell in with Scott's group, which now finally included the *McCalla*. *Helena* and *Duncan* had been away three days. The task group had taken so long getting to Point C they missed a crack at a Japanese supply run the night before (October 9-10). They raced north, but, receiving no word of Japanese ships approaching, turned back. So *Helena* and *Duncan* had not missed much.

Everyone in Scott's group sensed the importance of the operation. They all knew it had to be big because there was an Associated Press correspondent on *San Francisco*.

Duncan picked up the guard mail from *Helena*. In the mail was a memorandum from Scott entitled "Memorandum for Task Group Sixty-Four Point Two." Which was odd because Scott's group was 64.3. 64.2 was R/Adm. Lee's group. Presumably, a typo. Or, perhaps, a purposeful error, part of a disinformation effort aimed at hiding battleship *Washington*.

The memorandum was a list of battle instructions reiterating what Scott had already told the commanders and execs: The task group would make daily 450-mile loops between three points in the ocean. Departing each morning from Point C, 65 miles south of San Cristobal Island, they would head west-southwest in the general direction of Indispensable Reefs, dropping south one mile for every mile they advanced west to keep outside air reconnaissance range. At noon, after each cruiser had launched a scout plane, the task group would turn northwest toward Point A. They would pass east of Rennell and Bellona Islands. Point A was 100 miles south of the southwestern tip of Guadalcanal. They were to arrive there at 1600, and the four planes launched at noon would rendezvous with them there. Then, as the sun set, they would start north. Point B was 27 miles south of the southwestern tip of Guadalcanal (and 100 miles from the landing beaches on the northwest coast). They were to pass Point B at 1900. If they still had no word of Japanese ships approaching, they would abort and return to Point C south of San Cristobal. The next morning they would set out again. This was to be their daily routine until they finally met the enemy.

As Task Group 64.3 steamed west-southwest toward Indispensable Reefs that morning, it was 86° and the trades were easterly. The ships were in "arrowhead" formation (five destroyers in a semi-circle 4,000 yards ahead of the cruiser column).

At noon, they slowed while each cruiser launched a plane. Then they resumed speed and turned northwest toward Point A.

Two and a half hours later, they were passing 20 miles east of Rennell Island. Ninety minutes after that, at 1600, they were at Point A. The four floatplanes launched at noon were circling. As the convoy slowed, each plane landed in its cruiser's wake. Once the planes were recovered, the task group started north again, zigzagging into evening. Radiomen hung on their sets for reports of Japanese ships.

With sunset, at 1815, a surge of anxious exhilaration swept over the crews. As the ships pressed north, rumors increased. There was no word of Japanese ships, but they steamed by Point B at 1900 and continued north. Rounding Cape Hunter, the southwestern tip of Guadalcanal, they steamed up the west coast for ninety minutes. At 2200 when Scott finally ordered them around, they were only 60 miles from Cape Esperance.

The general feeling was more disappointment than relief. After the tension of steaming north for ten hours, turning back felt like failure. "WE ARE TURNING BACK BECAUSE THE JAPS TURNED BACK," Lt. Bryan lied over the PA in an attempt to keep up morale. What they were all thinking was that they were coming back tomorrow.

At dawn on October 11, the task group was back at Point C off San Cristobal, where it was raining off and on. At 0924, they started west-southwest toward Indispensable Reefs.

At 1030, a B-17 reported two cruisers and six destroyers in Bougainville Strait. They were 200 miles northwest of Guadalcanal but were headed southeast. Was it the report they were waiting for?

A short time later, a Marine scout plane reported the same convoy—two cruisers surrounded by six destroyers in an oval. Later in the morning when an Australian Coastwatcher reported the convoy, it had progressed 30 miles into New Georgia Sound.

Messages for R/Adm. Scott began flooding in, until radio circuits jammed. A noon dispatch from Ghormley directed Scott to attack the "two cruisers and six destroyers standing toward Guadalcanal."

*   *   *

The two "cruisers" were, in fact, Imperial Navy seaplane tenders, *Nisshin* and *Chitose*, operating as a supply group under the command R/Adm. Takaji Joshima.

V/Adm. Gunichi Mikawa, newly in command at Rabaul, had initially placed such importance on this night's supply run that he assigned three light cruisers to cover it, in addition to six destroyers and long-range Zeros and Bettys. But then Mikawa remembered that he owned the sea at night—the Americans had never made a serious attempt to stop a Japanese supply run— and, reconsidering, he decided that the three cruisers should bombard the airfield.

The cruisers were units of R/Adm. Aritomo Goto's 6th Cruiser Division. While R/Adm. Joshima was unloading men and supplies off Tassafaronga, R/Adm. Goto was to take his three cruisers east along the coast to a point 12 miles west of the airfield. From there, they were to lobType 3 (fragmentation) shells at the field, firing at low angles with fuses timed to ignite 30 feet above the ground. Mikawa hoped to knock out enough American planes to shut down the airfield for at least a few days.

R/Adm. Gotō's new mission quickly took priority over the supply run. Because the new plan required surprise, Gotō's departure was delayed until after dusk. Mikawa had directed the 11th Air Fleet to orchestrate a series of air battles over Guadalcanal during the afternoon to keep U.S. search planes grounded. 11th Air initiated a two-pronged attack: a fighter sweep at noon to draw American planes up, and then, as they were landing to refuel, a second wave of bombers to demolish them on the ground.

*   *   *

R/Adm. Scott's task group was 193 nautical miles south-southeast of Guadalcanal at noon when they slowed to launch floatplanes and then turn north. It was raining.

Air battles over Henderson Field began shortly after noon. CACTUS radio broadcast a play-by-play from the moment Henderson radar picked up seventeen bogeys incoming. The Japanese fighter sweep drew more than fifty U.S. planes into the air; thirty-nine F4s and a dozen or more P-39s and P-400s. The second wave of Japanese bombers appeared piecemeal. Most of the American fighters were able to land, refuel, and take off again before the majority of bombers arrived.

The rain stopped early in the afternoon. It turned into a lovely day. The sea was calm. The sky was clear. "Better than any barbershop calendar," remembered Ens. George Weems, the first lieutenant on *McCalla*. Lt.(jg) Charles Cook, an assistant engineering officer on *Helena*, remembered, "The horizon was empty except for a massive cumulus cloud towering to the east." As nice as the day became, it remained oppressively humid on the ships until the decks steamed off.

Buchanan's fire-control radar conked out early in the afternoon due to moisture in a coaxial cable. Cdr. Wilson reported the problem to Capt. Tobin by flag, who reported it to R/Adm. Scott by flag, but Scott did not reply.

Shortly after that, *Farenholt*'s surface-search radar went out. Ideally, Capt. Tobin should have transferred with his staff to another destroyer. He chose not to, probably because he did not want to annoy Scott by wasting time transferring when both of them thought radar was useless.

The task group arrived off Rennell Island at 1430, which was slightly ahead of schedule. They were only about 35 miles from Point A and had ninety minutes to get there. To kill time, Scott ordered a jog to the west.

Scott wanted to wait until it was a little darker before proceeding north this time. So he had the task group skirt west

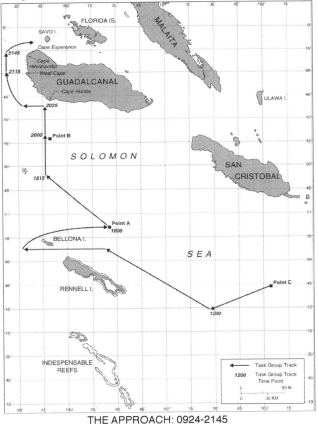

THE APPROACH: 0924-2145

between Rennell and Bellona Islands, then swing around the western end of Bellona before heading for Point A. The detour added 10 miles and killed a half hour.

All afternoon, executive officers were readying their ships for battle. Junior officers and chiefs readied their departments, following the provisions in their departments' battle bills more or less. Like all Navy regulations, battle bills were written for the lowest common denominator. Officers were expected to follow the provisions with a grain of salt. For instance, deck force's battle bill instructed that all inflammable gear be jettisoned. But, if first lieutenants threw all the files, paper, and lumber overboard, a warship would be hard to manage *after* the battle. As with all Navy regulations, some common sense on the part of officers was expected. If the officer jumped wrong, it was his neck.

CACTUS flashed an uncoded message to all commands: "6 DDS 2 CRUISERS BEARING 305 DISTANCE 210 FROM GUADALCANAL COURSE 120." The Japanese convoy had advanced 75 miles since first reported. Successive plottings had determined that it was increasing speed.

R/Adm. Scott was feeling like he did before the Savo fiasco. Like at Savo, he had little information about the approaching force. He had reports of seven to twelve ships of differing types. Some mentioned only destroyers. One said heavy cruisers. Many were contradictory. Scott had more questions than answers. It was clear these were fast ships. That sounded like a supply run.

Scott's approach went according to plan until late in the afternoon when they lost radio contact with two groups of scout planes. One group had been launched the previous evening and had spent the night at Tulagi. The others were the planes launched at noon. Both had been ordered to rendezvous with the task group at Point A at 1600, but Scott had changed his mind and now wanted them all to land atTulagi. A flag radioman had been trying to raise them for hours.

When the task group arrived at Point A at 1600 not a plane was in sight. They steamed in slow circles for a while. Scott was in no hurry. He did not want to get much closer to Guadalcanal until it was darker.

According to the Admiral's staff's calculations, they were ahead of schedule. From Point A, it was 180 miles to Cape Esperance, which would take six hours at the planned 29 knots. That would put them at Cape Esperance at 2200. It was important they arrive there *after* the Japanese. If they arrived before, they could get trapped against the shore themselves. In late morning, the staff was estimating the Japanese ships' arrival time at 2300, but, given the Japanese convoy's increasing speed during the day, subsequent guesses were 2230, 2200.

It was better to be ahead of schedule. Scott could always slow down or zigzag later if he needed to kill time. As they steamed slowly westward into the setting sun, Scott directed Tobin to tighten up the screen. The destroyers closed in to 2,500 yards.

At 1607, Scott issued the long-awaited intercept order to begin the approach. Flags on *San Francisco* signaled: "WE ARE GOING IN. JAP FORCE BELIEVED TO BE TWO CRUISERS AND SIX DESTROYERS."

* * *

Sharks began following the ships at dusk. Sharks knew to wait for the garbage the mess threw overboard in the evening.

The men were expecting a long night. Most coming off watch at 1600 headed for their bunks to try to catch an hour of sleep before early supper.

Wickstrom was thinking he could be dead by morning, and he had $30 in his pocket so joined in the crap game in the after crew compartment. Even though he had never shot craps before, he was up $300 by supper.

A lot of the men spent the hour before supper writing home. Lt.(jg) Fowler wrote a note to Pat. He wrote it as if from the grave. He told her he loved her more than anything in the world and his only regrets were not knowing her longer and not marrying her sooner. He told her to be strong and not think about him too much. He said she would always have the baby to remember him by. He folded the letter into an envelope that he shoved into a drawer. He then went and asked Wharton to mail it to Pat if anything happened to him.

Every man bathed and shaved before supper. They all understood the importance of cleanliness in case of wounds; they were under orders not to grow facial hair. They were very consciously dressing for battle. Most donned their best dungarees and "liberty" shoes. They all took their wallets and all their money. Wharton stuffed the roll of bills from the ship's store account into his pocket. Every man carried a penknife. The Annapolis graduates all wore their Academy rings.

The floatplanes launched at noon suddenly appeared overhead. Scott ordered them on to Tulagi, but they replied that their gasoline was contaminated and they had to land. So the task group slowed, and, in the fast-fading light, the four little planes set down in their cruisers' wakes. *San Francisco*'s plane smashed into the cruiser's stern and was a total loss.

Capt. Tobin directed *Buchanan* to rescue the plane's crew and sink the plane. Scott did not question Tobin's choice of *Buchanan*, even though he knew *Buchanan*'s FD radar was out. When *Buchanan* dropped out of the screen, *Duncan* moved up to about 38° on *San Francisco*'s bow to cover both stations as the task group resumed steaming north.

Buchanan recovered the pilot and observer and shot up the plane with 20mm fire until it sank. At 1725, when *Buchanan* started north again, the fast-moving task group had been gone ten minutes.

Supper was at 1745. The men ate quietly. In the wardroom on *Duncan*, the silence was broken only by Lt. Bryan asking LCdr. Taylor for permission to be on the bridge until the battle started. The exec's battle station was at after conn, which was on top of the after deckhouse where the stacks blocked your view. Bryan wanted to be up where the action is. He told Taylor he could be more use to him up on the bridge as an extra pair of eyes while they were maneuvering in formation at high speeds. He did not need to remind Taylor that the only officer on the bridge with him was the communications officer, who was a twenty-three-year-old reserve. Taylor told Bryan he would be relieved to have him up there.

Most of the air reconnaissance patrols scheduled from Henderson Field that afternoon were kept grounded because of the on-going air battles. Few patrols went out later in the afternoon because Maj.Gen. Geiger did not want to risk night landings by pilots who were overtired. There was no late search to the northwest, which was the most likely approach route. The last recon report was at 1810. It located the Japanese supply convoy 110 miles northwest of Guadalcanal.

General quarters began as soon as supper ended. There was no signal. Men knew to report to battle stations after chow. The officers left the wardroom without a word.

When Lt.(jg) Fowler got up to the roof of the bridge, Torpedomen Papacoda and Edwards were already at the director making adjustments, and Doty, the talker, was testing the phone circuit. Their circuit connected to the captain's talker on the bridge, the talker in the I.C., the talker on the torpedo mount, the talkers on the K-guns, and the talker at the depth charge rack.

The sun set at 1815. They were 50 miles south of Guadalcanal. The blue-tipped peaks of the mountains were visible on the horizon. The sea was calm with moderate swells. There was a 1,000-foot ceiling of broken cumulonimbus clouds.

Everybody was wearing a life preserver, either a big, gray, kapok lifevest or a pneumatic preserver, which was a canvas-covered inner tube that was worn deflated around the waist. Most of the men were wearing the bulky kapok vests. Officers all wore the pneumatic preservers, also men who had battle stations in tight quarters like the bridge or the I.C. Everybody was wearing bulbous helmets and carrying gas masks.

On the main deck, spademen, hot shellmen, and loaders were lining up shells underneath their main battery guns. Up in the mount of gun #2, Gunner's Mate Dunn, Seaman Roy Boehm, and Seaman Arthur Fischer were watching the sun go down. That close to the equator, the sun appeared to plunge headlong into the sea. Boehm remembered, "Sunsets in the Pacific are redder and more violent and more *everything* than anywhere else in the world." The last flickers of sunlight were mesmerizing.

The sky was a crystal dome of fading colors. In the shimmering afterglow, it became overcast. A massive thunderhead towered in the east. A slender new moon rose low in the west.

After the sun set, a wave of anxious anticipation swept over the crew. Men obsessively retested their gas masks and checked again to make sure their lifevests had a working flashlight, a fathom of line, morphine syrettes.

Most men had interior battle stations, either below deck or inside the bridge superstructure. Almost forty men had battle stations in the engineering spaces below. About twenty-five were jammed in the pilothouse.

The captain was very much in charge on the bridge. Only he, Bryan, and Beebe were allowed to move. Both Taylor and Bryan were bursting with nervous energy and were in perpetual motion. Taylor was continually jumping up from his chair in the pilothouse and walking out onto the port bridgewing, always followed by his talker and the War Diary recorder. (Chief Storekeeper Whitney Chamberlain was the captain's new talker, replacing Chief Paige who had hated the job.) Bryan was constantly shifting between the navigation table and the starboard wing. Beebe was always running up from the coding room with another decoded message.

At 1845, the two older cruisers shut off their old SC radars as ordered. Shortly after that, word came on *Duncan* for gun crews to load. All over the ship, men rolled up their sleeves and began rubbing gray flash-burn paint on their arms and faces and hands. It was nasty greasy stuff so they put off applying it until the last minute.

The task group had been on alert for days. Everybody was dazed from lack of sleep and eyesore from submarine watch. Bryan came around checking to make sure everyone was awake. The moment he was gone, men in gun crews and repair parties curled up at their stations to sleep. Men were sprawled all over the deck and gun mounts.

Shortly after 1900, the slender new moon plunged back into the darkening sea. In the short tropical twilight, darkness comes on fast. Ships' silhouettes faded into dark shadows. With surface visibility down to 4,000-5,000 yards, lookouts could only make out one or two ships in the limited field of their binoculars.

The captain summoned Lt.(jg) Fowler and torpedo director operator Papacoda to the bridge. They met with Taylor and Bryan on the port wing to discuss torpedo settings.

The torpedo problem was far less complex than the gunnery problem because you could see the "torpedo triangle." You knew your own torpedo's speed and could see your target and estimate its speed, so you could visualize the crossing angle and could usually estimate the lead angle near enough to hit something as big and slow-moving as a ship. There were only two torpedo questions: depth and speed.

They were after cruisers, so the depth setting easy. For cruisers, according to doctrine, torpedoes were to be set to run at 20 feet.

The speed setting required guesswork. Torpedoes had three speeds—low, medium, and high—and each corresponded to the distance that the torpedo would travel at that speed: at low speed, 8 miles; at medium speed, 4 miles; at high speed, 2 miles. So captains had to guess how close they would be able to get to their target. The longer the range the more precise the plotting of the target's course and speed needed to be. Torpedomen always pushed for the highest speed because it meant the shortest range. Torpedomen always wanted to be as close as possible. R/Adm. Scott had said he would try to get them "within lethal range." To torpedomen, that was inside 2 miles, though they preferred 1 mile. 1,200 yards was ideal. Any closer and the torpedo might not have time to trigger.

Everything argued for high speed, except the captain's uncertainty. Taylor could not imagine how he could get them within 4,000 yards when visibility was 4,000-5,000 yards. Surely the Japanese would spot them within 4,500 yards. If they set the torpedoes at high speed and only got to within 5,000 yards, the torpedoes would run out of juice and just sink.

When word spread that the torpedoes were to be set on high speed, everybody knew the captain was going to try to take them within two miles of a Japanese warship. "The guys all took out their rosaries," Fischer remembered. Many of them had premonitions that *Duncan* would never return.

Most seamen harbor an abiding fear of the sea. The thought of losing their ship and being dunked in the ocean was horrifying. Boatswain's Mate Charles Milek, who was regular navy but could not swim well, was worried that he would not make it in the water, especially given the weight of his money belt. Milek was a gambler who had about $6,000 in his poke. "You take the belt, Louie," he said to DeLucca. "If anything happens to me, it's all yours." Knowing what a weak swimmer Milek was, DeLucca was thinking he might get lucky.

By 2000, the task group had steamed past Point B and was 25 miles south of Cape Hunter. With each sweep on the new circular radar scopes on *Helena* and *Boise*, Guadalcanal's southwest coast was to the north. The U.S. column appeared as a line of seven dots extending through the center of the scope in a southeast-to-northwest direction. (The short count was because *Buchanan* was missing.)

Knowing that *Buchanan's* surface-search radar was out and that she was steaming blind, R/Adm. Scott assumed LCdr. Wilson would be having trouble locating the task group. But he was not about to break radio silence to help him.

At 2025, off Cape Hunter, Scott ordered a slight change of course to the west to get them away from shore while steaming north.

Lt.(jg) Beebe burst into the pilothouse with yet another message. Taylor read it by the light of the dim red bulb of his flashlight. Messages almost never had anything to do with the *Duncan*.

At 2100, the task group set Readiness Condition One, which required the engineering plant be split. Below deck, pipes were isolated with a pump on each.

At 2115, off West Cape where the coast turns north, Scott reduced speed to 25 knots and ordered, "Corpen 000." He was ordering the cruisers to follow the destroyers around the turn and onto a course due north.

The turn order elicited the usual pre-turn jitters in the

pilothouses. Whenever ships in formation were about to turn, there was always confusion about whether they were to come onto the new course by following the leader or turning simultaneously. It came down to two words—"corpen" or "turn"—and there was always doubt whether they had heard correctly. (If the order had been "Turn 000," they should all have put their wheels over at once.)

Farenholt in the van swung onto the new heading. The two destroyers on the outside of the arrowhead raced to regain their stations in the screen, and the two destroyers on the inside slowed to maintain theirs. Each cruiser in succession turned in the same water where the cruiser ahead had turned. When the turn was completed, Scott ordered formation speed increased to 29 knots.

Their new northerly course paralleled Guadalcanal's west coast 10 miles offshore. They could not see the island, but they could smell the hothouse fragrance of jasmine. The nautical chart showed a coral-bordered beach with trails leading inland toward 2,800- foot peaks close behind the beach. The chart was full of quaint-sounding place-names—Wanderer Bay, Tangarare Mission, Tuvutu, Lambi Bay. At the north end of this stretch was Cape Esperance, the island's northwestern-most point.

There was no moon, and patches of clouds and surface haze dimmed any illumination from stars. They were wrapped in impenetrable blackness. But darkness is a relative thing; the eye discerns objects because they appear a little blacker than the background. As eyes adjusted, familiar outlines emerged—deck, masts, bow.

With the blowers off, it was eerily quiet on deck. There was only the rumbling hum of the machinery below and the hiss of the bow cutting through the ocean.

Readiness Condition One dictated the maximum degree of watertight integrity. All connecting doors were closed and dogged tight, forcing officers and chiefs to move from station to station by circuitous routes. Battening down the machinery spaces also meant closing the big vents on deck so they would not take on water and flood out if they were hit.

Men below were always gripped by an uneasy sensation when the hatches were dogged down over their heads. Closing the vents shut off all ventilation below. In the boiler rooms, where temperatures normally hovered over 130° *with* ventilation, the temperature was soon approaching 160°. Watertenders gulped salt tablets and wiped sweat out of their eyes so they could see the gauges. "You couldn't breathe below," Quinn remembered. "Men were gasping." The air was damp and stale. It felt as if the bulkheads were closing in.

The men of the forward repair party were down in the dark mess hall, where it was over 120°. Lt.(jg) Smyth was allowing one man at a time on deck to get some air. They were supposed to return in a couple of minutes, but it was such a relief being on deck that each man took a little longer than the man before him to return below.

Men became quieter as time wore on. Unnecessary talk dissipated energy.

They were still awaiting word from the Admiral. Nothing was official until Scott made the decision to engage. Men on deck kept an eye on the flagship for the faint signal light.

At 2145, off Point Hihirinambo where the coast turns northeast, word came: "WE ARE GOING IN. SCOTT."

Speed was reduced to 25 knots. They set a 043° [north-northeast] course. Cape Esperance was 14 miles ahead.

Bryan's voice came on the PA: "WE ARE ROUNDING THE NORTHWEST CORNER OF GUADALCANAL WHERE THE JAPS ARE MAKING THEIR LANDINGS." He read Scott's message, adding, "UNLESS THEY CHANGED COURSE AFTER DARK WE'LL MEET THEM BETWEEN 2300 AND MIDNIGHT."

*　*　*

Time seemed weighted. Minutes passed like hours.

On each cruiser, a single-float monoplane, manned by a pilot and an observer, waited on the catapult. These last four Curtis Kingfishers were tasked to search out their assigned sectors and illuminate Japanese ships with parachute flares. *Salt Lake City*'s plane drew the cove off the landing beach at Tassafaronga, the key assignment. Upon learning of their assignment, the observer, Radioman Claude Morgan, tossed in a few extra flares for good measure.

Minutes before 2200, the formation slowed to 20 knots to launch planes. Everyone knew then that a battle was expected within an hour.

When they slowed, *Buchanan,* which had been trailing the convoy for almost five hours, was finally able to rejoin the formation.

Only *San Francisco* and *Boise* got their planes up. *Helena*'s TBS was on the blink so she missed the launch order, and *Salt Lake City*'s plane crashed.

As *Salt Lake City*'s plane was shooting off the catapult, one of the loose flares that the observer had tossed in ignited. Feeling his ankle burning, he glanced around and, seeing that the plane's tail was on fire, scrambled out of his seat and crawled forward and whacked the pilot, Lt. William F. Tate, Jr., on the back of the head, shouting, "Land! Land!" The plane hit the water 500 yards off the cruiser column. Morgan and Tate were able to swim clear before the plane erupted in a towering column of fire fed by high- octane gas and float lights.

On *Helena*, Capt. Hoover was growing increasingly anxious to get his plane off. Hoover thought the Japanese ships were probably already at Tassafaronga. He could not understand what the Admiral was waiting for. Seeing *Salt Lake City*'s plane go down in flames 600 yards ahead, he phoned Scott for permission to launch. He got no reply.

The fire from the burning floatplane flared fiercely. Everyone assumed the pilot and observer could not possibly have survived. The fire lit up the sky for a full three minutes before dying out. R/Adm. Scott was sure it was seen by everybody within miles.

Ten minutes after the plane fire died out, Capt. Hoover on *Helena* was still trying contact R/Adm. Scott. *San Francisco* never answered, and no other ship heard *Helena*. The fire was out for fifteen minutes before Hoover finally ordered their plane dumped overboard.

Three minutes later, at 2223, with Cape Esperance 12 miles to starboard, R/Adm. Scott issued the code word "DOUBLEHEADER," the order for the formation to single up in column.

Farenholt took the van. *Duncan* fell in 500 yards astern *Farenholt*, and *Laffey* fell in 500 yards astern *Duncan* (and 500 yards forward of *San Francisco*). The cruisers in column—*San Francisco*, *Boise*, *Salt Lake City*, and *Helena*—closed up to 600 yards in "dog formation" (slightly offset from the ship ahead to facilitate signaling). Destroyers *Buchanan* and *McCalla* fell in at the rear. The nine warships formed a column 4 miles long. From flagship *San Francisco*, which was a little forward of the middle, Scott was unable to see either end.

At 2225, with the task group in battle formation, Scott ordered a new track—075° [east-southeast]—to round Cape Esperance, which was now about 9 miles to starboard. The new bearing headed them straight at Tassafaronga, where at that moment a Japanese tender was off-loading and two destroyers were steaming close by.

Lightning flashed on the horizon to the northwest. In the moment of the flash, it was like daylight for a second, and you could see the coastline of Guadalcanal and the dark mountains behind the shore. A breeze from the island was full of jungle smells. Seeing land seemed to make the smell of jasmine even stronger.

Without the lightening, lookouts could not see much against the dark background of the shore. Even the new SG radar was ineffective this close to land. Worse, the scout plane that crashed had been assigned to light up the cove at Tassafaronga.

Faced with impenetrable blackness, Scott started second-guessing his decision to approach Tassafaronga straight on. Approaching from seaward made them fat targets silhouetted against the lighter sea horizon.

The floatplane fire changed the tactical situation for R/Adm. Scott, who now had to assume he had lost the element of surprise, his one advantage. In terms of a battle plan, he did not have much else. He soon stopped feeling like the aggressor. Within an hour of the fire, he had started to think that he was leading them into a trap. The ships they were looking for could be laying in wait for them against the shore. Scott was expecting Japanese guns to open up on them any moment.

Farenholt made a FC radar contact 7 miles to the northwest. Capt. Tobin dismissed it as either a radar malfunction or Russell Island, and did not report it. Twenty-five minutes later, a lookout on *Farenholt* spotted two blue lights on the beach at Tassafaronga. Tobin did not report them because he assumed lookouts on *San Francisco* would see them, but lookouts on *San Francisco* did not see the lights.

At 2250, *San Francisco*'s plane reported a sub tender and two destroyers off the beach at Tassafaronga: "ONE LARGE, TWO SMALL VESSELS ONE SIX MILES FROM SAVO OFF NORTHERN BEACH GUADALCANAL." Scott presumed "one large, two small vessels" meant one cruiser and two destroyers, but did "one six miles" mean one was 6 miles from Savo or were all three "one six" [16 nautical miles] from Savo? Scott assumed they were hostile because they were in Japanese territory. Thinking he was stalking two cruisers and six destroyers, Scott thought he had one cruiser and two destroyers accounted for.

Scott assumed that the missing "cruiser" and four missing destroyers were still approaching. This increased his feeling of vulnerability. Afraid of getting trapped between warships against the beach and warships approaching from seaward, he decided to set a course toward Savo Island and wait there for the missing cruiser and destroyers. He knew that, as long as he kept to the northwest, he could deal with the ships off Tassafaronga later. "If no interception was made on this course," Scott explained later as if he had planned it like this all along, "I intended to double back to the southward and make another run along the coast."

At 2307, Scott ordered the change of course to the northwest by column movement. The column was stretched along the north coast of Guadalcanal from rear destroyer *McCalla*, which was 7 miles off Cape Esperance, to van destroyer *Farenholt*, which was 5 miles off the beach at Tassafaronga (and only about $6^{1/2}$ miles from Savo).

Farenholt turned hard to port until she was headed to the west of Savo. *Duncan* turned about a minute later, at 2308. *Laffey* turned a minute after that. Creating a new battle plan on the fly, Scott decided to allow the second group of Japanese ships to slip by, and, when all eight were against the shore, he would come around and do battle to port. He liked his odds—his four cruisers and five destroyers versus two cruisers and six destroyers.

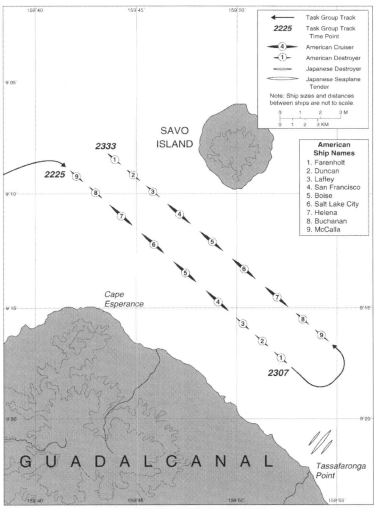

THE NORTH COAST: 2225-2333

A voice on *Duncan*'s gunnery circuit repeated over and over in a soft chant, "Pass the word. This won't be a dummy run."

Unless a ship was hit, the two repairs parties, forward and after repair, had nothing to do at GQ. Forward repair's battle station was down in the mess hall, and after repair's was on deck aft near the machine shop. After almost $4^{1/2}$ hours at GQ, Lt.(jg) Smyth gave up trying to keep the forward repair men below. Now, they were all up on deck. Most were huddled at the port side of the exterior passageway between the bridge superstructure and the forward deckhouse.

Wickstrom was with the after repair men. He was thinking how much going into battle was like any other training exercise. "We had drilled so much that when it came to it we didn't have to think about it," he remembered. "It was another drill."

Fear made some men silent. Others could not stop talking. DeLucca, the talker in #3 handling room, read to men on his battle circuit from a *Popular Mechanics* article about sharks. It said some sharks have 700-pound livers. Milek's voice came back, "Wouldn't want to meet up with him." Chief Chamberlain, the captain's talker, broke in, "Cut out the chit-chat."

Impending battle crystallizes a sense of spirituality in some men. In #2 handling room, 2nd powderman Rosalio Rizzi, a nineteen-year-old from New York City's Hell's Kitchen, blew a mournful tune on his harmonica. Some men whistled. Others sang quietly to themselves. A sailor on top of the afterdeck superstructure sang "Amazing Grace" straight through in a voice clear as a bell, and all over the after half of the main deck men stopped to listen.

At 2330, *Duncan* was $4^{1/2}$ miles due west of Savo when her surface-search radar found a contact 15 miles to the west. No ship had reported it, so Taylor dismissed it as a phantom. The navigation crew began plotting it, and the fire control crew started searching to the west with the fire-control radar.

The 5-inch guns suddenly slewed to port. That was the first indication the crew had that something was up.

Part III

THE BATTLE OF CAPE ESPERANCE
2333 October 11-0200 October 13

We make war as we can, rather than as we should.

- Michael Howard

Chapter 6
"WERE WE SHOOTING AT 12?"
2333-2350 October 11

Show me a hero, and I'll write you a tragedy.

—F. Scott Fitzgerald

Inside *Duncan's* pilothouse, it was hot and close and clammy. The bridge crew stood very still, shoulder to shoulder. Tempers were short. The only light was from the shielded lamp on the navigation table, where Lt. Bryan hovered over Chief Lehman's shoulder nervously watching the navigation crew plot the contact. Bryan gnawed on the last knuckle of his left pinkie when he was nervous. It had to be a ship because it was moving. Bryan thought they should have come around already, if they hoped to cross the Japanese T. "When are we turning? Why haven't we turned? We should've turned," he pleaded to no one. Bryan thought it was already too late. He was frustrated, and he was not shy about expressing it, or his opinion of the Admiral's tactical sense. "What's he doing? What's he thinking? Come on. What're you waiting for?!"

On the torpedo mount on top of the after deckhouse, Chief Boyd paced the catwalk, clutching the mallet he would use to fire torpedoes if remote control failed.

At 2333, Scott came on the TBS: "THIS IS CTF [commander task force]. EXECUTE TO FOLLOW. LEFT TO COURSE 230."

"Left to course 230"—a simultaneous port turn: all ships were to turn on the execute. That elicited a burst of applause on *Duncan's* bridge. Chief Lehman was shouting that the new bearing would put them on track to cross the Japanese T. Everybody assumed the Admiral ordered the simultaneous turn to bring them around faster. Even Bryan was cheering.

The TBS was silent for about thirty seconds. It seemed like an eternity. During the prolonged silence, second-guessing began and doubts set in. Had the Admiral misspoke? He had *never* ordered a simultaneous turn. He said only column turns. But he clearly said, "Left to course 230." That was a simultaneous reverse turn order. If he intended them to turn simultaneously, then the execute order should be "230 turn." Or, if he intended a column turn, "230 corpen." But no execute order followed. The bridge crew began to suspect that the Admiral meant to order a column turn. Some were placing bets that a correction was coming.

Unaware of the proximity of Japanese ships, R/Adm. Scott intended his task group to come around in the safer, more-leisurely column movement. He thought he had ordered a column turn. He broadcast the execute himself. It was in code.

As decoded using Voice Card Key Baker, it said simply: "FROM CTF: EXECUTE."

The flag radioman relayed the order to *San Francisco*'s pilothouse as "230 turn," a simultaneous turn. Scott was shocked when he felt *San Francisco* suddenly turning to port.

Putting the rudder over on the execute was the order from the old signal book. It was also what they were all used to from screening *Wasp*; ships screening carriers *always* turned on the execute.

When the flagship started turning, the formation was thrown into confusion.

On *Boise*, six hundred yards astern *San Francisco*, Capt. Edward "Iron Mike" Moran assumed the Admiral had misspoken, so he was surprised to see *San Francisco* turning. He was more surprised van destroyer *Farenholt* was *not* turning because *Farenholt* was the one ship that should have turned on the execute whichever the order. Capt. Moran had little more than a minute to decide—follow the flagship or the van destroyers? If he followed the flagship, the van destroyers would be pitched out formation, and, if he followed the van destroyers, the flagship would be left alone. Hundreds of years of naval tradition told him to follow the flagship. At 2335, *Boise* countermarched. That set the example for the ships astern.

Farenholt was maintaining radio silence, so nobody noticed the TBS was malfunctioning. They did not hear the turn order or execute.

Duncan continued to follow *Farenholt*, and *Laffey* continued to follow *Duncan*. After about a minute, LCdr. Hank on *Laffey* came on the TBS calling *Farenholt*. He got no response. In about thirty seconds, he tried again. Then a *Laffey* radioman took over, and he called *Farenholt* repeatedly.

On *Duncan*, Quartermaster Johnson at the wheel was focused on *Farenholt*'s dim blue wake light. "That old blue wake light," Johnson remembered, "that's all I had to steer the ship by."

After a couple of minutes of unnerving silence broken only by *Laffey*'s repeated calls to *Farenholt*, Taylor jumped out of his chair and walked out onto the port wing. Chief Chamberlain, his talker, and Yeoman Haveman, the War Diary Recorder, hurried out after him.

On the port wing, Taylor looked aft to the southeast. He could see the shadows of the cruisers two miles back doubled around the turn. He looked around at *Farenholt* plowing toward the northwest.

At 2336, a radioman on *Farenholt* suddenly responded. The *Laffey* radioman calmly told him to "kindly inform Capt. Tobin the cruisers are turning." There was a very short silence. Then Capt. Tobin came on, screaming: "Come About! Execute!"

Farenholt turned hard to port at 2338. Viewed from *Duncan*, her wake seemed to boil as her silhouette spread out to port.

In the three minutes that it took to get a response from *Farenholt*, the three van destroyers at 25 knots had steamed another mile away. Now, they were almost 5 miles northwest of Savo, which was $1^{1/4}$ miles out of position.

Capt. Tobin had heard no contact report, so he took the cruisers' turning as simply another turn. If he needed to, he could regain the van in about twelve minutes at high speed, but he did not want to do that, not with a battle imminent. His hope was that LCdr. Wilson had led *Buchanan* and *McCalla* to the new van. In that case, he would take *Lansdowne*, *Duncan*, and *Laffey* to the rear of the column. Tobin ordered *Farenholt* to stop until they could see if *Buchanan* was astern *Helena*.

About a minute after *Farenholt* turned, *Duncan* reached

the turning point. Helmsman Johnson spun the wheel counter-clockwise, struggling to keep *Farenholt*'s blue stern light in sight.

Duncan's surface-search radar was still holding the contact to the west, but fire controlmen had been unable to locate it with the fire-control radar. And no other ships had reported it. Taylor dismissed it as a radar glitch.

As Taylor understood Tobin's order, the van destroyers were going to regain the van. It is what van destroyers did when formations made simultaneous turns. According to doctrine, van destroyers were to speed away from the column at a 25° angle to a point 1,000 yards off the flank, where they were to turn and steam parallel to the column until they were able to regain the new van.

Duncan was three-quarters around the turn when lookouts shouted that they were overrunning *Farenholt*. "Engines one-third," Taylor yelled. "Helm starboard." Johnson spun the wheel back clockwise to dead ahead. Engines slowed.

Farenholt was idling off the port bow. Taylor studied her, trying to divine what Capt. Tobin was up to. *Farenholt* had slowed onto 275° [west], which was "approximately parallel," as Taylor explained later, to *Duncan*'s course. Seeing *Farenholt* slowed in the direction of *Duncan*'s contact, Taylor now thought Tobin was jockeying prior to launching on a torpedo run. All of sudden, Taylor believed their radar contact, and he hurried into the pilothouse to tell Bryan.

Inside the pilothouse, the gyro repeater was clicking as *Duncan*'s bow came around. Taylor pushed through to the navigation table where he and Bryan whispered together excitedly. Both were naturally aggressive and going into battle for the first time.

Everything in their professional careers had led to this moment. Men nearby sensed their exuberance. The compass repeater's clicks slowed as the bow lolled onto a westerly course.

Suddenly, fire controlmen were shouting that they had a contact. It was at the same range and bearing as the contact the surface-search radar had been holding for eight minutes. With both the FD and FC radars on it, Taylor thought he knew why the cruisers were turning: they had the contact but were maintaining radio silence. It probably never occurred to Taylor to break radio silence to report his contact. Taylor was expecting *Farenholt* to take off on a torpedo run at any moment.

Farenholt was stopped in the turn for about a minute before lookouts spotted *Buchanan* still astern *Helena*. Tobin ordered LCdr. Seaward to take *Farenholt* to the van by the unengaged side, which, as far as they knew, was to starboard. [Tobin explained in his after-action report: "Up to this time there had been no contact of enemy forces in the vicinity," and, given that Scott was expecting to meet the enemy to port, starboard was the "unengaged side."]

At 2340, Seaward ordered *Farenholt* to flank speed on a course 25° west of the column's bearing.

On *Duncan*, portside lookouts were watching the cruisers turning 2¼ miles to the southeast. The black mass that was *Salt Lake City* was just entering the turn when forward lookouts started shouting that *Farenholt* was moving.

"Prepare to come left to course 255," Taylor ordered. "Ahead full." (255° is 25° west of the 230° course the U.S. column was on.)

At 2341, as *Duncan* surged ahead, Taylor walked out onto the port wing.

In the pilothouse, Bryan picked up the PA mic and pressed the button to speak but hesitated. Then he said, "This is it." That was all he said.

"THIS IS IT." The words resonated throughout the ship. "THIS IS IT."

Laffey turned in the water where *Duncan* had turned, but, by the time *Laffey* rounded the turn, *Duncan* was gone. Mystified, LCdr. Hank ordered *Laffey* to follow in *Duncan*'s wake.

The night was so black every time Chief Chamberlain stepped out onto the port wing he had to stop and blink a few times before he could even see where the lookouts were. Over his phones, he was hearing a steady stream of radio and radar reports, and he was relaying them to the captain in a monotone:

guns #3 and #4 loaded with starshells; torpedo director on target; guns #1 and #2 on target.

A minute into the run, at about 2342, Chief Lehman warned LCdr. Taylor that they were going to get caught in a pincer between the two fleets if they kept on this course. Taylor should have turned to starboard then and prepared to fire his torpedoes to port, but maybe he thought it was too late to change.

Chief Chamberlain had alerted the starboard lookouts to the threat to starboard. They reported back that it was too dark to the west to see anything.

Helena came on the TBS at 2342 and warned of as many as nine ships at 12,000 yards bearing 285°. "It was more in the form of information rather than a directive for action," *Duncan*'s chief fire controlman, Carl Koehler, remembered.

The flag radioman on *San Francisco* replied, "Roger."

At flank speed, *Farenholt* was at about 40 knots which was 6-10 knots faster than *Duncan* and *Laffey* and twice the speed of the formation. At 2343, after two minutes at flank speed, *Farenholt* was almost 1,000 yards ahead of *Duncan* but was still a mile short of where rear destroyer *McCalla* was turning. *Farenholt*'s TBS was working sporadically. She copied *Helena*'s message. Tobin was dubious, but, if it was true, they were between the lines and still had ten minutes to the van, assuming the Admiral did not speed up. Tobin chose to play it safe and ordered *Farenholt* to slow down to clear the line of fire by allowing the column to pull ahead.

Almost two minutes after *Helena*'s report, *Boise* re-reported *Helena*'s contact as five "bogeys" at relative 65° [65° off *Boise*'s starboard bow] at 11,000 yards.

Again, except for an acknowledging "Roger," the flagship was silent.

Slowing, *Farenholt* was about 1,000 yards west of the column and almost parallel to *McCalla*. Hearing *Boise*'s report of five "bogeys," Tobin told Seaward to take *Farenholt* to the rear of the column fast.

When forward lookouts on *Duncan* reported that *Farenholt* was turning eastward toward the U.S. line, Taylor walked out onto the port wing to see for himself.

Fire control radar was to aim the main battery. Normally, it locked onto the largest or closest target. *Duncan*'s FC was locked on a target that was aft to starboard and closing fast. Closing ranges were being called out.

Lt.(jg) Fowler, searching aft to starboard through the telescope on the torpedo director, was seeing only blackness. At 10,000 yards, lookouts reported that maybe they were seeing something. Fowler was still not seeing anything, even at 9,000 yards.

The fire-control computer continued struggling to calculate the target's speed and bearing. Once it achieved these two solutions, the information would be transmitted to the torpedo director electronically. All the gears inside the torpedo director would then combine these numbers with other data—*Duncan*'s speed and course, sight angle on the target, speed setting of the torpedo—to produce a firing solution. The solution would be in the form of an angle: the angle at which torpedoes should be fired in order to meet a moving target minutes in the future.

In less than a minute, the target was at 8,000 yards. Then 7,000. Fowler still could not see it.

The silence in the pilothouse was the sound of everybody holding their collective breath. They all knew they were meant to be following *Farenholt*. It was 2344, two minutes after Chief Lehman told the captain they were going to get caught in a pincer. Successive plottings showed that the Japanese were going to intersect the U.S. line between *Boise* and *Salt Lake City*.

If Taylor had turned to starboard two minutes earlier, they would have had a perfect setup to port. Now, it really was too late. If they swung to starboard now and re-angled the tubes to port, they would lose the setup that the computer was still calculating and have to start again. Taylor probably recognized his mistake by now, but he knew the Admiral was counting on him to get his torpedoes off. Taylor was silent as *Duncan* steamed past *Farenholt* at 30 knots.

When word came over the phone circuits—"WE ARE NOW ENGAGING A 10,000- TON ENEMY CRUISER"—the feeling swept over them that they were on a suicidal charge. Another surge of nervous chitchat flooded the battle circuits until Chief Chamberlain again barked, "Knock off the bullshit!"

On *San Francisco*, Scott was trying to make sense of *Helena* and *Boise's* reports. Both had reported ships bearing toward Savo Island, which seemed to make no sense. Scott was awaiting ships bearing for Tassafaronga. He assumed *Helena* and *Boise* were reporting the van destroyers, and he got on the TBS and called Tobin to make sure the van destroyers were to starboard.

At 2344, a minute after *Boise's* report, Scott got Tobin on the TBS. His first question was "Are you taking station ahead?" It must have been the tone in Scott's voice that told Tobin that the Admiral *expected* him to be taking station ahead.

Farenholt was headed for the rear of the column at flank speed, but Tobin replied, "Affirmative. Moving up your starboard side." He quickly ordered LCdr. Seaward to come around and make for the van.

Men on *Duncan's* bridge were shocked to realize that Tobin thought *Duncan* and *Laffey* were behind him.

The second Scott was off the TBS, *Helena* came on again with an "Interrogatory Roger" (permission to open fire).

In the cramped I.C. on *Duncan*, Wharton was nervously eying the rangefinder- repeater. The tension is even worse when you can *see* the range closing. They were at 6,000 yards when Wharton grabbed the phones. He got Chief Chamberlain and said, "Jesus, it's really getting down there."

"Still no word from the Admiral," Chamberlain replied.

"Well, better hurry him up," Wharton said.

At 5,000 yards, *Duncan* lookouts confirmed visual contact on a large formless smudge moving right to left on the bow.

The flag radioman re-reported *Boise's* contact, giving the range as 14,000 yards when *Duncan* had it at 4,000. That was the moment *Duncan's* bridge crew realized Scott did not have the contact.

"Prepare to make torpedo attack on enemy cruiser to starboard," Taylor said quietly in an almost fatalistic tone.

On the bridge roof, the crew at the torpedo director could hear

Chamberlain down on the wing calling the order into his phones. Doty did not even bother to repeat it but simply said, "Stand by."

"Stand by," Papacoda echoed.

A few miles to the west, the three heavy cruisers of R/Adm. Goto's 6th Cruiser Division were steaming southeasterly at 26 knots, screened by two destroyers. Heavy cruiser *Aoba*, Goto's flagship, was in the van with destroyers *Fubuki* and *Hatsuyuki* in a rough T-formation, the two destroyers 20° and 3,600 yards ahead to port and starboard of the cruiser. The two other heavy cruisers, *Furutaka* and *Kinugasa*, were in column astern *Aoba* at 1,300-yard intervals.

The U.S. column was stretched across the Japanese line of advance. R/Adm. Scott had achieved the theoretically impossible—he was crossing the Japanese T. Except he did not know it.

Wharton could see on the radar repeater that *Duncan* was heading between the U.S. line and some large ships to the rear of the Japanese formation. He phoned Chief Chamberlain just as Capt. Hoover came back on the TBS.

Having waited almost a minute since his "Interrogatory Roger," Capt. Hoover demanded again, "Interrogatory Roger." The northern-most Japanese van destroyer, *Hatsuyuki*, was 10° abaft *Helena*'s starboard beam at 3,600 yards, point-blank range for a cruiser. Alarmed by Scott's silence, Hoover asked again for permission to open fire and requested acknowledgment.

The flag radioman came back, "Roger," which meant either Yes or Message Received.

Hoover must have decided it gave him enough wiggle room to intentionally misunderstand because within seconds he ordered Open Fire.

At 2346, a *Boise* searchlight sliced through the dark. A machinegun on *Helena* started firing.

About thirty seconds later, now 2347, the 6-inch main battery guns forward of *Helena*'s bridge opened up on the Japanese van cruiser.

The night exploded.

Tracers streamed off in shallow arcs. Each cruiser's tracers

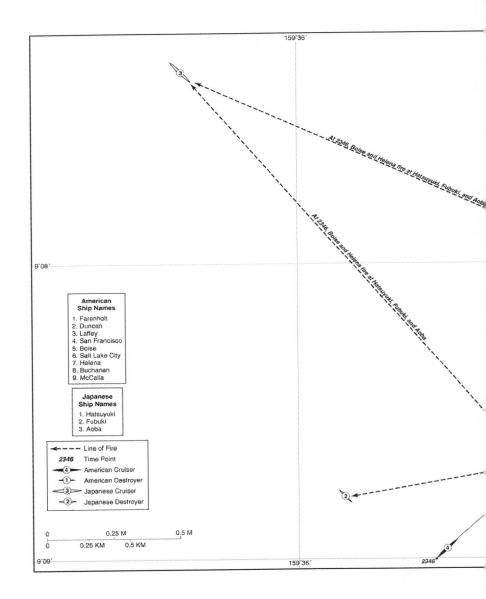

CROSSING THE T: 2346

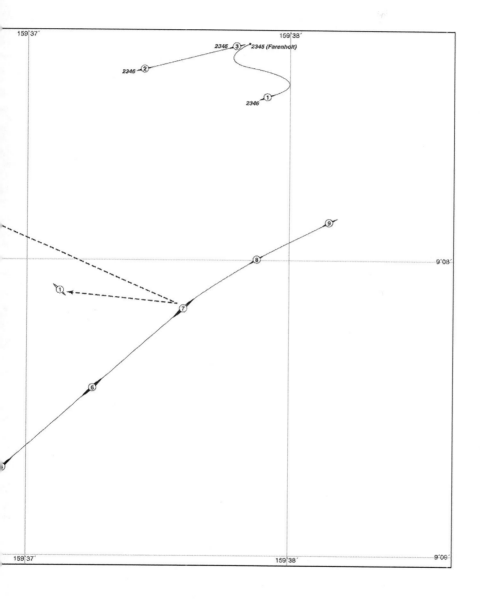

were a distinctive color. It was a violent rainbow.

Within thirty seconds, *Boise* and *Salt Lake City*'s main batteries had opened up on *Aoba* at 4,000-4,500 yards.

Duncan was half a mile abeam *Salt Lake City* when the old cruiser's 8-inch guns fired. Men on *Duncan's* deck were dazzled to see the 265-pound projectiles flying off like big orange balls, their trajectories almost flat as they converged on *Aoba*.

More than five minutes into *Duncan's* torpedo run (and almost two minutes after *Helena* opened fire), *Duncan's* computer finally achieved a torpedo solution on the target aft to starboard. The torpedo director radar-locked on the target and began automatically tracking it.

Salt Lake City fired a starshell. That first bloom of incandescent blue light revealed several Japanese warships. It was a shock to see how close they were.

In the flickering, blue-white light, Taylor watched the 7,500-ton *Aoba* moving right to left across his bow at 3,500 yards. Taylor must have known he would never again have such a fat target illuminated so close in front of him. Impulsively, he switched targets, shouting up at the torpedo director, "There's your target, Mr. Fowler."

Lt.(jg) Fowler took his eye off the telescope to see what the shouting was about and saw the Japanese van cruiser bathed in blue light in front of them. He quickly switched the director off radar control and swung the telescope around onto *Aoba*.

Up in the main battery director, Lt. Hauck had been searching through the slewing sight for the target aft, which radar showed at less than 3,000 yards. When the first starshell burst overhead, he swung the slewing sight around to look at *Aoba*, which was at 3,200 yards. As the sight swung around, the four main battery guns on automatic swung onto *Aoba*.

The telescope on the torpedo director had a tiltable mirror that held the target as *Duncan* rolled. From a mile-and-a-half away, Fowler could see men on the cruiser's decks with horrifying clarity. "All set up," he shouted. "Less than a minute to target. Stand by to fire one."

"Stand by!" Papacoda echoed.

The torpedo tubes were out 55° to starboard. Torpedoman Edwards set the dial for the center tube to fire first. Papacoda double-checked him, then shouted, "Ready to fire five torpedoes high speed."

"Prepare to commence firing at target bearing 45 relative," Taylor shouted. *Helena* shells targeting *Aoba* sailed close across *Duncan*'s bow. Over the phones, Chamberlain told Lt. Hauck to stand by. Torpedoes, as a weapon of surprise, had to be launched before guns opened up or the gunfire would alert the enemy (and also momentarily flashblind torpedomen). Taylor ordered the main battery to open up after the first torpedo was fired and while they were still forward of *Aoba*'s beam.

Hauck swung the slewing sight aft to starboard and resumed searching for their original target. He could not find it because it was so close.

Taylor was studying *Aoba* through binoculars when the first U.S. shells hit her. He saw two 5-inch shells from *Helena* explode high in *Aoba*'s bridge.

The three ships in the Japanese van maneuvered wildly as shells splashed around them. The destroyer to the south, *Fubuki*, put out smoke and swung hard to starboard, while under fire from secondary batteries on *Boise* and *Salt Lake City*. *Aoba*, the cruiser in the center, and the northern destroyer, *Hatsuyuki*, both swung hard to port.

While she was coming around, *Hatsuyuki* briefly came parallel to the U.S. line between *Helena* and *Farenholt*. She fired a 5-inch salvo at *Farenholt*, and one shell hit *Farenholt*'s mast. Then a shell from *Helena* knocked out *Hatsuyuki*'s after battery. *Hatsuyuki* continued coming around, trailing smoke.

It was almost a minute into the battle, and *San Francisco*'s guns were still silent. Her forward fire-control radar had *Fubuki* at 4,600 yards, and Capt. McMorris was pretty certain she was hostile, given her position and that she was under fire by secondary batteries on *Boise* and *Salt Lake City*. Without requesting permission from the Admiral, he ordered Open Firing.

R/Adm. Scott was thinking the only ships to the west were his van destroyers, so when *San Francisco*'s batteries opened up his

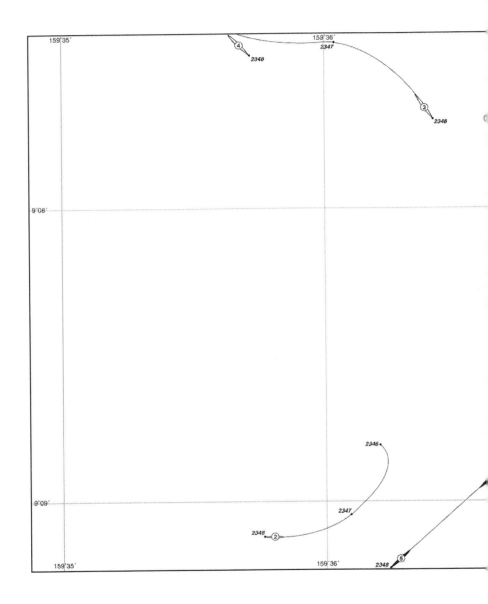

DUNCAN'S TORPEDO RUN: 2346-2348

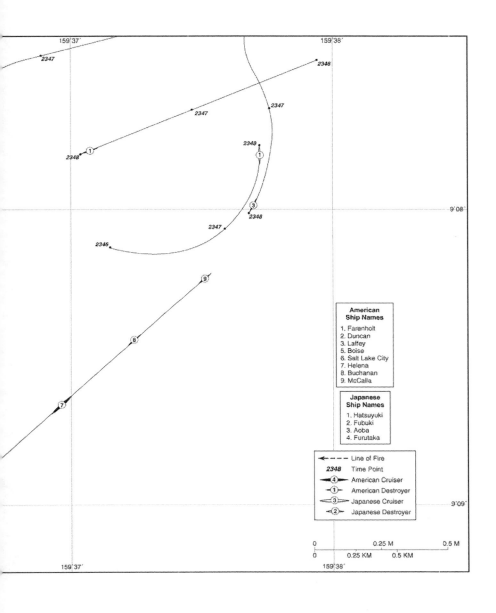

159°37′ 159°38′

2347

2346

2347

2347

2348 ① 2348 ①

9°08″

③
2348

2347

2346

⑨

⑧

⑦

**American
Ship Names**

1. Farenholt
2. Duncan
3. Laffey
5. Boise
6. Salt Lake City
7. Helena
8. Buchanan
9. McCalla

**Japanese
Ship Names**

1. Hatsuyuki
2. Fubuki
3. Aoba
4. Furutaka

◄━ ─ ─ ─   Line of Fire
2348   Time Point
━◄④━   American Cruiser
─◄①─   American Destroyer
━◄③━   Japanese Cruiser
─◄②─   Japanese Destroyer

0   0.25 M   0.5 M
0   0.25 KM   0.5 KM

9°09″

159°37′ 159°38′

first thought was that they were shooting at his destroyers. He grabbed the TBS mic, shouting, "Cease firing! Cease firing!"

On *Duncan*, everybody on the bridge was so riveted by the sight of *Aoba* swinging toward them that nobody noticed *Hatsuyuki* to the east coming up from half a mile astern.

More than a minute into the battle Scott was still shouting "Cease firing!" There was no noticeable letup in fire. It was virtually impossible to hear anything on the TBS while the guns were firing.

Another barrage exploded on *Aoba*'s bridge, and the cruiser reversed course again, swinging back to starboard. 6-inch shells from *Helena* targeting *Aoba* were sailing low over *Duncan*.

To keep the torpedo tubes lined up on *Aoba* as she was swinging away, Taylor had to swing to port into *Helena*'s fire. He probably figured they could get off five torpedoes in thirty seconds, and he could swing away to starboard before receiving too much friendly fire damage.

"Left full rudder," Taylor ordered. "Prepare to fire torpedoes to starboard." "Full left rudder," Lehman echoed. Johnson spun the wheel counter-clockwise, and *Duncan* swung in sharply toward the U.S. line—and into *Helena*'s fire. "Fire when ready!" Taylor shouted.

Laffey was swinging sharply in an emergency turn. Taylor watched as *Laffey* raced off toward the rear of the U.S. column. He could see *Farenholt* half a mile to the east racing again for the new van. "We're on our own," Taylor said aloud but as if to himself.

"Yes, sir," Chamberlain replied.

"Tell Mr. Bryan."

Most of the men on deck aft were watching calmly as 5-inch shells from *Helena* arced toward them. Some were surprised at their own detachment as glowing, red-hot shells flailed in through the night. The first shells passed low overhead. Few men even bothered look around to see what the target was. When shells started bursting close around them, exploding the water with brightly-colored spotting dyes, it came to them all at once that *Duncan* was being targeted. *Helena*'s shells were all shorts or overs so far, but *Duncan* was being "straddled," so it was only a matter of time before they were hit.

All the U.S. destroyers were firing starshells now. The night had become an eerie blue midday.

Oddly, the Japanese ships had not opened fire, except for sporadic machinegun bursts. R/Adm. Gotō had ordered them to hold fire because he thought he had run into R/Adm. Joshima's supply group. One of the first shells that exploded on *Aoba*'s bridge mortally wounded R/Adm. Gotō, and he stepped overboard into the sea.

Up in *Duncan*'s main battery director, Lt. Hauck was searching for their original target when he found *Aoba* again. He was so relieved to find a Japanese cruiser he thought she was their original target.

Wharton was less concerned with the target than the range. He remembered, "When you see [the range] get around 3,000, you say, 'What do we have to do, wait until we see the whites of their eyes?'"

R/Adm. Scott was shouting—"Cease firing! Cease firing!"— over the TBS. Every U.S. ship was still firing.

At 2349, three minutes into the battle, Lt.(jg) Fowler saw a shot at *Aoba* and punched the fire button. "Fire one!" he shouted.

The impulse charge was like a barely perceptible push that was felt throughout the ship.

"One fired," Doty reported. "120 seconds to target."

Within seconds, Lt. Hauck up in the main battery director shouted, "Fire!" Sobelman, the pointer, turned the firing key, which allowed voltage to the guns. Then he turned the key back, which closed the breeches. When the firing pins touched the primers, the two forward 5-inch guns exploded.

The first salvo was like a bomb in your brain. It did not matter how prepared for it you were, you were always dazed and deafened and, if you were on deck, momentarily blinded.

At 2,600 feet-per-second initial muzzle velocity, the shells' trajectories were flat. Fire Controlman Koehler, the rangefinder operator, was watching *Aoba* for 5-inch shell bursts. All he saw were 20mm tracers winking out in the cruiser's superstructure.

Seaman Fischer was watching *Aoba* from the mount of #2 gun, and he saw both shells hit into the ocean short of *Aoba*. "I was mesmerized," Fischer remembered. "These two beautiful red shells hitting the green waves. It was like a water ballet."

"Short 200! Short 200!" A spotter in the mast was screaming.

Lt. Hauck shouted, "Spot up 200." Koehler lengthened out the range 200 yards on the rangefinder. The two forward guns slewed up imperceptibly.

The fire control crew could not believe they missed. They were firing broadsides. Three thousand five hundred yards was point blank for big guns. All the men in the gun director were suddenly defensive and blaming one another. Two hundred yards was a big miss at that short range. Fire-controlman First Class Sobelman, the pointer, and Chief Paige, the trainer, both insisted that they had the cruiser in their cross-hairs. Sobelman kept saying his line-of-sight was on the cruiser's bridge. "I'm dead nuts on the bridge," he said.

Duncan fired again. Then again. Fifty-three pounds of smokeless powder every three or four seconds until the gunfire became a steady roar. The second and third salvos exploded into *Aoba* near the waterline. Koehler saw the dull reddish-brown flashes of 5- inch shell bursts.

In about fifteen seconds, *Duncan's* two forward main battery guns had fired four salvos at *Aoba* under director control.

After the third salvo, smoke from the two forward guns was so thick LCdr. Taylor's view of *Aoba* was obscured. Chief Chamberlain saw warships "on both sides and ahead of us, and it was hard to determine which was which." *Aoba* was swinging hard away and already a near-impossible up-the-kilt shot. Taylor was suddenly afraid that *Aoba* was too close to ships in the U.S. van. He told Chamberlain to ask Hauck if he was on the enemy or one of our own ships. When Hauck came back that he was not positive, Taylor told him to hold fire.

Lt. Bryan took advantage of the lull to phone Taylor and urge him to maintain course and come and see what was to starboard.

Lt. Hauck, hearing the hold-fire order, swung the slewing sight to starboard and searched again for their original target. He quickly located it at less than 2,000 yards. The second Japanese cruiser, *Furutaka*, was steaming closer and closer. At 1,600 yards, Koehler said, "What're we going to do, board 'em?"

The lull in main battery fire lasted about twenty seconds. Then the two forward main battery guns started firing again, in local control.

Ens. Andrews was back at after conn, and he did not know what was happening. The first thing he knew the gunner's mate on the 1.1 shouted, "Jap destroyer off the starboard quarter." He saw *Hatsuyuki* at about 1,000 yards by the flashes from her forward guns firing at *Duncan*.

The two after 5-inch mounts on *Duncan* quickly cut out of automatic. Gun #3 opened up on *Hatsuyuki* with starshells, while the talker tried to raise the main battery director. Gun #4 switched to armor-piercing shells before pouring rounds at *Hatsuyuki*.

San Francisco stopped firing at *Fubuki* finally, and R/Adm. Scott took advantage of the sudden silence to call Capt. Tobin again. "How are you?" He asked.

"OK."

"Were we shooting at 12 [DesRon 12]?" Scott asked, revealing his worst fear.

"I don't know who you were shooting at," Tobin replied.

Alarmed, Scott ordered the destroyers to flash their recognition lights.

In *Duncan*'s pilothouse, Lt.(jg) Beebe was walking toward the electric panel on the bulkhead as Taylor was pushing through toward the starboard wing. Chamberlain was relaying a report from gun #3 that a Japanese destroyer was off the starboard quarter.

Out on the starboard wing, Lt. Bryan was watching the wake of their torpedo drilling after *Aoba* and gnawing on the knuckle of his pinkie. When Taylor joined him, Bryan nodded off 30° to starboard. Taylor looked off and saw *Furutaka* as another large blur materializing.

Bryan glanced up at the mast to see the recognition lights flash.

Recognition lights were three lights displayed vertically on the mast. Tonight's colors were green-on-green-on-green. Bryan saw them blink on and off once, twice...

Two 5-inch shells from *Hatsuyuki* to starboard exploded on *Duncan*. One exploded at the base of the forward stack, and the other high in the mast.

Within seconds of the first torpedo, Lt.(jg) Fowler shouted— "Fire Two!" The moment he pushed the firing button, the shell that exploded in the mast rained shrapnel on the roof of the bridge. Everybody on the roof was knocked down by shrapnel or the blast.

The concussion from the explosion in the mast caused Lt. Bryan to bite off the tip of his pinkie.

Both shells from *Hatsuyuki* were devastating, but nobody inside the bridge heard either over the forward guns firing. They were surprised when they heard the after 5-inch guns open up.

For a few minutes, time stood still; everything happened so fast men's brains short- circuited in processing the overload. Seaman Carlson, ammo passer on the 1.1, first heard "a 'bang' forward" (*Hatsuyuki*'s first shell hitting the base of *Duncan*'s forward stack), then "a 'whanging' sound' of the first torpedo being fired," next the "whirl of the #3 mount toward [*Hatsuyuki*]. Hardly had this happened, we were hit hard forward and repeatedly."

Shipfitter Wickstrom with the after repair party remembered, "The starshells lit up the whole bay. At the same time, we got hit on our stack."

The forward stack began toppling as if in slow motion. The stack fell slowly aft, first knocking down the gig, which fell onto the forward repair men who were below in the exterior passageway. Boatswain's Mate First Class Dernehl was cut in two by the gig falling on him.

The stack continued toppling aft to starboard, tangled in cables and twisting. At one point, it dipped into the ocean, which sent it flying aft faster. Startled men on the roof of the after deckhouse, seeing the stack rolling toward them, tried to scramble out of its way.

A fireball erupted from the forward fireroom through a hole in the deck where the stack had been. The gun crew in the 20mm on 0-1 level and the men in the clipping room were driven from their stations by a rising cloud of steam. The three mess attendants who had been manning the clipping room—George Allen, Matthew Moreland, and Samuel Jones—dropped down through the ammo passing scuttle into officer country.

Machinegun rounds from *Hatsuyuki* were ripping into *Duncan*'s starboard side. Down in the I.C., the main gyro was vibrating from all the gunfire. Chief Colbeck was stepping over to adjust it when a 20mm round tore in through the starboard sea bulkhead near the overhead. The shell ricocheted off machinery and exploded next to the hatch where Electrician's Mate Christensen was standing. Christensen took the full force of the blast and was killed instantly. Everyone else in the small compartment was knocked senseless.

At the same time, a 20mm round from port entered the forward fireroom. It tore through the electric board and exited through the starboard bulkhead. Nobody was injured, but the electric board blew out. The board blowing out tripped the generator, so boilers #1 and #2 were disabled. The talker reported the situation to Chief Magee in the forward engineroom. Magee told them to secure the boilers and evacuate.

On the roof of the bridge, Lt.(jg) Fowler was laying on the deck at the base of the torpedo director, semiconscious. He had a gaping neck wound, and his chest was drenched in blood. Instinctively, he struggled to his feet. He grabbed the torpedo director and managed to pull himself up. He reached for the firing button and pushed it. Nothing happened. He pushed it again—nothing. Losing consciousness, he collapsed back onto the deck.

All at once, nothing was functioning. "The steering control was knocked out," Johnson, the helmsman, remembered. "After we got hit we couldn't conn anything from the pilothouse. We were hard to port. We had 20° left rudder."

Flames blazed around the torpedo tubes. Chief Boyd thought he ought to fire off the torpedoes before the warheads exploded

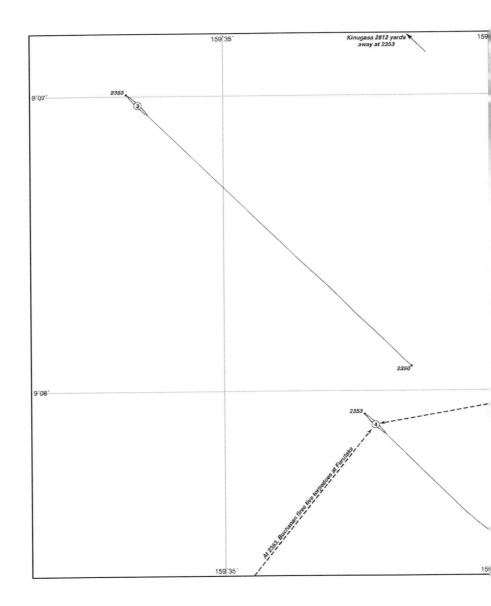

159°35′

Kinugasa 2812 yards
away at 2353

159

9°07′

2353

③

9°08′

2350

2353

④

At 2353, Buchanan fires five torpedoes at Furutaka

159°35′

15

DUNCAN OUT OF CONTROL FIRES AT FURUTAKA: 2350-2353

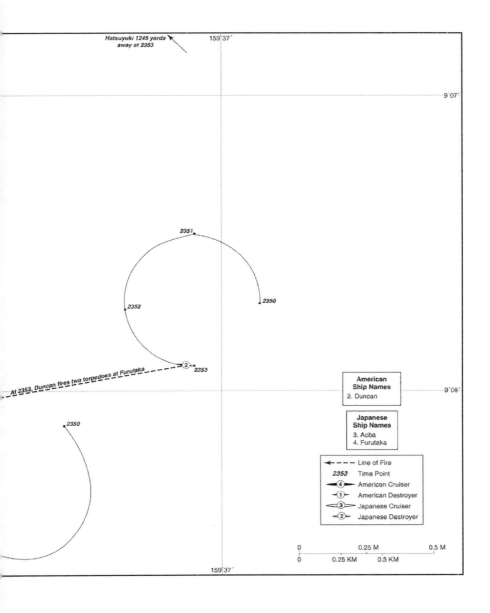

Hatsuyuki 1245 yards
away at 2353

159°37'

9°07'

2351

2352

2350

2353

At 2353, Duncan fires two torpedoes at Furutaka

2350

9°08'

**American
Ship Names**
2. Duncan

**Japanese
Ship Names**
3. Aoba
4. Furutaka

— — — Line of Fire
2353   Time Point
◄●④●►   American Cruiser
◄①►   American Destroyer
◄③►   Japanese Cruiser
◄②►   Japanese Destroyer

0   0.25 M   0.5 M
0   0.25 KM   0.5 KM

159°37'

in the heat. Torpedoman-striker Dan Ragsdale was dead in the mount, crushed by the stack. The phones were out. The electrical connection to the torpedo director was dead. Flames and sparks and thick, heavy smoke drifting aft made it difficult to see more than a few feet.

Chief Boyd was about to jettison a torpedo when he caught a glimpse through the smoke of *Furutaka* to starboard at about 1,200 yards.

At 2348, two minutes after Scott started calling for cease firing, *Helena*'s main batteries stopped firing at *Duncan*, after firing at her for one full minute without ever hitting her. Secondary batteries on *Helena* continued to fire at *Duncan*.

From *Boise,* lookouts could see three burning ships: two to the left [*Fubuki* and *Aoba*]; and one far to the right [*Duncan*]. With her forward stack gone, *Duncan* looked like a Japanese *Amagiri*-class destroyer, and her continuing left turn was carrying her between *Furutaka* and the U.S. line.

At 2348, the minute *Helena* stopped firing at *Duncan*, *Boise* lit *Duncan* and took her under fire for another minute.

It was between 2348 and 2349 that all hell broke loose on *Duncan*. Boatswain's Mate John Vandonkelaar, who was in the after repair party, remembered the stack going over, then "*Boise* put a light on us."

Lt. Bryan had left the bridge to return aft to his battle station at after conn. LCdr. Taylor was still out on the starboard wing watching *Furutaka* materialize out of the blackness to starboard when *Boise*'s searchlight lit *Duncan,* and the light spilled over, illuminating sections of *Furutaka*. Taylor saw the second Japanese cruiser's superstructure lit with shocking clarity—the heavily raked stacks (the forward stack much larger), the turtle appearance of the up-take forward of her leading stack, the sloping appearance of the after deck. Her turrets were trained in, and her decks looked relatively empty. She was 1,300 yards astern *Aoba* and was swinging to starboard, as if trying to insert herself between the wounded *Aoba* and the U.S. line. Lookouts on *Duncan* then spotted a third Japanese cruiser, *Kinugasa*, swinging to port 1,300 yards to the west.

Seeking shelter from *Hatsuyuki* to starboard, *Duncan*'s forward repair party was huddled at the port side of the exterior passageway when two 5-inch shells from *Boise* hit amidships to port. When the smoke cleared, forward repair men lay dead the length of the passageway. Only Machinist's Mate Olek stumbled to his feet. The air was damp with steam that was billowing out of the giant hole in the deck. Seeing three more shells hurtling in from *Boise*, Olek started to run to starboard, but he only got a few steps before he stumbled over Chief Morton's body.

Kinugasa, the third Japanese cruiser, was firing at a U.S. cruiser when *Duncan*'s bridge superstructure got in her line of fire. An 8-inch *Kinugasa* shell tore into *Duncan*'s radio room on 0-2 level from starboard and drilled upward, exploding in the code room with a deafening concussion, and, continuing upward, exited the port side at bridge level.

Men aft could see the disaster that was unfolding forward. "When the chartroom got hit, that's when all hell started breaking loose," Wickstrom remembered. "Ammunition was exploding. This was all happening amidships and forward."

All the after repair men were running to their tool locker. Except for Watertender Boyle, who became unhinged and hid in a ready locker where 20mm ammo was stored. Two more shells from a second two-gun salvo from *Hatsuyuki* hit into *Duncan* from starboard. The first shell drilled through the deck and started fires in the galley and the exec's office. The second shell was a dud that hit into the chartroom behind the pilothouse. Nobody on the bridge even noticed it because they were all so dazed from the explosion of the 8-inch round seconds earlier.

A 5-inch shell from a third salvo from *Hatsuyuki* hit into the main deck amidships to starboard one inch from the forward engineroom bulkhead, and it drilled down into the fireroom. A huge explosion below blew a steel deck plate into the air that almost crushed Olek.

The talker in the forward fireroom had just reported to Chief Magee that they were battling a small fire and would evacuate as soon as "everything's straightened out." When the 5-inch round exploded in from overhead, boilers jumped six inches off their beds and high-pressure, superheated steam cut men to ribbons.

Men stationed below could not always hear the shell hits, but they could smell them. In the after engineroom, Lt. Kabat and Chief Machinist's Mate Harry Solomon smelled burned gunpowder and knew they were hit. Solomon ordered the vent blowers shut off. The engineroom talker lost contact with the forward fireroom and could barely hear the forward engineroom or the after fireroom.

On deck, after repair men were running forward, tools in hand. They were stopped by the wall of steam rising from the huge hole in the deck where the forward stack had been. This was a far bigger salvage problem than they ever faced in training. Half-heartedly, they broke out a firehouse and hooked it up, but, when they turned on the water, there was none because there was no power. They were all standing around discussing what to do next when Seaman Louis Cruz was hit in the leg by shrapnel from ready ammo that was exploding across the deck.

When the forward fireroom was disabled, Chief Magee in the forward engineroom went through a series of steps aimed at keeping the generator and pumps running. It was another training exercise they had done a hundred times: close the bulkhead stop to #1 and #2 boilers; open the auxiliary steam stop from aft; cut the emergency electrical power from #2 generator.

In #2 gun mount, Fischer saw Dunn's face blanch, and he looked around in time to see a Japanese incendiary round drill through the deck into officer country. Dunn shouted, "Let's get out of here!"

Officer country was deserted when the round crashed in. It tore forward, setting fire to everything, and crashing out through the forward bulkhead into #2 handling room.

The incendiary round broke through the bulkhead into the handling room. There was only a minor concussion, but the compartment was showered with sparks. Shellmen Joseph Fallon and Edward Ferreira dove out through the shell hole into officer country. Powdermen Rosalio Rizzi and George Goodman remained at their stations while the incendiary round sizzled at their feet. Severely burned, Rizzi continued passing powder cartridges up to the mount while Goodman, dazed, continued sending shells up the hoist.

One level down was #2 magazine, an airless little space where John Kemp, James Duncan, and Edward Bowers, the unpopular short-order cook, were busily opening powder cans and passing the brass cartridges up to Rizzi. Hearing the incendiary round crashing in above, Kemp slammed the hoist trap shut before the concussion and smoke traversed down. Then a much bigger shell exploded into the handling room.

At 2350, seconds after the incendiary round, an 8-inch round from *Salt Lake City* exploded into #2 handling room through the port bulkhead. Instantly, the handling room evaporated in a tremendous explosion.

The explosion ten feet from the bridge blew up the forward part of the ship. All four men in the forward 20mms were killed, including Seaman David Fowler, the divinity student who was the best machine gunner of them all. Gunner's Mate Robert Taylor lived just long enough to tell Seaman Wood his two big regrets: leaving his wife and not seeing Australia.

The handling room explosion blew open the hatch in #2 gun mount. The concussion blew shellman Leo O'Brien's head off. Hot shellman George Ginder, who had been standing behind the trainer's seat, was knocked to the deck inside the mount, mortally wounded. Gun captain Dunn was blown out of his seat, and he landed down on the fo'csle with two broken legs. Fuse-setter Stanley Dubiel had been sitting with his legs dangling down into the handling room hatch, so his legs were horribly burned and he was screaming.

On the bridge, everyone was violently knocked to the deck. Starboard wing lookout James Flaherty felt the deck drop out from under him. Inside the pilothouse, Chief Chamberlain was thrown against the bulkhead and knocked unconscious.

Up in the main battery director, Koehler had "the sensation that the director jumped a foot or two in the air." Sobelman remembered it felt "like a dog took the ship and shook it."

The explosion in #2 handling room caused *Duncan* to tremble from end to end. Even men aft were knocked off their feet. Men on the after gun platform did not hear the explosion over the noise from #3 gun, which was in rapid fire at *Hatsuyuki*, but Carlson, who was holding onto the tub shield in the 1.1, was jarred to his knees. They all knew they were hit hard forward. Thick, oily smoke poured over them, smoke full of ash and cordite particles that made it difficult to breathe.

At 2350, *Boise*'s gunnery officer saw an explosion envelope *Duncan*, and he ordered cease firing. By then, some of the after 5-inch guns on *Boise* had been firing at *Duncan* for almost four minutes.

On *Duncan*, the two forward main battery guns were firing in local control. In the mount of #2 gun, trainer Fischer and pointer Boehm still had their eyes on their sights, and loader Shurney down on deck was still throwing shells into the gun like he was on automatic. The gun was swinging around, still firing. "A cam on the outside ring of the mount was supposed to come up and stop it and release the trigger mechanism," Fischer remembered, "but we're still firing." Suddenly, in his gun sight, Fischer saw "the captain smoking his cigar." It was supposed to be impossible for the gun to come all the way around and point aft. Fischer's first thought was that he was seeing things, but he looked up and there was Taylor on the starboard bridgewing with a cigar in his mouth. Fischer choked, "Cease fire!"

A large-caliber shell hit the base of #1 gun mount. It exploded on the cog wheel gears that the mount turned on. Unaware they were hit, the mount crew continued firing. Then spademan Raymond Whelan noticed he was wounded. He looked around and saw fire pouring out of #2 handling room and the pilothouse. He tapped Gunner's Mate First Class Davenport on the shoulder. Davenport took one look and shouted, "Cease firing!"

The #1 gun had been firing continuously since the first salvo. Even after power failed, the #1 gun squeezed out four or five more rounds in local control. Yet it fired no more than twelve to fifteen rounds total. Given the rate of fire of a 5-inch gun at about fifteen shells per minute, *Duncan*'s entire battle could hardly have lasted a minute.

Chapter 7
"AMERICAN DESTROYER"
2350 October 11-0200 October 12

Heartily know, When half-gods go, The gods arrive.
—Ralph Waldo Emerson

Everybody on *San Francisco*'s bridge was silent watching *Fubuki* swinging away. When suddenly she came parallel to them at 1,400 yards, looking as if she was steadying on a torpedo-firing course, everybody started screaming. It was 2351.

Down on the flag bridge, R/Adm. Scott was out on the starboard wing looking for destroyer recognition lights when *San Francisco*'s searchlight lit *Fubuki*. Seeing a destroyer type he instantly recognized as Japanese, Scott ordered open firing for the first time. It was five minutes into the battle (and four minutes since he first ordered cease firing).

San Francisco fired four ten-gun salvos at *Fubuki* while the Japanese destroyer increased speed and swung away sharply. A shell from the fourth salvo exploded on *Fubuki*.

As van destroyer *Farenholt* was racing south for the new van, she crossed *Duncan*'s wake. Capt. Tobin was shocked to learn *Duncan* was ahead of him.

On *Duncan*, men were slow to recover from the handling room blast. Inside the mount of #2 gun, both Ginder and Dubiel were writhing on the deck. Fischer and Boehm remained in their seats. A broken hydraulic pipe was pumping hot recoil oil into a hole in Fischer's leg, but he was so dazed by the blast he did not feel it. Boehm suddenly jumped to his feet. He grabbed Dubiel and shoved him out through the spent shell hatch in the floor of the mount, which dumped him onto the roof of the forward deckhouse. As the gun was pointing aft to starboard, the mount hatch opened to port, so Boehm was able to step out onto the deckhouse roof.

Still dazed, Fischer got up out of his seat. He did not notice the hole in his foot until he put weight on it. He was just starting down the ladder to the fo'csle when he saw Ginder getting to his feet inside the mount. That was the last anyone saw of George Ginder.

Climbing down to the fo'csle, Fischer could see ready ammo was cooking off and firing across the deck. The instant he set foot on deck, a 20mm round hit him in the shoulder and knocked him out.

Half the men on bridge level were unconscious or dead. The pilothouse was filled with steam and funnel smoke and chemical smoke from smoke generators and burning flags. It was a heavy caustic smoke laced with the searing rasp of cordite. The ventilation ports were open, but fires were raging around the bridgewings. From inside, it looked as if the whole ship was engulfed in flames. The bridge crew still manned their stations, gasping and choking, eyes burning. Chief Chamberlain, dazed from a concussion and flashblind, sat on the deck manning the phones, though few connections remained. The captain was out on the starboard wing shouting down to men on the fo'csle to abandon.

Down in the I.C., the crew, deafened and disoriented, was slowly coming to their senses. It was pitch-black. Wharton's first thought was that he was blind. He could hear distant explosions and the quieter, closer, more-ominous sound of running water. Then he noticed there was an inch or two of water on the deck. The air was so thick and acrid from burning wiring he could not breathe without choking. In the dark, it is difficult to know how badly injured you are, but he felt like he was covered in blood. Fire Controlman Hess noticed a power light on the I.C. panel, and he went over and picked up a phone and got Chief Chamberlain. He told him the I.C. was hit. Chamberlain's voice came back groggy, "Rescue the pay accounts." (The pay accounts were in the burning exec's office next door.) Then the last fire control circuit died, and the power-failure bell started ringing. Fire Controlman Combs cut the gyro to battery, which stopped the ringing. The water on the deck was beginning to slosh around. Somebody tried to open the hatch, but it was jammed.

Lt. Bryan tried to get aft to his battle station but was barely able to get off bridge level. He had to feel his way it was so dark. The deck was littered with bodies. The ladders were all wrecked. Bryan made it down two levels but was stopped on 0-1 deck by the fire geyser erupting from the forward fireroom.

At 2353, seven minutes into the battle, a lookout on *Boise* spotted a destroyer to the west that looked like a *Livermore*-class. *Boise* put a searchlight on it, and lit *Farenholt* 400 yards out steaming for the van.

Fire controlmen on the second Japanese cruiser, *Furutaka,* saw *Boise*'s searchlight and made it their aiming point. *Furutaka*'s forward batteries opened up on *Boise* with incendiary shells first.

An after 8-inch gun on *Furutaka* tried to fire on *Duncan,* but the two ships were so close, less than a thousand yards, that *Furutaka*'s gun was unable to depress enough to hit *Duncan* anywhere but up around the main battery director barbette.

The Japanese ships were all firing flashless cordite so there were no muzzle flashes. All you could see were flickers of blue flame. *Boise* lookouts never saw *Furutaka* until she was firing at them.

On *Duncan*'s torpedo mount, Chief Torpedoman Boyd watched as they surged closer and closer to the Japanese cruiser. *Furutaka* was headed directly at *Boise* and was firing at *Boise.* Then *Furutaka* was suddenly straddled by shells from *Helena* and *Salt Lake City.* Boyd aimed the torpedo tubes by eye, and, when *Duncan* was about 800 yards from the cruiser, Boyd struck the firing pins with his mallet. *Bang, whoosh, bang, whoosh*— two torpedoes leaped into the dark. "40 seconds to target," Boyd shouted.

At 2354, R/Adm. Scott was informed that the Japanese ships were withdrawing, and he ordered a course change to 310° (a little north of west) to pursue them. He then dictated a terse dispatch to V/Adm. Ghormley and Maj.Gen. Vandegrift: "ENGAGING HEAVY CRUISERS."

Scott's change of course only elicited more grumbling on *Duncan*'s bridge because, again, he had not order a simultaneous

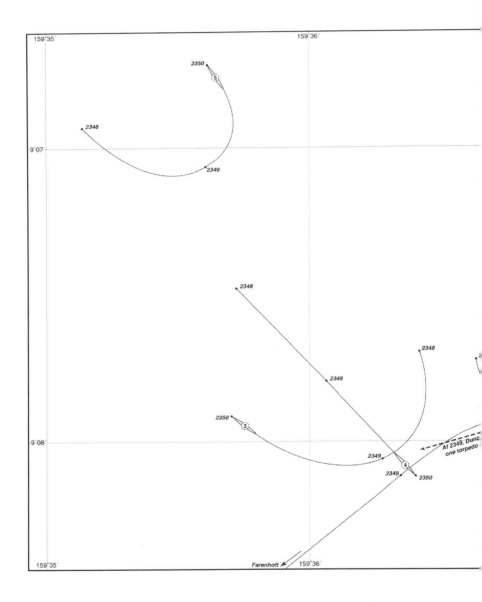

DUNCAN FIRES AT HATSUYUKI AND AOBA: 2348-2350

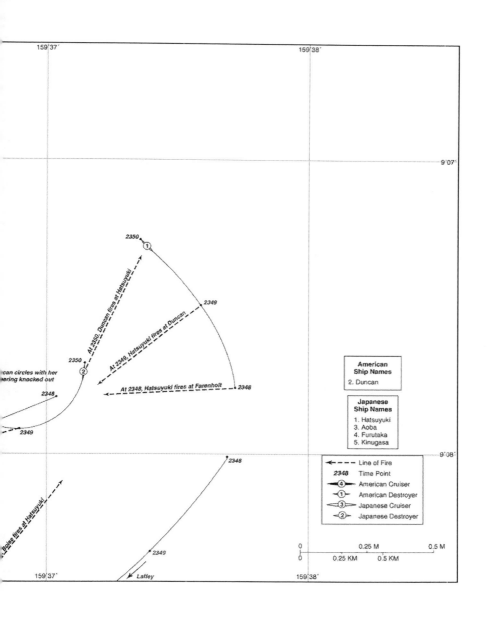

159°37′ 159°38′

9°07′

2350
① 2350

At 2350, Duncan fires at Hatsuyuki

2349

At 2349, Hatsuyuki fires at Duncan

can circles with her
...ering knocked out

2350
② 2350

At 2348, Hatsuyuki fires at Farenholt 2348

2348

2349

Boise fires at Hatsuyuki

**American
Ship Names**
2. Duncan

**Japanese
Ship Names**
1. Hatsuyuki
3. Aoba
4. Furutaka
5. Kinugasa

9°08′

◄---- Line of Fire
2348 Time Point
◄④► American Cruiser
◄①► American Destroyer
◄③► Japanese Cruiser
◄②► Japanese Destroyer

2348

2349

Laffey

159°37′ 159°38′

0   0.25 M   0.5 M
0   0.25 KM   0.5 KM

turn to bring them around faster. And he had not ordered an increase in speed so that they might catch them. Some men were openly suggesting that Scott did not want to catch them.

Furutaka was ablaze from a barrage of shells that hit her amidships. She was swinging to starboard under withering fire from three U.S. cruisers while two *Duncan* torpedoes closed on her.

Then, as *Furutaka* came parallel to the U.S. line at about 2,000 yards, *Buchanan* fired a spread of five torpedoes at her.

On *Duncan*, Chief Boyd was loudly counting down as the two ships surged closer and closer. Blue lights floated lazily overhead casting eerie shadows among the swinging ships. "...four-three-two-ONE."

At that moment, six 8-inch shells from *Salt Lake City* struck into and around the wounded Japanese cruiser. One explosion close by *Furutaka*'s port side sent up a column of water higher than the others. Men on *Duncan*'s after deckhouse thought it was one of their torpedoes, and they started celebrating.

Furutaka's forward guns continued firing at *Boise*. At 0000—midnight—*Boise* was straddled eleven times in quick succession and then was hit four times in twenty-six seconds.

Furutaka's forward main battery guns went silent, and, in the sudden, eerie quiet, muffled explosions like firecrackers in a tin can could be heard coming from deep inside the cruiser. Very slowly, *Furutaka* split apart, and she was consumed in a great red- orange-yellow explosion that appeared to lift her several feet off the sea.

The excited celebration aft on *Duncan* was cut short by another in-coming shell from the American line. It was a dud that tore into the machine shop sideways. The concussion inside blew bolts off the hatch.

R/Adm. Scott was watching *Boise* when she was hit. She was in flames but was still in rapid fire when she veered off into the dark and he lost sight of her. A minute after that, Scott ordered cease firing.

Furutaka was a fiery glow behind a dense cloud of smoke. *Boise* continued firing at her for two minutes after Scott's cease fire order, until 0003 when lookouts saw *Furutaka*'s stern upend.

Farenholt was still racing south to regain the van. Her temperamental TBS caused her to miss Scott's turn order again, so Tobin was unaware that *San Francisco* had turned west, and *Farenholt* steamed across *San Francisco*'s bow.

Seeing a destroyer ahead of them to the west, *San Francisco* took *Farenholt* under fire.

Hit three times, *Farenholt* cut sharply to port as *San Francisco* swept past her. *Farenholt* quickly came around and raced to the new van, and she was soon leading *San Francisco* west at 20 knots.

Seeing *Boise* swing out of column in flames shook Scott. The U.S. column was a shambles. Ships were so spread out radarmen could not make out the column. Scott was not sure how many ships he still had. He ordered them to close up and to flash recognition lights.

San Francisco lit *Fubuki* again. The Japanese destroyer was near vertical, propellers spinning in the air.

Searchlights on the U.S. cruisers were sweeping the sea ahead and to starboard. *McCalla* fired a spread of starshells. All around, the sea was empty.

* * *

Southwest of Savo Island, *Duncan* was circling out of control and losing power. The bridge had lost power almost completely. Steering, engine order telegraph, recognition lights—all were out. Most battle circuits were dead. Chief Chamberlain had repeatedly called the after steering engineroom to have them straighten out the rudder, but he never heard a reply. LCdr. Taylor, unable to issue orders or receive reports from beyond the walls of flame, was effectively relieved of command.

Bridge messengers were sent forward and aft, and both returned. One was blocked by the fire in #2 handling room and the other by the fire in #1 fireroom. When Bryan returned, the fight went out of out of Taylor, and he said to Bryan quietly, "Abandon ship." It was twenty minutes since they had started on the torpedo run.

"We've been hit! The bridge is on fire!" Chief Chamberlain shouted into the phones. "Abandon ship!"

Some stations heard him. The steering engineroom, the station furthest away that he had been trying to reach so urgently, heard him clearly and replied, but Chamberlain did not hear them.

On the roof of the bridge, Lt.(jg) Rhodes was dead at the 20mm director. Lt.(jg) Fowler lay motionless on the deck beside the torpedo director. Papacoda and Edwards checked him out and decided he was dead. The surviving men on the bridge roof were recovering from the shock of the blast, wandering around, disoriented. None of them heard an order to abandon. There was a lot of shouting down on the bridgewing. Papacoda went and looked down. He saw men below cutting down halyards in preparation for lowering wounded over the side.

Chief Paige, climbing down from the main battery director, stopped on the roof of the bridge when he heard someone moaning in the dark. He found Lt.(jg) Fowler laying on the deck asking for help. Sobelman came over to see where Paige went. When he saw Fowler, he grabbed two morphine syrettes from the cabinet on the director barbette, and he gave Fowler a shot in each leg. Then he took a compress from his belt and tied it around Fowler's neck to try to staunch the bleeding. Fire Controlmen James Bilbro and James Queen joined them, and Paige told them to cut down halyards.

On the main deck, men were abandoning while men below were still manning their stations or struggling to escape them.

In the dark I.C., the men could feel the water was rising around their feet. Christensen's body was starting to float. "If we weren't steaming in circles, that hole would be below the waterline," Ham remembered. They tried to cut through the bulkhead into the exec's office, but the bulkhead was red-hot from the fire on the other side. At that point, some of them gave up. Others went to work on the hatch. They were all gasping in the smoky airlessness. Lt.(jg) Wharton became unhinged. He kept saying that nobody knew they were there and that it was hopeless and they were all going to drown like rats. He started to scream for help at the top of his lungs. His screams were unnerving in the dark in such a small space.

In the forward engineroom, Chief Magee released the men in the lower section, and they all exited up through the hatch into the machine shop. But then, as soon as they were gone, fire flared up between the upper and lower sections, cutting off that route of escape for the remaining men. They were forced to battle through the fire in the upper section to get to the ladder to the deck. They were involved in this effort when Chief Magee sensed the ship slowing. Glancing at the gauges, he saw that their speed was down to 15 knots and that the pressure from #1 flushing pump was down to 5 pounds (from 120 pounds). "Okay, let's cut it off and take it aft," Magee said suddenly. The men all quickly returned to their stations. Bethune cut off the steam forward while others cut it in aft. Then they resumed battling the fire. The heat was intense. All of them were on the verge of collapse by the time they cut a path to the ladder. The first man up tried to push open the hatch but was only able to push it up enough to see that there was debris piled on top of it.

On top of the forward deckhouse, Boehm was passed out. He finally regained his senses and began making his way around the mount. It was difficult going because it was so dark and what remained of the deck was unsupported from below and sloping forward. He found Dubiel unconscious at the bottom of the shell scuttle. He put a lifejacket on him and lowered him to the fo'csle.

Down in the I.C., the men working to unjam the hatch came to realize there was something outside in the passageway jammed against it. They took turns shaking the hatch violently. Finally, it budged a little. After a while, the object outside was partially dislodged, and they managed to get the hatch opened enough that the smallest man was able to squeeze out. He cleared away the debris outside. The object that had been jamming the hatch was the charred remains of Watertender John Puzines, the Navy wrestling champion. When the hatch was pulled open and air rushed in, Lt.(jg) Wharton rushed out, shouting, "Abandon! Abandon!" Chief Colbeck delegated two men to carry Christensen to sick bay.

Boehm's only thought was to get aft and see if anybody was alive and who was in command. He left Dubiel unconscious in a heap on the fo'csle and started making his way aft along the port side, but he did not get far before he saw fire amidships shooting out 50 yards to port. Returning to the fo'csle, he walked around forward of #1 gun and then headed aft along the starboard side, but again he did not get far before he saw fire amidships shooting out 50 yards to starboard.

Men from the I.C. began arriving in the mess. There were no medics there. They laid Christensen on a table. Then they all stood around assessing their own wounds. Combs was the most seriously injured. He had wounds in his side and shell fragments in one arm. The others had mostly scrapes and scratches. Wharton was riddled with little shrapnel cuts and was completely unnerved. When he suddenly announced that he was going up to see the captain, the others just stared after him as he walked to the ladder and started climbing up.

Wharton came up through the scuttle. He emerged in the exterior passageway, which was littered with bodies. Incoming shells were still splashing around the ship. Ready ammo was popping off. Wharton could see that the bridge superstructure was demolished. He shouted down through the scuttle, telling the others to go forward to the fo'csle. Wharton decided he wanted to check out his stateroom. Smoke was billowing out of the hatch to officer country, but Wharton took a deep breath and scrambled down the ladder. Below in the passageway, paint and linoleum were burning fiercely. Wharton remembered bitterly senior officers telling them paint did not burn. Seeing flames blowing out of his stateroom, he raced back up the ladder.

In the mess, the men from the I.C. were moving into the passageway toward officer country when Chief Colbeck heard someone calling from on deck. He went over to the ladder and, looking up, saw Lt.(jg) Broccolo looking down. Broccolo told him he had Chief Pharmacist's Mate King, who was wounded. He said he needed help lowering him to the mess. Colbeck told him they were supposed to be abandoning. Chief King begged Doc Broccolo not to leave him. Broccolo told Colbeck he had to attend to his chief. King's back was riddled with shrapnel, and he screamed in pain as Broccolo lowered him into Colbeck's arms. They laid him on a table in the mess face down. Broccolo then took a quick look at Christensen and pronounced him dead. Colbeck suddenly felt the need for air. He told Combs he was going topside to see what was happening. Combs followed him up.

The passageway was scattered with debris and bodies. Colbeck and Combs, stepping carefully to starboard, went around the bridge superstructure. A small fire was burning in the wardroom. Colbeck grabbed a CO_2 tank and quickly extinguished it. They could see the wall of fire forward blowing out of #2 handling room and the fire aft erupting from the forward fireroom. That section of the main deck was completely cut off.

Colbeck and Combs returned down to the mess, where Doc Broccolo was picking pieces of shrapnel out of Chief King's back. Colbeck ask him if there was anything they could do. Broccolo shook his head hopelessly. "I don't have the right instruments anyway," he sighed.

Colbeck looked into the I.C. and saw that some console lights were on, indicating that a phone circuit was operating. He went in and phoned the bridge. Signalman Sam Albright answered. Albright said the forward part of the ship was ablaze and the crew was abandoning.

Colbeck told Broccolo the crew was abandoning. Broccolo said they would be along in a moment.

Colbeck and Combs headed forward. They had just entered the passageway when a shell exploded behind them in the galley. It killed ship's cook Emil Johnson and started a fire. Moments later, a second shell exploded in the mess. That shell killed Lt.(jg) Broccolo and Chief King and turned the mess into an inferno.

Carlson was up on the main deck, checking out bodies amidships when he encountered Lt.(jg) Wharton. "What's happening?" Wharton asked. Carlson thought it was an odd question under the circumstances. He told him Taylor and Bryan had abandoned, but Wharton did not believe him. "Taylor would never abandon," he said. "I'm going up to see the captain." He removed his side arm and thrust it into Carlson's hands.

Scaling scorched ladders and debris, Wharton made it up to 0-1 level. He went inside the radio room. Two bodies were sitting upright at their desks, hands on the keys. Wharton managed to climb up one more level to 0-2 deck. The heat there was intense from fire that was still raging up on the bridge. Wharton looked in the coding room. The smoke inside was suffocating, but he saw Ens. Lane sitting at his desk with his head missing.

When Fischer regained consciousness, he found himself laying on the fo'csle. Opening his eyes, the first thing he focused on was a vision of the captain on the bridge, pointing off and shouting, "Abandon ship! Abandon Ship! Land on the port bow!" Lifting his head, Fischer looked around. All around, men were abandoning.

Mess Attendant Shurney was standing alone, gazing down absently into the fire in #2 handling room. Boehm walked over to him, and they stood together, staring down into the fire in silence. Rizzi's body was standing upright in the inferno. "I can't swim," Shurney said to Boehm forlornly. At that moment, a piece of shrapnel hit Shurney's lifejacket, and it burst into flames. Men ran over. They grabbed Shurney and wrestled him to the deck and held him there while somebody pissed on him. That put the fire out, but Shurney was sore about it for days.

Boehm tried to get a handybilly (portable pump) started, but shrapnel had punctured the motor. Everybody else on the fo'csle was staring up at the bridge. They could see men jumping off the bridge. "Now that really tells you something when you see your officers jumping off the bridge," Albert Viering remembered.

"Well, okay then," Davenport said. "Let's get off the ship."

Boehm went back to where he had left Dubiel. He found Dubiel still unconscious. He dragged him to the side and lifted him up. Destroyers had rounded fo'csles that extended outward, so Boehm had to really heave him. Dubiel safely cleared the side and vanished into the dark.

The few men remaining on bridge level were anxious to get

off. The fire below in the coding room was eating at the deck beneath their feet. "You better leave while you still have time," LCdr. Taylor kept saying over and over. Chamberlain was handing out lifejackets, shouting, "Get a kapok jacket, boys." Most of them had pneumatic belts on but were happy to take an extra. They were waiting in line out on the starboard wing for their turn to go down the halyards that were hanging over the side. Lt.(jg) Beebe, Quartermaster Johnson, and Signalman Benson followed each other down. Some choose not to wait and leaped 40 feet to the sea.

Duncan was losing speed, but she was plowing along at about 15 knots. "About as soon as I hit the water she was gone," Beebe remembered.

Men were still piling up through the forward hatch onto the fo'csle. The three mess stewards from the forward clipping room were among the first onto the fo'csle and were among the last to go. For half an hour, they stood together clutching their mattresses while loudly trying to talk themselves into jumping.

The last men onto the fo'csle were from the I.C. When they came up and saw the fierce foreground blaze in gun #2, they thought #2 magazine was cooking off.

Still obsessed with getting aft, Boehm made one final attempt. He went down through chief's quarters, where a fiery glare reflected down through the hatch. Feeling his way, he headed aft. He ran into patches of fire. The heavy, green, battleship linoleum in the passageway was burning and the linseed oil in the paint. He was choking on the fumes, and his eyes were burning from the thick oily smoke. Officer country was burned black. By then, Boehm could see that the mess hall was ablaze, so he turned back.

When Boehm came back up onto the fo'csle, the last men were abandoning. They were sliding down fire hoses or jumping. Only Shurney was refusing to go. Davenport warned him that he was going to blow up with the ship. Shurney said he would rather blow up than drown. Then Davenport ordered him off the ship, and Shurney refused.

Davenport tried to wrestle him to the lifeline, but Shurney

was so big and strong Davenport had to call for help. Half a dozen men rushed over. "We literally kicked his hands off the rail and threw him over the side," Fischer remembered.

Boehm and Palmer found Gunner's Mate Ray Whelan on the deck, and they asked him if they could do anything for him. Whelan said, "Oh, hell, pick me up and throw me over the side." Together, they picked Whelan up and threw him overboard. Palmer jumped after him. Boehm was about to jump when he noticed flashes from gunfire over the horizon. He looked around and did not see any ships, but he saw the silhouette of land to starboard. Then he noticed that *Duncan* was circling. He knew that meant nobody was steering from after conn. He took a few steps back and got a running start, and he hurled himself into the night.

Fischer was the last man on the fo'csle. He stood at the lifeline staring down at a big shark swimming in the bow wave. Fischer's lifejacket suddenly burst into flames, "only now there was nobody left on the forward deck to piss on me. I went over and did a big belly flop," Fischer remembered. "I waved to *Duncan* as she went by. I could see Captain Taylor on the bridge."

Johnson, the helmsman, felt a lot safer once he was in the water. Watching *Duncan* circle off across the seascape "like a burning death-ship," he was thinking if he had stayed on board one minute longer he was going to be blown up.

Koehler wound up in the water with a sonarman. They spotted something on fire approaching and realized it was *Duncan* coming around again. "The cutwater of the *Duncan* missed us by something less than 10 feet," Koehler remembered, "and the bow wave carried us well clear, a hundred feet or more by the time the fantail got by."

Fischer was just appreciating the warm, calming water when he saw *Duncan* coming. He remembered, "I know that ship passed me twice doing 15-18 knots."

The sea was littered with flotsam. When Boehm floundered to the surface, he banged against a wooden spar the size of a telephone pole that must have come from a Japanese ship. He grabbed onto it before he noticed a bedraggled Japanese sailor clinging to the other end. Boehm felt for his sheath knife, but it was gone. He eased off his end of the spar and the Japanese sailor eased off his end, and they both swam off in opposite directions.

As he was swimming away, Boehm glanced over his shoulder and saw *Duncan* "blazing like a Viking's funeral pyre" bearing down on him. Swimming hard to get out of her way, he swam right over Dubiel, who was floundering and raving out of his mind. As *Duncan*'s blazing prow loomed over them, Boehm grabbed Dubiel's lifejacket and backstroked as hard as he could, and "the ship rushed by so near I thought I could reach out and grab her," Boehm remembered. The wake drove them under. When they surfaced, "the world had grown quiet and warm and peaceful."

Out on *Duncan*'s starboard bridgewing, Lt. Bryan urged the last men over the side. Lt. Hauck went and stood beside Chief Chamberlain, who was flashblind and still recovering from a concussion. Hauck offered to jump with him. They were discussing it when Chamberlain lost his grip and fell. He hit a life raft below, injuring his ankle.

Olek finally made it to the stern. He felt so beat up he almost passed out. He flopped onto the deck next to the depth charge rack. Looking up, he saw eerie blue light and thought it was the light you see when you are dead.

Up on the roof of the bridge, Chief Paige was overseeing the trussing-up of Lt.(jg) Fowler. They lifted him up and carried him to the starboard side. After they had lowered him to the bridge wing, Sobelman, Queen, and Bilbro slid down the halyards. Paige chose to go down a ladder, but he found that the starboard ladder was blown away, so he went down the portside ladder. Down on the port wing, fires were smoldering. To get to the starboard wing, Paige had to climb through the wreckage in the wheelhouse. He saw men dead at the chartdesk.

Emerging out onto the starboard wing, Paige went over to help with Lt.(jg) Fowler. Stepping gingerly, they carried him to the lifeline. Only part of the wing was intact, so the deck sagged under their combined weight. They lowered Fowler to the main deck. Sobelman, Bilbro, and Queen slid down the halyards after him.

The starboard wing was deserted now, except for Paige and three sailors who were chatting together over by the pelorus (compass repeater). Paige walked over to them. Signalman Albright was sitting by the pelorus, and Fire Controlmen-strikers Floyd Burnham and William Dunlop were trying to talk him into abandoning with them. As Paige got closer, he saw that Albright was covered in blood and doubled over in pain, and he was begging them to leave him alone. Albright looked up brightly at Chief Paige. "Hey, Chief," he said with a big smile. Paige could now see that Albright was holding his intestines in his hands. He told Burnham and Dunlop to go down and help with Mr. Fowler. He waited until they were gone. "Come on, Sam," he said finally. "You know I can't leave you." Albright looked embarrassed by all the fuss he was causing. Paige was trying to think of something inspirational to say to him. Albright broke the awkward silence. "Get off, Chief," Albright said. "It's all right. You go. Don't wait for me. I'll be along." Paige nodded. He had decided Albright was better off where he was than in the water. So he left him there, leaning against the searchlight. As Paige was walking away, Albright called after him, "Take care of yourself, Chief."

Back at after conn, Ens. Andrews did not know what was going on forward because all his phone circuits were dead. He could see that the forward section of the ship was smothered in smoke. *Duncan* was steaming at about 10 knots and swinging hard to port. Shells had pretty much stopped coming in, but Andrews could still hear the distant rumble of the U.S. guns; the U.S. battle line was about 4 miles to the southwest.

Ens. Andrews climbed down to the main deck, which was all but deserted. Only one man was in sight, Watertender Boyle, and he was hysterical and running in circles. When he saw Andrews, he froze for a second and then ran toward the lifeline. He was about to jump overboard when Andrews pulled his pistol and shouted, "You abandon this ship before the order is given and

I'll shoot you in the back." Another sailor came by, and Andrews told him to go and find out which officers were alive and who was senior.

Much of the crew was still manning their stations. Eventually, individuals took it upon themselves to tell others to abandon. Carlson shouted down the scuttle to the 1.1 clip room and told them to clear out.

Bewildered men were gathering on the afterdeck. When DeLucca came up from #3 handling room, he could hardly believe his eyes. "That ship was burning like a gas tank," he remembered. "We were all nerved up, but there was nowhere to run. You just had to wait for somebody to say, 'Abandon Ship.' Instead, they called for a rescue crew."

The first order of business was to get the fires out, especially the blaze in the forward fireroom. A bucket brigade formed spontaneously. Men from after repair were quickly joined by black gang and after gunners.

Before long, every man aft was employed in a rescue crew or bucket brigade or was searching in the dark for survivors. Everybody was told to check and make sure none of the bodies lying around were alive. Slovenec volunteered to put on an asbestos suit and go down and look for Doc Broccolo in the mess. The 1.1 crew dumped gasoline and kerosene and flooded the 1.1 magazine and the after 20mm magazine.

DeLucca put on a flash suit, and he reported to Chief Motor Machinist's Mate Borcykowski at the forward engineroom. Borcykowski was also wearing a flash suit. "All the forward guys [#1 engineroom crew], all gone," Borcykowski told him. [In fact, seven died, but four had escaped.] Borcykowski said the forward engineroom was too hot, but he said he thought they could get into the forward fireroom. DeLucca started down after him, but, halfway down, Borcykowski practically ran over DeLucca trying to get back up. Tearing off his hood, he gasped, "No way I'm going down there with all that steam and fire. If anybody's alive down there, they would've yelled. Nobody yelled."

Forty-five minutes after the first shell hit *Duncan*, the three men manning the after steering engineroom were still manning their stations. Quinn thought they had been forgotten. Finally, Ens. Andrews shouted down to them to abandon.

When Quinn came up onto the afterdeck, Ens. Andrews, Chief Holt, Chief Boyd and others were discussing how they were going to save the ship. Andrews thought he could navigate from after conn. He planned to steer to Savo Island and beach the ship. He thought the island was to the northeast. "It couldn't be more than five miles," he said. Chief Boyd took some men down to disengage the steering.

A quick check forward had determined that Lt. Kabat was the senior officer on board. He was still at his battle station in the after engineroom. Andrews climbed back up to after conn and called the after engineroom. He was surprised when the engineroom talker answered. Andrews told him to inform Lt. Kabat that the captain and exec might have abandoned and that he could be the senior officer so he should come aft and assume command.

A few moments after Kabat left, the engineroom talker got a panicky call from the after fireroom reporting that the main feed water pressure was too low to feed two boilers. Choking on the smoke and fumes, Chief Solomon ordered the vacuum dragline opened and the #2 emergency feed pump started.

Lt. Kabat emerged topside at about 0030, which was about an hour after R/Adm. Scott had ordered the fateful turn. The last starshell and parachute flare had long-since fizzled out. Kabat was momentarily night-blind. As he stood on deck waiting for his eyes to adjust, he listened to men around him abandoning. The ship's engines were pounding. He could feel that their speed was dropping and he sensed that they were circling. *Duncan* had already completed two 360° turns.

When Lt.(jg) Wharton climbed down from the bridge, almost everyone was gone from the main deck amidships. Three sailors were by the lifeline. Wharton walked over to them. One had a mangled arm and leg, and the other two were helping him over the side.

"This's a pretty fix," Wharton said. "Where's the captain?"

"Swimming to that island over there," one replied.

"The exec?"

"Swimming with him, I guess."

"Mr. Hauck?"

"Swimming."

"Mr. Fowler?"

"He's wounded. He's being carried by somebody."

More sailors in search of a leader were gathering.

"Well, christ, who's in charge around here?"

"Looks like you are, Mr. Wharton."

"We have to go," Wharton said. "Keep your shoes and socks on."

It was only about six feet to the water, but some of them were afraid to jump. Wharton pushed them. Wharton took a long last look around at the devastation. Then he dove in. Underwater, he "heard the throb of the propellers go by."

While Lt. Kabat was waiting for his night vision to return, men rushed up to him with damage reports. As his eyesight returned, the first things he saw were the fire on the bridge and then the firelight reflecting on the water. Assuming command, he ordered everybody topside. "Abandon Ship," he shouted. He then headed aft to inform Ens. Andrews.

The feed pump in the after fireroom was not pumping enough water to feed even one boiler, so Chief Solomon ordered the distilling plant shut down. Then word came from Lt. Kabat to secure the machinery. Solomon ordered #3 and #4 boilers secured. Motor Machinist's Mate John Hernday cut the main steam valve.

Watertender Boyle had recovered from his panic and joined the fire brigade. He heard muffled cries coming from the dark behind him, and he went to investigate. The cries were coming from beneath the pile of burning debris that had once been the gig. Boyle shouted for help and started pulling flaming pieces of the gig off the forward engineroom hatch.

Colbeck and Combs were floating about twenty feet from the ship, which was now barely moving. From their vantage, *Duncan* looked like a vast stage upon which numerous scenes were unfolding. Flames were leaping up all over the forward section, lighting up the night. Directly in front of them—stage center—the bucket brigade was throwing water onto the inferno in the forward fireroom. There was darkness aft, but men could be seen gathering on the fantail.

Lt. Kabat found Ens. Andrews aft surrounded by men who were all heatedly expressing their opinions on the situation. No one believed anybody was alive on the bridge. When Kabat informed Andrews that he had ordered Abandon Ship, Andrews told him that he thought he could steer from after conn and beach *Duncan* on Savo. Kabat rescinded his Abandon Ship order.

The men who went down to the after steering engineroom managed to wrestle the rudder amidships. Andrews climbed up to after conn and got the ship "heading for Savo, I guess. I tried to head for where I thought the island was. We'd lost power but were still going a little bit."

Lt.(jg) Coley and Chief Watertender Holt debated whether they could still get steam up. The after fireroom was intact, but the main steam valve had been cut, which popped the safety, and that cut off the flow of fresh water to the boilers. When the feed water tanks emptied, the boiler tubes would melt. But Chief Holt thought if they moved fast they could get salt water into at least one boiler.

Water was supplied to boilers by suction. Holt's plan was to initiate suction using a handybilly to pump seawater into a boiler. The men who went down into the fireroom first checked the gauges. They discovered that all the water had already drained out of both boilers.

Wickstrom up on deck got a handybilly started. "We had the one suction hose over the side and then the $1^{1/2}$-inch fire hose going down below," Wickstrom remembered. But the handybilly kept losing suction because the hose connection was loose, so they shut it down, and Ehrenberg ran aft to the machine shop and got the spanner wrench. In a couple of minutes, they had the pump running again.

When Lt.(jg) Coley judged that the tubes were probably full, he ordered the boiler lit. The cold brine quickly began to boil.

The pressure started to rise. But the water was boiling away faster than the handybilly was pumping it in so the pressure inside the boiler soon exceeded the pressure of the water coming down, and, since the boiler now had no check valve, steam eventually blew back up the hose. That clogged the handybilly, which promptly conked out. When water stopped flowing into the boiler, suction was lost, and, with the flow of steam interrupted, the fire boxes grew hotter and hotter until the boiler tubes melted.

They were down in the fireroom less than ten minutes. When they returned on deck, the ship was losing what little headway she had.

Duncan sloughed to a halt. "And there we are," Andrews remembered. "Dead in the water."

*   *   *

Salt Lake City fired a final salvo at *Aoba* at 0025. That ended the battle, which had lasted thirty-nine minutes—from *Helena*'s first round to *Salt Lake City*'s last.

The Allied task group steamed west after the Japanese warships, but Scott's heart was not really into the chase. He could see *Salt Lake City* by her fires. *Boise* was not responding to TBS calls. Neither was *Farenholt*. Nobody had even noticed that *Duncan* was missing. It was assumed she was with *Farenholt*.

They followed the retreating Japanese northwest for fifteen minutes. Then, at 0040, R/Adm. Scott ordered a withdrawal to the south. Capt. Hoover thought they should have kept chasing them until every last Japanese ship was sunk. Many assumed they were going to search the northwest coast of Guadalcanal before withdrawing, but they steamed right past Cape Esperance and continued south.

They were passing Cape Esperance when Scott delegated rear destroyer *McCalla* to go back and search for *Boise*. She had not been heard from for an hour.

McCalla swung out of column and headed back north.

McCalla was not gone five minutes before *San Francisco* picked up a very weak signal from *Farenholt* that *McCalla* radiomen missed: "TWO HOLES AT WATERLINE BUT FARENHOLT SEAWORTHY [and *Duncan*] SEVERELY HIT AND MAY BE SINKING OR SUNK."

* * *

Chief Colbeck was floating comfortably about twenty feet from *Duncan*, but he was feeling guilty that he was not on board contributing in the epic struggle that was being waged before his eyes. He said to Combs, who was floating beside him, that he was going back on board. Combs was wounded, so he was not happy with the idea, but he did not want to be left alone in the ocean, so he floundered after Colbeck, trying to swim with his one good arm. They quickly reached the stern, and Olek threw them a line and pulled them aboard.

A top-to-bottom search of the ship had revealed that most of the crew was overboard. Shoes were neatly lined up along the deck as if the owners expected to return. A few wounded were found, but they all had medical problems too serious to help. Many dead were counted: eight in the exterior passageway, five in the mess, four in the forward 20mms, one on the torpedo mount, seven in the forward fireroom, two in #2 handling room, four in and around #2 gun mount, five in the radio room, one in the coding room, one on the signal bridge, one on the starboard wing, one on the port wing, five in the wheelhouse, and two on the roof of the bridge.

The fires on the bridge were subsiding. Wickstrom put on a flashsuit and was able to climb all the way up to the bridge. He saw the unexploded *Hatsuyuki* shell in the chartroom. "I knew it was Japanese," he remembered, "because it was in the starboard side."

On the main deck, the bucket brigade was not getting anywhere with the blaze in the forward fireroom. "It was like pissing on a volcano," Bethune remembered. Coley finally called off the effort and told them all to report to the fantail.

Lt. Kabat was worried about the two torpedoes still on board. He thought they might work loose and kill somebody. He sent Chief Boyd up to the mount to fire them off. He delegated Torpedoman Watson to set some of the depth charges to explode at 30 feet and some at 300 feet. [What he should have ordered was the exact opposite: set the depth charges on safe and remove the detonators.]

The remaining officers, chiefs, and senior petty officers broke into groups and headed below to survey the physical damage to the ship. Battle lanterns hung all over second deck now. The survey teams systematically searched every compartment below the waterline looking for leaks or other signs of structural failure. They found none.

From the fantail, it looked as if everything forward of the bridge was on fire. There was a rumor that the forward magazine had not been flooded, so it was likely to blow any second. Andrews felt strongly that they would all be better off in the water. He reminded Kabat of the photograph in *Life Magazine* of the *U.S.S. Shaw* exploding at Pearl Harbor after fire got into her magazine.

When the survey teams returned topside, Coley tried to tell Kabat that the ship could be salvaged. As he was reporting to him, the fire in #2 handling room flared ominously, so all Kabat wanted to discuss was how to most expeditiously abandon.

"This is it," Kabat told the remaining men, mostly all after repair and black gang. "We haven't got enough men," Kabat said. "We've got to get out of here or we'll be burned to death ourselves."

Some men were delegated to go below and open up the sea cocks. Others were sent to retrieve the small arms from the saillocker. One man went down to #4 handling room and broke out powder cans to be used as flotation devices.

Chief Boyd shouted down from the torpedo mount that he could see Savo Island. Savo has a distinctive, volcanic-cone silhouette. He fired the two remaining torpedoes in the direction of the island.

Quartermaster David Nicoll noticed Lt.(jg) Coley at the rear mast hauling down the American flag. Nicoll went over to him and said, "You can't do that. The United States Navy never strikes her colors." Coley quickly hauled the flag back up and struck the commission pennant instead.

The men who went down to the saillocker returned with the weapons—a Thompson submachine gun, four 30-caliber rifles, and four pistols. They handed them out to anybody who wanted one.

Lt.(jg) Coley called the remaining men together. Of the twenty-three men who had remained on board and fought the fires, sixteen were still on board.

"Our boilers are gone," Kabat said. "Our boats are gone. Our rafts are gone. We're going down. It's every man for himself." There were two explosions far off to starboard as Boyd's torpedoes hit Savo. "Okay, good," Kabat said. "That means there's land over there. Head there."

"That was almost five minutes," Boyd shouted. "That puts that island at about 3 miles."

"If the tide's against you," Kabat said, "don't try to swim against it. Keep your clothes on, especially your shoes. You're going to want to have them in case you get ashore. That coral will tear hell out of your feet. When she goes down, get the hell away or you'll be sucked under. Well ... okay, let's go then. Abandon ship! Abandon ship!"

"Hell," Watson snorted, removing his lifejacket, "what's three miles?" Tossing his lifejacket on the deck, he performed a perfect swan dive that barely left a ripple.

"Don't anybody else try that!" Coley shouted. The rest of them pulled the straps on their lifejackets tighter. At about 0130 on October 12 (local time), the last sixteen men started over the side.

Once the decision was made, most were eager to go. Quinn was worried about getting sucked under by the ship, so he went quickly. Some men cannonballed into the sea with a spirited yell. Others hesitated. Fred Donelle was afraid because he could not swim. Chief Colbeck had to order Carlson off. In a grand gesture, Carlson took all the coins out of his pocket and tossed them into the sea before jumping. Andy Slovenec refused to abandon. "I think it's a dumb idea," he told Ens. Andrews. Every time Andrews would order him off, Slovenec would reply, "No, let's stay on." Andrews screamed, "Get your ass off this ship!" Slovenec said, "Okay, wait, wait. Lemme just go to my locker. I gotta get some clothes and stuff." Whereupon, he just wandered off. Andrews screamed after him, "Get back here!" But Slovenec was never one for taking orders, and Andrews was past caring.

Colbeck and Combs dived into the sea together for the second time that night. Seaman Robert Dunn went in clutching the Tommy gun. "*Duncan* was leaning over pretty good," Bethune remembered. "I was relieved to get off the ship. I thought she was sinking." George Bacsik, an escapee from the forward engineroom, was one of the last off.

When Slovenec finally returned topside, Ens. Andrews was still waiting for him. Slovenec was wrestling a rolled-up mattress that had a huge bulge in the middle where he had tied all his belongings. Without a word, he walked to the lifeline and tossed the mattress overboard and jumped after it.

Only a few men remained. Most were stalling because they were afraid of the water. Dawson and Ziegler would almost get up their nerve before hesitating, but they finally jumped. Nicoll was so terrified that Coley offered to jump with him. They threw a piece of timber over the side, but, when Nicoll stalled again, Coley pushed him. Before Coley jumped, he glanced at his watch. It was 0136.

Chapter 8
THE SOUTH SEAS SWIM CLUB
0200 October 12-0200 October 13

Dark hills at evening in the west,
Where sunset hovers like a sound
Of golden horns that sang to rest
Old bones of warriors under ground,
Far now from all the bannered ways
Where flash the legions of the sun,
You fade—as if the last of days
Were fading, and all wars were done.

—*Edwin Arlington Robinson*

Because they had abandoned at different times while *Duncan* circled, survivors were spread over 16 square miles of ocean between Savo Island and Guadalcanal.

The more confident swimmers, like Watson and Bryan, were swimming the crawl toward Savo. The rest were just floating, mostly in groups. Men in larger groups tied themselves together with manila lanyards. Those wearing kapok lifevests were riding high in the water. Almost all were in good spirits.

Coley and Nicoll were sharing a piece of timber and riding it like a canoe. Andrews, who had just turned twenty-one, remembered, "The water was warm. I was a good swimmer. My first thought was I wouldn't have to deal with those Title B chits." Fischer heard "Maytag Charlie," an Imperial Army scout plane, "putt-putt-putting overhead." Palmer floated on his back staring up at the sky that was suddenly filled with stars. It was Columbus Day, so DeLucca improvised a song for the occasion: "In 1492, Columbus was looking for land./It's 1942, now I'm looking for land."

The sea was thick with oil and flotsam and survivors. "It was a mess out there," Papacoda remembered. "There were Japs in the water all over the place, and they was hollering. That was scary."

Most of the fire controlmen were in one large group. "We were all in pretty good shape," Sobelman remembered, "except for Mr. Fowler." Sobelman, as the highest-rated man, delegated Dunlop and Queen, the two lowest rated, to watch after Fowler.

Fire controlmen were an elite group and, as individuals, were notoriously opinionated. Before long, they were discussing the battle. None of them understood what had happened, but all had strong opinions. They agreed it was suicidal taking on a Japanese cruiser on their own initiative and single-handed. They all thought Taylor and Bryan were glory-seekers looking for medals. "He had to do what they told him—get his torpedoes off," Sobelman argued, putting himself in Taylor's place. "He can't embarrass the Admiral."

All of them were mortified by their own performance. Their first salvo, at point blank range, was 200 yards short. Sobelman was very defensive because he was aiming the guns. "I had the bridge dead nuts on," he insisted. Sobelman thought battery alignment was the problem—the projectiles were not coming out of the barrels at 2,600-feet-per-second. Battery alignment was Chief Colbeck's responsibility. Chief Colbeck was not there to defend himself. Sobelman thought Colbeck screwed up—failed to set the correct air data (temperature and humidity) into the computer or misdialed the powder temperature. "I know it didn't happen on my watch," Sobelman insisted.

Clinging onto powder cans and rubbish, the last men off the fantail steadily paddled away from the ship. After about twenty minutes, seeing they were only a couple of hundred yards off, they got discouraged and stopped paddling and just floated there looking at *Duncan*. The fires were subsiding. She did not look like she was about to sink. Ens. Andrews suddenly announced he was going back on board. He was probably expecting somebody to volunteer to go with him, but nobody did. "You should've thought of this before," Slovenec groused.

It took Ens. Andrews about ten minutes to paddle back to *Duncan*. When he got to the port side, he porpoised up and tried to grab the edge of the deck, but it was way out of reach. He swam to the stern. He tried to grab the propeller guard, but even it was out of reach. He swam around to starboard, where he found a line hanging down. He tried to pull himself up it, but the line was wet and his hands kept slipping.

The group from the fantail, waiting for Ens. Andrews to return, talked about how *Duncan* could suddenly go down. They were worried about the depth charges. They had all seen what depth-charge concussion did to men in the water. They were all very relieved when they saw Andrews paddling toward them. They resumed paddling away, only now with more urgency. They were all anxious to get far away from *Duncan*.

"You know what was rough out there?" Seaman Warren Craig remembered. "Being alone." Bethune remembered, "It was dark as hell. I'd strapped my knife to my wrist so I wouldn't lose it." Men with knives were very glad to have them, especially the men who were alone. "The trouble with being alone," Craig remembered, "is you're thinking for one person. I wanted to kill myself." In agonizing pain with a broken leg, Whelan was alone and certain he was going to die, and he was trying to figure out how to kill himself without a knife.

Their shoes were quickly waterlogged. Their pants got heavier and heavier. Carlson ditched his pants, shoes, and socks. Sobelman urged the men with him to keep their pants and shoes on, but most of them ignored him. He pleaded with them to at least keep their socks on. He told them sharks were attracted by white feet.

Fischer was driven by his vision of the captain on the bridge pointing toward land. He had decided he was better off on his own, and he dropped his shoes and pants but quickly regretted it, especially the pants. "Man, those white shorts and my white skin," he remembered. "The water was very phosphorous. Every time I kicked, the white in those bubbles looked too inviting." He was thankful he still had his socks on. He had a moment of dread when he heard someone splashing behind him. "I thought it was a Jap and nobody was going to know what became of me. I put my knife in my mouth. It was [Seaman James] Duncan panicking because he couldn't swim."

Signalman Francis Benson could barely swim, but he

killed a Japanese sailor in the water and cut off one of his ears. Somebody asked him, "What'd you do that for?" Benson replied, "I want proof."

* * *

McCalla retraced the task group's track north to where *Boise* was last seen—"latitude 9- 97S; longitude 159-28W," or "12 miles bearing 295 [west] from Savo Island"—and started searching there. A light was spotted on the southeast horizon. It appeared to be a fire, so they headed that way. Radar was picking up blips from the Japanese ships withdrawing to the northwest. Sonar was picking up soundings that could have been a ship sinking or a sub. LCdr. Cooper was afraid it was a sub, so *McCalla* zigzagged southeastward for five or six miles. By then, they could clearly see a ship on fire close to Savo Island.

The *Duncan* survivors were so low in the water they could only see the tip of *McCalla*'s mast. Lt.(jg) Beebe thought she was Japanese. So did the men in the life raft that Quinn was clinging to, and they took a vote and decided they would rather drown than be captured. "We all played dead," Quinn remembered.

McCalla closed to 2,500 yards from the burning ship. LCdr. Cooper was afraid to get closer because he thought she was grounded on Savo. They put a searchlight on the hulk at 0220.

Carlson, who was now sharing his piece of timber with Chief Holt and some firemen and a seaman, remembered the searchlight beam shot "straight out of the blackness abaft the *Duncan*, across the waters, then upon the very still ship itself." They debated whether to call out and decided to keep quiet.

Mystified, LCdr. Cooper studied the strange-looking vessel. She was an eerie sight. With the intermittent explosions, it was surreal. They could not make out any numbers on her bow because flames enveloped her forward, and they could not see the numbers on her stern because of all the smoke that was aft. She clearly looked doomed. There was no sign of life. It was obvious she was not the *Boise*. She appeared to be a destroyer.

LCdr. Cooper first thought she looked Japanese, but, after studying her for a while, he began to see familiar *Livermore* lines. Then he decided she was the *Farenholt*. A lookout reported seeing "485" on her stern, but nobody else could see any numbers. Cooper doubted she was *Duncan* because there was too much discrepancy in her position, even accounting for drift. And, as far as they knew, *Duncan* was not even missing.

LCdr. Cooper ordered his exec, Lt. Floyd Myhre, to take a salvage party and board her if it did not look too dangerous. If she was American, they were to destroy the coding machine and set some depth charges to blow her up in case Japanese approached.

Word came over the PA: "THE SHIP WILL SEND A BOAT TO THE BURNING VESSEL." The salvage party consisted of Lt. Myhre, Ens. George Weems, and three petty officers (pharmacist's mate, gunner's mate, and signalman), plus the small boat crew (two seamen and a fireman). The whaleboat was lowered at 0300.

Lt. Myhre was nervous that she might be Japanese. They all sat quiet as they motored slowly toward the hulk. Two or three times, they shut off the motor and listened for voices. "Numerous minor explosions were heard at intervals," Ens. Weems remembered. 500-600 yards off, they cut the motor. They could hear splashes from glass falling in the water. The whaleboat drifted toward the hulk. The ship's numbers were veiled in smoke and shadow. Lt. Myhre was afraid that the forward magazines could explode. When they were a few hundred yards off, he decided that was close enough. Ens. Weems volunteered to swim to the ship and identify her.

Weems swam for about ten minutes before he noticed that a strong current was carrying him. "I just floated with it," he remembered, "swimming cross-current only just enough to make sure I would track toward the ship. I wanted to leave as small a wake as possible." When he was about 50 yards off, he thought he saw somebody on board. "I distinctly saw a man standing at the rail, with a rifle in his arms—not pointing it at me, just holding it in readiness. He was so intent and immobile. I stopped swimming and just floated, to avoid attracting attention. I began to make out features of the ship. She had depth charge racks in a position like ours. (I was drifting down onto the stern). Her turrets looked different. Finally I saw white markings on the stern, and became pretty sure she was a sister can. That 'guy' on the fantail, however, discouraged my disclosing myself until I was certain." Weems was about 25 yards away when he clearly saw "485" on the stern. He sang out, "On board the American destroyer!" No answer. "I swam up to the stern and found my 'sentry' to be a davit for depth charges, his 'rifle' being the block and tackle." He could not reach the propeller guard. Noticing that the ship was listing to starboard, he swam to the starboard side. There was a line hanging down, "so I tarzaned my way up it and crawled aboard ... No one was aft so I yelled back to the whaleboat, '4-8-5'. After several tries I got a faint answer, 'O.K.'"

There was little damage aft, but, as Weems walked forward, he saw "steam escaping, fire hoses led out, buckets, etc. All the guns were trained out. The deck was littered with all sorts of clothing and gear—mostly shoes and trousers piled neatly where their respective owners had left them when going over the side." As he continued forward, he came upon scenes of increasing devastation. Dead bodies were everywhere. The forward stack was on its side. The ship forward of the forward engineroom was gutted. Heat had melted ladders, decks, bulkheads. Everything else combustible was burned. Most of the fires were burning themselves out. The only fire burning fiercely was the motor whaleboat. What had appeared from a distance to be a mass of flames forward was "a series of small fires, everywhere."

Weems's primary assignment was to destroy the coding machine. It was a struggle to pull himself up the demolished inside ladder. He was barefoot and quickly regretted not grabbing a pair of shoes. On 0-1 level, the deck was hot, and he gashed his foot on "the sharp edge of a plow-like furrow" carved by an 8-inch shell. He managed to get up to O-2 level. He went in the coding room and found the coding machine "pretty well blottoed."

Weems climbed back down to the main deck. He returned to the fantail and checked the depth charges. A few were set for 30 feet and a few others for 300 feet. He shouted into the dark, "She can be salvaged!"

Within a few minutes, the whaleboat pulled alongside. Weems reported to Lt. Myhre on the ship's condition. Myhre was still worried about the fires forward, and he decided they should abandon temporarily. Reluctantly, Weems climbed into the whaleboat. They motored off 200-300 yards. "We did hear more explosions," Weems remembered, "but nothing alarming."

After leisurely swimming the crawl for less than an hour, Torpedoman Watson splashed up onto a beach on the southwest coast of Savo Island. Finding himself alone, he laid down in the warm sand and promptly fell asleep. He was startled awake by the sound of Lt. Bryan splashing ashore. Bryan could not talk, only grunt, because he was preserving the severed tip of his pinkie in his mouth. He sat beside Watson, and they listened to survivors splashing in the dark.

After a few hours in the water, many of the survivors were becoming desperate. "I thought I'd take my .45 home and have a .45 for nothing," Ens. Andrews remembered, "but after a couple of hours that .45 was getting heavy. I loosened the thing and let it drop. I felt better after that."

Dunlop woke up with a start. He glanced over at Lt.(jg) Fowler just as Fowler was slipping out of his life preserver. "Hey, Mister Fowler's lost his preserver," Dunlop shouted, grabbing him before he went under. Sobelman swam over, and, removing his pneumatic belt, he strapped it around Fowler. "Now see that one doesn't come off," he snapped.

Sobelman had pointed at the vague shape of an island and urged the men with him to head there, but it is difficult to get a group of men in the water moving in the same direction. "We had five guys," Lt.(jg) Beebe remembered, "and one couldn't swim, even though he was career Navy. Getting that group moving in a coordinated pattern was too much to ask. I figured we'd do better if we all stayed together as a group, as far as keeping the sharks away. We had lanyards so we all fastened onto each other with snap hooks."

The last men off the fantail had been paddling toward where they thought Savo was. After a few hours, they realized they were not getting any closer. Ens. Andrews was no longer even pretending he knew where Savo was. He finally divided them into pairs and headed them off in all directions. "Dawson and Slovenec, you men go that way," he said. "Me and Ziegler, we'll go this way."

Slovenec could not see a thing. "Look for the darkest part," he told Dawson, "that's gotta be Savo."

Boehm was still towing the semi-conscious Dubiel when he spotted "an ink blot against the stars on the horizon" and decided that was where they were meant to be headed.

Despite his serious wounds, Fischer paddled like a man possessed toward where he had seen the captain pointing. He paddled by many survivors floating on the current.

All of them were becoming increasingly weak and demoralized. Most had given up even trying to stay together. Wickstrom let go of the raft that he had been holding. Hess set off alone to try to swim to where he thought land was. Hess swam past the group of fire controlmen, and they tried to talk him into staying with them. "But Hess was a hard-headed German," Sobelman remembered. That was the last anyone ever saw of Ernest Hess.

Dunlop and Queen slept with Lt.(jg) Fowler floating between them. When they awoke, they discovered that they had floated away from the group and were alone. They drifted for another hour or so. Then they came upon the three mess stewards from the forward clipping who were floating comfortably on air mattresses, chatting and laughing. One volunteered his mattress for Lt.(jg). Fowler. They had a monumental struggle getting him onto it his body was so limp. Once that was accomplished, it became socially awkward because neither the two whites nor the three blacks were keen to spend the night with the others. Finally, Mess Attendant Allen offered to look after Mr. Fowler, and Dunlop and Queen, hugely relieved, quickly paddled away.

Turning an officer over to the care of mess stewards was not unusual. Mess attendants normally felt closer to the officers than to the enlisted men, and the officers often felt closer to the mess attendants than to the other enlisted men. Some of the East Coast-types bonded more strongly with mess attendants than with fellow officers. "A lot of us felt as close to the mess attendants as anyone," Lt.(jg) Wharton remembered.

Throughout the night, survivors drifted apart and came together in new couplings. LCdr. Taylor and GM2c Whelan wound up together, two of the unhappiest men alive. Both were consumed with thoughts of suicide. Taylor, who was in despair over the loss of his ship, was certain his career was finished, and Whelan, who was in terrible pain, thought he was just awaiting his inevitable demise.

Lt.(jg) Wharton came upon Seaman Lappin who was floating alone. He was semi- conscious and was slipping out of his lifebelt.

About an hour later, Lt.(jg) Coley and Seaman Nicoll came upon Wharton and Lappin. Wharton was holding Lappin up. Both Coley and Nicoll had two lifebelts, so they each took one off and hooked it around Lappin. When Coley got a close look at Lappin, he could see that his lower jaw was gone. He told Wharton that he thought Lappin was dead. Wharton became furious. He insisted Lappin was sleeping, and he ordered them to leave.

Men trapped together by circumstance become easily annoyed with one another. Fireman Dominic DeOnofrio kept saying Hail Marys all night. That drove a lot of men away. Carlson's piece of timber gained passengers all night until there were half a dozen men clinging to it, including Seaman Russell Dazen who kept cheering on the others with a continuing chant of "Kick, men, kick, kick! Don't give up! Keep it up, men!" Dazen finally ran down, Carlson remembered, "like an old Victrola" at about 0400.

Dubiel was in and out of consciousness as Boehm was towing him toward Savo. He was silent for long periods, then would suddenly wake up screaming, "Mom, are you there?!" or "Look out! Look out!"

DeLucca was floating with a fireman named James Rosenfelt.

Rosenfelt was a big fat kid who was not a good swimmer, and he had a stomach wound so he was struggling. All night he had been bumping and grabbing DeLucca, until DeLucca finally snapped, "Stay away from me, Rosey. I can't hold you up." Rosenfelt replied softly, "Okay, Louie." And he floated away. That was the last anyone saw of James Rosenfelt.

As dawn approached, all the survivors were actively trying to make landfall, paddling desperately toward shadows. Slovenec and Dawson were encouraged to see the silhouette of a volcanic cone emerging from the dark.

Everybody saw Japanese destroyers *Shirayuki, Murukumo,* and *Hatsuyuki*. They had been sent back to search for *Furutaka* and *Fubuki*. The three Japanese destroyers spent the night rescuing *Furutaka* survivors.

Shortly before dawn, Lt. Myhre finally became satisfied that the fires on *Duncan* had subsided enough that they could safely board her. When they got aboard, the first thing they did was put the two after 5-inch guns and the two machineguns in operation, in case they needed to defend themselves.

Most of the fires were burned out but still smoldering. Myhre signaled to Cooper: "THIS SHIP HAS BEEN ABANDONED. CAN BE SALVAGED. SEND REPAIR PARTY. CAN BE TOWED FROM STERN. DEEP WATER AFT. AM TAKING SOUNDINGS FORWARD. SHE IS ROLLING FREELY."

McCalla returned to *Duncan* at 0600 when it was still very dark. *McCalla* put a searchlight on *Duncan*. The beam illuminated out hundreds of yards, revealing dozens and dozens of survivors in the water. On the spot, Cooper decided that rescuing survivors should be his priority. He shouted to Myhre that he was going over to Savo and start rescue operations.

Fischer was so close in the water he heard them shouting. "They were talking *English*," he remembered. "They had the searchlight on. I yelled and yelled, but nobody heard me."

Cooper radioed Scott: "HAVE LOCATED DUNCAN. SHE HAS BEEN ABANDONED. AM SEARCHING FOR SURVIVORS THEN WILL ATTEMPT TO TOW DUNCAN."

Scott replied: "REPORT IMMEDIATELY BY RADIO IF

YOU NEED SERVICES OF ANOTHER DESTROYER."

Cooper then radioed Maj.Gen. Vandegrift on Guadalcanal: "AM SEARCHING FOR SURVIVORS NORTHWEST SAVO ISLAND. REQUEST AIR COVERAGE DAYLIGHT."

As the black night slowly turned to a gray-velvet predawn, DeOnofrio stopped the Hail Marys and started cursing the Japanese.

Boehm, towing Dubiel, stopped periodically to retch seawater and switch arms. Salt water had swollen his face. "My eyes felt like they were dipped in acid," Boehm remembered. "My vision was blurred. My tongue felt like a dry sea cucumber stuffed down my throat. I feared it would block my windpipe."

At first light, Carlson could see a beach on Savo, and he could still see the *Duncan* with the "bluish, smoky haze [rising] above her." All night, Carlson had been growing increasingly annoyed as his shoring timber picked up more and more passengers. Finally, it was so over-crowded he chose to swim alone to Savo.

Fischer was sure he was getting close to Savo, until first light revealed how far he still had to go. "I thought it was a small island," Fischer remembered, "but it's a tall island."

As the day slowly dawned, exhausted survivors could suddenly see where they were. Cape Esperance on Guadalcanal was to the south, and Savo, the small island with the cone-shaped volcano, was to the northeast. Which landfall was nearer depended on when they had jumped off the ship. At 20° rudder, the ship was circling in a diameter of about one mile. In the two hours between the first man off and the last, she had circled almost three times.

McCalla began picking up *Duncan* survivors at first light. Most were east of Savo within what LCdr. Cooper described as "a roughly rectangular area approximately eight miles north and south and two miles west." There were a lot of Japanese survivors in the area, but they were not as widely scattered.

The first survivors *McCalla* picked up were Lt.(jg) Fowler and the three mess stewards. When LCdr. Cooper first saw them, they were being circled by "many tremendous sharks [that were] making no attempt to attack." Fowler was lifted aboard *McCalla* in the wire-mesh stretcher at 0630. He was in shock but semi-conscious. Lt.(jg) L.V. Potter, *McCalla*'s doctor, would spend the better part of the next two hours cleaning his wounds.

Shortly after dawn, *McCalla* ran in among some Japanese, and Cooper sent the gig out to capture some. They put up ferocious struggles before two young officers were forcibly rescued.

With daylight, the water seemed suddenly colder. And the dawn brought a horrible new fear—sharks. "Jeez, I hated to see that sun come up," Bethune remembered. "The sun comes up, the sharks come out."

Almost all the *Duncan* survivors had untied themselves, and the tide had separated them. Most of them were out of sight of one another.

DeLucca thanked his lucky stars he had kept his shoes on. He was afraid to kick them off because he had a hole in his sock. He was clinging onto a shiny powder can when he heard somebody screaming, "Shark fins! Shark fins!" DeLucca quickly let go his powder can and swam away.

All night, Seaman Elvin Scott had been clinging onto a raft that was full of wounded men. He had thought the man next to him in the water was sleeping, but, at dawn, he saw that the man's lower half was gone. Scott let go the raft and drifted away.

Seaman Gerald McCleary was clinging onto a raft when a shark gashed his ankles and buttocks. McCleary hit it with his fist, and the shark swam away.

Papacoda and Edwards were very worried about sharks because Doty was bleeding from his stomach. A shark slithered up to them, but it was less interested in Doty than the shiny powder can Papacoda was clutching. "I punched the shark," Papacoda remembered. "We're all splashing like crazy."

Seaman Warren Craig had never seen a shark and did not know to be afraid. "I didn't know what it was," Craig remembered. "The only thing I saw was Japs and sharks, but I was too dumb to be scared."

Four or five fins circled Boehm and Dubiel. "I had never experienced such utter fear," Boehm remembered. "The casual, detached way they approached set my heart pounding. Thank God Dubiel was blissfully unconscious." Thinking that any show of panic might induce a shark to attack, Boehm tried hard to maintain a steady stroke. The sharks circled closer. One darted in and bit Boehm's foot, and he felt a scratching, tingling sensation. He kicked frantically. His foot was bleeding. The shark circled ten feet away. Boehm thrashed the water, which drove the shark under. That was worse. Boehm saw the dark shape below him getting larger. He started spinning like a top. The shark surfaced, brushing "sand-paper rough" against his leg. Boehm screamed, and then Dubiel screamed as he was wrenched from Boehm's grip. Boehm thought Dubiel "must have had some awareness at the last instant as his body exploded out of the water." Dubiel "twisted violently in the white froth." His scream broke off as he was dragged under, and a "red smear stained the sea." Boehm thrashed and kicked and did not stop until he was too tired to care. He floated, exhausted, resigned to his fate. Seconds passed, then minutes.

On board *Duncan*, the salvage party closed all the watertight valves and doors and fittings. Half an hour after dawn, a couple of Marine planes from Guadalcanal flew over, and they all ran to the after guns.

Marine boats and planes were all over the sound at dawn. The planes were swooping low and dropping smoke bombs near survivors to aid the small boats in finding them.

On the beach on Savo, Bryan, Watson, and others who had landed during the night watched the Higgins boats and planes on the southwest horizon. Bryan did not know who was occupying Savo, so he was worried about them all standing out on the beach in plain sight. When it was an hour after dawn and still no planes had come that far north, Bryan decided that they would all be better off back into the water. His order did not go over well at all, but they all eventually went back in, bitching every step of the way.

A lot of the men from the bridge found themselves close to Guadalcanal at dawn. Most decided to wait to be rescued. Koehler had two packs of cigarettes in a condom and a couple of boxes of matches.

Everybody was leery about going ashore. "If there's Japs there, they'll kill us," somebody said. "If there's Marines there, they'll kill us," somebody replied. The Marines had had unhappy experiences with Japanese crawling ashore and faking they were Americans by answering with the name of a ship when they were challenged. Reportedly, Marines were now shooting first. They discussed which was worse: Japanese, Marines, or sharks?

When Palmer saw *McCalla*'s mast, he thought she was Japanese, until he noticed that Marine planes were not diving on her. Koehler realized *McCalla* was American when he saw two Marine planes fly over her without drawing any gunfire. Johnson remembered when he first saw *McCalla* she was "hull down [just visible over the horizon]. I figured she was picking up survivors because she would move ahead, stop, move ahead, stop."

On board *Duncan*, approaching planes repeatedly interrupted the salvage party's work. All hands would drop what they were doing and run for the guns. The planes were always friendlies. In between plane scares, the salvage party cleared walkways, destroyed confidential items, rigged phones, prepared emergency steering, rigged emergency pumps. *Duncan*'s most serious problems were the smoldering fires and the seawater that was flooding into the forward fireroom.

They first set about extinguishing the fires. There were half a dozen minor fires and one big fire. It was on the main and second decks around chiefs' quarters and #1 magazine. Once they got a handybilly going, they quickly extinguished all the small fires.

The smoke and heat from the big fire were so intense the only way to even get close to it was from above. So they ran a hose forward onto the fo'csle and down into chiefs' quarters. They battled that fire all morning.

The forward fireroom was flooding through a 5-inch shell hole in the port side. The hole was too far below the waterline to get to from the outside, and escaping steam inside the fireroom made it too hot to work in there for very long. From the outside, they plugged all the shell holes around the waterline that they could reach. Inside the fireroom, they successfully shored up the forward bulkhead. But the flooding continued.

The lifevests that the *Duncan* survivors were wearing were becoming waterlogged. Men who had once ridden high were now so low they were being hit in the face by waves. "The water was slapping you in the face, slapping you in the face," Craig remembered. Kapok lifevests were supposed to be good for twenty-four hours, but, after only six hours, a lot of them were worrying about their lifevests' limit.

Many survivors were converging on Savo. Boehm met up with Viering, Cruz, and Bethune just offshore. "We were so close we could see people walking on the beach," Viering remembered. The tide was taking them out, then bringing them back in. "I'm swimming like hell," Bethune remembered. "I got sores under the arms." A plane flew 20 feet over their heads waving its wings. Boehm heard a voice—"Here, Boats, give us your hand."—and, thinking he was delirious, whirled around. A Higgins boat was idling 10 feet from him.

Early Higgins boats were difficult to get in and out of because they had no bow ramp. The kapok in Boehm's lifevest was so heavy it took two Marines to lift him aboard. Bethune remembered, "I'm bleeding under the arms from the lifejacket being too tight. It just tore the skin off. I was red like a lobster. That sun beats on the water. Cruz's leg was bleeding where he had a 20mm through it. I didn't even notice he was wounded."

Fischer was just off the beach at Savo, but he was so weak from loss of blood and exhaustion he was ready to give up. Then a swell lifted him and he saw two young boys playing in the sand not more than a few hundred yards away, and he shouted. They looked up as he sank behind a swell. Fischer could feel that he was losing consciousness. "Then I hear them coming— *hoy, hoy*—two boys maybe 8-9 years old in a little dugout with an outrigger paddling and chanting in unison, '*Hoy*,' with each stroke." They tried to pull Fischer aboard. His waterlogged lifevest was so heavy they almost capsized the little outrigger. They pushed Fischer off and quickly rowed away. Then they returned with one boy standing at the bow. That submerged the bow enough that Fischer was able to roll himself aboard.

The little outrigger had about an inch of freeboard as the boys paddled to the beach. They dragged the outrigger up onto the beach and ran off, leaving Fischer to drag himself out of the water. He crawled up the beach to dry sand and collapsed. When he opened his eyes, the two boys were hovering over him with a rusty tin can full of fresh water. Fischer drank it all. Another boy came with a coconut, which he smashed open with a rock. He cradled Fischer's head and poured milk into his mouth. Fischer remembered it as the sweetest taste he ever experienced. Within ten minutes, he had diarrhea. Shortly after that, he went into shock. When he awoke, a U.S. Marine was leaning over him, explaining that he had given him morphine. Fischer began to cry. Marines carried him out to a Higgins boat and passed him over the gunwale. He was laid on the deck. Looking around, he saw familiar faces, including Boehm, Viering, and Palmer. A Marine wrapped him in blankets. Fischer could not stop crying.

*   *   *

Since before dawn, *Duncan* survivors had been watching planes dropping smoke and *McCalla* zigzagging. They could see that a rescue was underway. Most thought they had been spotted more than once. "All morning planes would fly over and dip their wings at you, then haul ass out of sight," Wickstrom remembered.

Wickstrom had floated off to be by himself, but he was hardly alone. Lt. Kabat was about 30 yards off, and Slovenec and Dawson were a bit further away. All of them were watching *McCalla*'s topmast. "You'd see the destroyer bearing down on you," Wickstrom remembered, "then see it turn around. Oh, jesus, they didn't see me, you're thinking."

Papacoda, Edwards, and Doty saw *McCalla* coming and were celebrating, but then she veered away. Papacoda was so mad he swore he was going to write the Navy.

After about eight hours in the water, Carlson and Green were picked up by *McCalla*'s gig. There were a lot of survivors in the gig, including Pharmacist's Mate Bruner Flowers. When Carlson climbed aboard *McCalla* and saw all the familiar faces, he was overcome with emotion. PhM2c Flowers walked straight to the wardroom and reported to Lt.(jg) Potter, who immediately put him to work caring for *Duncan* survivors.

Torpedoman Ham had been swimming alone toward Guadalcanal since before dawn. The tide was against him, so he was still pretty far off shore when a plane flew over him and dipped its wing. Ham saw a Higgins boat coming toward him. Then he saw a shark. It was very close. He thought, Is this how it's going to end? The shark must have heard the boat coming because it swam away.

All morning, small boats had been pulling alongside *McCalla* and unloading survivors. Most were found alone or in pairs. The largest group was thirty-one men who were in and around three life rafts that were tied together.

Many of the survivors were too weak to climb up the ladder to *McCalla* and had to be lifted aboard in the wire-mesh stretcher. Seaman Craig was lifted aboard by stretcher and was carried to the wardroom. "A guy sticks his finger under my tongue and puts whiskey in there," Craig remembered, "and when I got done out of there I'm drunk."

Fischer was lifted aboard, but, once on deck, he got a second wind, and he hobbled to the wardroom on his own. He had shrapnel in one shoulder and a gaping hole in his knee, and he was severely dehydrated. Lt.(jg) Potter left a patient to check him out. He told Fischer his injuries were not serious enough to require immediate attention. Flowers gave Fischer a shot of Old Overholt, the Navy's medicinal whiskey, and assigned him a bunk in chiefs' quarters.

McCalla was getting a lot of help from the Marines on Guadalcanal, including medical supplies and medical personnel. All morning, Higgins boats brought out food and clothes. Shoes were especially welcome because *McCalla*'s decks were very hot.

DeLucca had thought he was about to be rescued half a dozen times. Finally, a PBY spotted him and threw down a flare, and, within minutes, a Higgins boat came over. "They had my exec,

Mr. Bryan, on board," DeLucca remembered. "He'd lost his little finger, but there was no blood. McCleary was in the landing barge. He had a shark bite his ass, but there was no blood. Milek was in there, too. He was so relieved to be alive he'd forgot about his money belt. I said, 'You son of a bitch, Milek, I was about ready to let this belt of yours drop.' He sat up, startled. 'You still got my belt, Louie?' There was almost $6,000 in it. He gave me a thousand on the spot. I would have traded it for one cigarette, and I didn't even smoke. When I got on the *McCalla*, I went up to the first familiar face and asked him for a cigarette. I took a few drags and that was it. I never smoked until then. That's when I started."

When Lt. Bryan got aboard *McCalla*, he went directly to the wardroom and took Dr. Potter aside and showed him the severed tip of his pinkie. Potter told Bryan he had too many more serious injuries to deal with. Flowers poured Bryan a shot of Old Overholt. Bryan swallowed it down in one gulp. On deck, Bryan walked to the lifeline and tossed the tip of his pinkie overboard.

When McCleary hobbled into the wardroom, he announced, "Shark bit me." Everybody laughed. Dr. Potter told him to sit down and wait his turn. McCleary sat down and took off his shoe, revealing teeth marks around his instep. Potter came over to look. "Bit my heinie, too," McCleary said, "but I hit him and pulled out." Everybody laughed. McCleary stood up and dropped his pants. 14-inch teeth marks encircled his rear end.

All morning, Yeoman Coninx had been wandering around the ship handing out paper and pencils to *Duncan* officers and chiefs and telling them they were to write up their stories about the battle. They were to turn them in to Lt. Bryan before 1600.

Lt. Hauck was interviewing survivors, trying to get them while their memories were still fresh. The memories were a little too fresh for a lot of them. Many were actively trying to forget. Some would be waking up screaming for weeks. Whenever Wharton thought about being trapped in the dark I.C. with the water rising, he broke into a sweat and started shaking. Boehm knew he would never forget Dubiel's interrupted scream when the shark dragged him under. But some of them found it helpful to talk. Some, once they started talking, could not stop. During their long struggle in the water, they were preoccupied with trying to stay alive and had not given much thought to the battle. It was only now, on board *McCalla*, that they noticed they were shaking.

It helped that they had all gone through it together—and survived. Surviving combat forges comradeship. Even the chasm between officers and enlisted men smoothed out to where a real bond developed among them. Privately, every survivor must have reflected on how he behaved under fire. If nothing else, they had learned a lesson in bravery and cowardice. "'Hero' and 'coward' are myths is what I learned," Fischer remembered.

Laughter is contagious, especially among men recovering from shock. They all saw gallows humor in what they went through. They laughed about Watertender Boyle who one minute was hiding in a locker and the next was in the bucket brigade rescuing trapped sailors from the forward fireroom. The funny part was that Chief Holt was recommending Boyle for a medal.

They were all severely dehydrated. The first men rescued by *McCalla* drank up all the water. "All I wanted was water, my tongue was so swollen," Olek remembered, "but I had to settle for black coffee." By the time Sobelman got on board, there was no water, no coffee, not even any medicinal whiskey.

Sobelman headed up to the bridge to try to get away from the crowd on deck. Lt. Hauck caught up with him on 0-2 level. Mostly he wanted to know about Mr. Fowler. They were trying to figure out who got him to the *McCalla* so they could give the man a medal. Sobelman was so thirsty he could hardly think straight. He told Hauck he thought it was Dunlop and Queen. Hauck said he heard it was Bilbro and Queen. Sobelman shrugged. That seemed to satisfy Hauck. He patted Sobelman on the shoulder. "Good job. Good job," he said.

When Sobelman got up to the roof of the bridge, he was surprised to see his former chief gunner's mate from the *Utah*: "It was old Smoothbore Smitty." Chief Smith was blasting away at sharks with a 30-06 Springfield. The water all around the ship was thick with sharks and Japanese.

Lt. Kabat, who was still in the water, suddenly felt a scratching, tingling sensation, and he lifted his left foot out of the water and saw that his foot was bleeding. "I need a knife," he shouted to Wickstrom, who was 30 feet away. "The sharks are attacking me." Slovenec and Dawson were close enough to hear him, and they could see the sharks. Kabat splashed frantically as if trying to lift himself out of the water. He had a powder can under each knee. One shark kept darting in. "It had a big round front end like a Buick," Slovenec remembered. Kabat would raise his fist and wait for it and hit it as hard as he could. The shark would turn and swim off about 20 feet, then come back and attack again. After each encounter, Kabat would raise his feet and arms to check to see what was left of him. The shark first tore off a piece of his left hand. Next, the big toe on his left foot was dangling. Then, a piece of his right heel was gone. "A shark," Kabat screamed. "A shark's eating me!" None of them had a knife. "Then this Dauntless comes over low," Slovenec remembered. "I'm pointing at Kabat. I put my hand in the water like a shark. Well, he spotted him and dove on him like to try to scare the shark. He comes back and waves at us and dives again. I guess he radioed the ship because pretty soon McCalla comes along."

McCalla charged in at full steam. "They're shooting into the water around us," Wickstrom remembered. "Kabat's screaming, 'Shark! Shark! Shark!'" Naked and clinging onto two shiny powder cans, he looked like bait. They threw a monkey fist to him, and they were pulling him in when two sharks hit him at once.

Nobody who witnessed it would ever forget his scream. Gunners were pouring small arms fire into the water around him. As the gig was racing out to him, men in the gig were shooting at the sharks. The two sharks kept darting in and out. "You could see the fins," Bethune remembered, "and you could hear that poor prick screaming for miles." A McCalla sailor named Ferrera, seeing the look on Kabat's face, thought for a second about doing him a favor by putting a bullet in him.

When the gig crew hauled Kabat out of the water, they were

so horrified by what they saw they headed straight back to the ship. Wickstrom was close enough that he was able to swim over and haul himself into the boat before it took off, but others close by in the water could not believe they were left behind. "I figured they could see us and would pick us up," Slovenec remembered. "Dawson was terrified of sharks now. When he saw the gig turn away, he asked me to kill him. I tell him, 'You know how to pray, Dawson? Talk to God. I made a deal with God. I says, Lemme live through this here, God, and You can pick me on land anytime. If I'm on land I don't mind dying, just not as shark bait.'"

Lt. Kabat was lifted aboard *McCalla* by stretcher. *Duncan* survivors collected on deck to watch as he was carried to the wardroom. "The sharks had took bites out of his leg, his arm, his ass," Bethune remembered. "He looked like a hundred pounds of hamburger. I predicted, 'That poor prick's not gonna make it through the night.'" [Kabat became a professor and lived another forty years.]

The night before, Wickstrom had turned his last $30 into $300. Having made it aboard *McCalla* without a scratch, he was feeling unnaturally lucky, so he headed aft looking for the crap game—and promptly lost his $300. He was sure he was swindled. "Guys on that ship were crooks," he remembered.

On board *Duncan*, the men in the salvage party had begun to suspect their efforts were futile. *Duncan* had too many problems—mechanical, water, oil, steam. It was so hot and steamy down in the after fireroom nobody could stay down there for more than a few minutes at a time. They struggled for an hour in the dark trying to light a boiler before they realized the tubes were toasted. It was hopeless without more pumps. They got a handybilly working, but it was low on gas. They tried to signal to *McCalla*—they could see her moving back and forth on the horizon – but they failed to get a message through. Lt. Myhre finally called off the effort to light the boiler. He told them all to make ready "lines, phones, anchor chain, etc." in preparation for towing.

Lt. Myhre had surveyed *Duncan* from top to bottom. He noted the helm was to port 20°, full left rudder. Two unexploded shells were found: a Japanese 6-inch round was sitting on a workbench in the machine shop; and, on the main deck, there was an 8-inch round on which some sailor had scratched *"Salt Lake City."* Overlooked were: a 5-inch dud round from *Hatsuyuki* amid the rubble in the pilothouse; and a 5-inch round from *Hatsuyuki* that exploded through the main deck amidships (evidence of which was subsequently obliterated by the explosion in the forward fireroom that blew a big hole in the deck). Myhre diagrammed thirty-three shell holes of assorted calibers—20mm, 40mm, 5-inch, 6-inch, and 8-inch. Many were ins and outs. Almost all had entered through the port side; therefore, from U.S. ships. At least five larger-caliber holes were in the port side. There were so many smaller-caliber shell holes to port that Myhre did not even try to count them all. One larger-caliber and two smaller-caliber shells were in the starboard side, and there were so many 20mm holes forward of the bridge to starboard Myhre did not count them.

Duncan's starboard list increased as the morning wore on. At about 1100, the ship made a sudden list to port. Men dropped what they were doing and ran because they thought she was settling. The forward engineroom was suddenly taking on water faster. Myhre thought the bulkhead between the forward fireroom and forward engineroom gave away, but the bulkhead was holding. One thought was that water might be entering through ruptured pipes, so they rigged a suction hose down the hatch, and they ran the handybilly until it ran out of gas. The leak was never located. The forward engineroom continued taking on water. The list to port kept increasing. *Duncan* was down a couple of feet at the bow when, at about 1145, came an ominous rumble from the forward fireroom. Men checked fore to aft, topside and below. At about noon, *Duncan* made a giant lurch. With that, Lt. Myhre ordered the salvage operation abandoned.

Ens. Weems was climbing into the whaleboat when he remembered the sword he saw in the commodore's stateroom. He ran up to O-1 deck and retrieved it. By the time he got back, water was sloshing over the port side.

Lt. Myhre wanted to watch *Duncan* settle, so they motored off about 300 yards and cut the engine. After a few minutes, a small craft was spotted on the horizon. It was about two miles away and was racing toward them. Myhre decided *Duncan's* machinegun battery "offered better protection than one Tommy gun," so they steamed back to *Duncan*. They were manning the after guns when a Higgins boat loaded with *Duncan* survivors pulled alongside. The bedraggled survivors were all staring up in stunned silence at their old ship.

The salvage party climbed into the Higgins boat, and the whaleboat crew returned to the whaleboat, and the two boats motored off. *Duncan's* port deck was awash.

Duncan floated for another twenty minutes. Her bow finally went under at 1242. She stood on her head a moment, then slowly turned turtle and nosed under with a half twist, cocking her American flag in the air. Myhre noted she went down in 500 fathoms six miles north of Savo Island.

The two small boats were a quarter of a mile away when a couple of the depth charges set for 30 feet went off. A moment later, 6 feet of *Duncan's* stern bobbed to the surface. It floated for a few minutes before sliding under. About twenty minutes later, the depth charges set for 300 feet went off in an explosion that rocked the ocean. Even though the two small boats were about a mile away, it felt as if they lifted clear of the water.

Zigzagging north in search of her salvage party, *McCalla's* sonar was picking up *pings* from *Duncan's* sinking hulk. They had been listening to *pings* all morning from *Furutaka* and *Fubuki* sinking and from Japanese sub I-12 that was stalking them. Suddenly hearing new *pings* (and unaware that *Duncan* was sinking), LCdr. Cooper thought a second sub was tracking them. He ordered even more zigzagging.

When the gig finally picked up Slovenec and Dawson, Slovenec was so weak he needed help getting aboard. "They had to pull me up," he remembered. "I wanted to take my mattress—I had all my stuff tied up in there—but they wouldn't let me. There was a lot of guys on there. The boat was full." Slovenec was feeling lucky after witnessing sharks attacking

Kabat from 40 feet away. He later discovered that his flashlight batteries were leaking, and he thought maybe the battery acid had kept the sharks away.

LCdr. Taylor and GM2c Whelan were still together when they were found. The small boat that rescued them cut a path through a churning mass of Japanese sailors and sharks around *McCalla*.

Taylor was so depressed he was in shock. LCdr. Cooper gave him his cabin, and Dr. Potter gave him something to help him sleep. Taylor went into the captain's cabin and did not emerge for hours.

Five Japanese in the water were holding onto one piece of lumber while a large shark circled them. The gig went out to rescue them, which galled a lot of ex-*Duncan* men. "They'd rescue them and give them clean underwear and food and an interpreter," Quinn complained, "instead of shooting the sons of bitches like they'd have done us." A sailor on the gig threw one of the Japanese sailors a line, but he refused to take it. "The Japs didn't want to come aboard," Craig marveled. When they tried to rescue another, he pounded his head on the lumber. Another tried to drown himself, but he could not stay down. Each time he bobbed up, they tried to grab him. After the sixth or seventh try, they got hold of him. He put up a terrific struggle. By the time they got him subdued in the boat, the gig crew was so exhausted they did not feel like trying to rescue any more.

McCalla now had four Japanese prisoners. The two captured early in the morning were down in the brig. The two captured late in the morning were forced to sit on the deck topside. *Duncan* survivors wandered by and gawked at them. "They had always showed us these little bitty fellas with buck teeth before we went over there," Palmer remembered. "These guys were great big burly fellas."

DeLucca was watching as one of the prisoners was led below. All of a sudden, a *McCalla* sailor came up behind him and hit him on the head with a big wrench. "The blood came blowing out of his head," DeLucca remembered. "They grabbed the sailor. The Japanese guy died, I think. That was murder. That guy was a prisoner." The surviving prisoner was quickly removed to the saillocker.

The Japanese were kept in the saillocker under armed guard for their own protection. Initially, *Duncan* men were assigned to guard them, until someone thought better of that idea. Then *McCalla* guards were assigned to watch the *Duncan* guards.

McCalla picked up the last *Duncan* survivor at 1209. *McCalla* was so low on fuel she was burning lubricating oil, which put out a lot of smoke. LCdr. Cooper was so worried about the Japanese submarine trailing them that he called off any further attempts to rescue Japanese. He ordered the *McCalla* south. He then sent a message to Vandegrift: "FIFTY OR SIXTY JAP SURVIVORS LATITUDE 902, LONGITUDE 15939 EAST. HAVE PICKED UP THREE AND AM PROCEEDING. REQUEST YOU CAPTURE REMAINDER."

Late in the afternoon, ex- *Duncan* men were allowed down to look at the prisoners. The three were sitting on the deck inside the saillocker. All three were officers—a lieutenant commander and two junior officers. Sobelman thought they looked "scared shitless." The ex- *Duncan* men mostly just stared at them.

Horsing around, DeLucca asked the ranking officer, "How come your uniform's different from them?" The man replied in perfect English, "I was an executive officer." DeLucca could not have been more surprised if an animal at the zoo spoke up. "The guy spoke better than I do," he remembered. "He asked me where I was from. I told him Dorchester, Massachusetts. 'Ahh, Fields Corner, Mattapan. I was in the Imperial Navy, but I was studying at Harvard.'" DeLucca was reminded of an incident years earlier when he and his father, a career Navy man, were on their way home from Boston on the train and they saw a Japanese-looking man taking pictures of the harbor, and his father grunted, "They aren't all here for nothing." DeLucca asked the Japanese officer, "What about all you Japs around Boston before the war? What were you doing? My dad says you were getting ready." The officer smiled. "Your father was right," he said.

Taylor emerged early in the evening, looking haggard. He was somewhat rejuvenated by a report that *Duncan* had sunk a cruiser *and* a destroyer. He went down to officer country before supper to visit with the injured officers. Kabat and Fowler were both too drugged to speak. Unfortunately for Wharton, he was only drugged enough to control his nerves. The only thing Taylor said to him was, "Where's all the money?" Wharton knew he meant the money from the ship's store. "Sir, the money's in the pocket of the pants they cut off me," he replied. He was just thankful the ship's-store book had burned because it was never balanced.

Taylor did not bother to go to chiefs' quarters and visit with the enlisted wounded. Not one senior officer did. "Bryan or Taylor, none of them, *never* came to see us," Fischer remembered, still bitter about it fifty years later.

Shortly after Taylor left officer country, Wharton noticed Fowler moving in his bunk. Wharton went in and sat beside him. "He was very much alive," Wharton remembered. "He might've been pretending to be asleep when the captain was there. After a while, he was talking. He knew he was dying. He had shrapnel all through his body. There wasn't enough needles and thread to sew anybody like that up. He was full of steel. It's hot so it cauterizes, but there was nothing the doctor could do. He was groggy with morphine but was talking about his wife and her letter and how she was having the baby and all. He knew it was a boy. He was sure of it. And he was so proud."

At dusk, the survivors who were ambulatory stood muster on the fantail. No official muster list survived, but the chiefs had compiled the names of all the men in their departments from memory. Out of a total complement of 248, only one name was forgotten. Chief Paige read out the names. When somebody answered, he put a check beside it. If nobody answered, he would say, "Anybody seen this guy?" If nobody had, he put an "X" by the name. One hundred and ninety-six men were present—nine officers and 187 enlisted. The officers had gotten the worst of it, percentage-wise. Of thirteen officers, four were dead, two were dying, and another was injured.

Fifty-two men were unaccounted for. Four officers were missing and known to be dead. Of 48 enlisted men unaccounted for, nine were known to have been taken to Guadalcanal. So 39 were unaccounted for, and 34 of them were known to be dead. In the end, five men were unaccounted for. Four of them—Hess, Rosenfelt, Ginder, and Dubiel—were seen in the water. They were all presumed to have drowned. In the end, only one man was missing without any explanation whatsoever—Seaman Elvin Scott.

Shortly after muster, the PA squawked—"NOW HEAR THIS. LAY UP TO THE BRIDGE."—and the names of the forty-four missing were read aloud. Most had never made it off the ship and everybody knew it, but there was always the hope that someone could be on Savo or might have been taken to Guadalcanal. When all the names had been called and nobody had answered, there was a dreadful silence.

That evening, two Marines on Guadalcanal borrowed a LCT and took it out for an unauthorized spin. They went to the north of Savo to see what they could find in the way of battle debris. What they found was Seaman Elvin Scott floating alone. It was dark by the time they got him to Guadalcanal.

The movie on *McCalla* that evening was Paramount's "The Fleet's In," a musical remake of an old Clara Bow vehicle. Ladies' man sailor (William Holden) on leave in San Francisco bets he can melt iceberg nightclub singer (Dorothy Lamour)— "Gobs of glee! A boatload of beauties! A shipful of songs!"

While the movie was playing, Taylor, Bryan, and Hauck huddled in the captain's cabin trying to reconstruct the battle. Senior officers were required to write after-action reports. It was imperative that they get their stories straight so that they not contradict one another; covering your ass, U.S. Navy-style, requires you first cover the ass of the next higher up.

Reconstructing a night naval battle is notoriously difficult under the best of circumstances because the combatant ships pass at high speeds and in the dark, so nobody really sees anything. This battle was even more difficult because the ship's log was lost and the yeoman charged with documenting the battle was killed and his notes were burned. What Taylor, Bryan, and Hauck had to go on were written statements from three junior officers and twenty-eight enlisted men, plus Bryan and Hauck's notes from interviews with survivors.

Ships maneuvering half a mile away glimpsed for an instant in the flickering light of a falling parachute-flare left witnesses with ghostly, dream-like images. They might have seen ships rolling over or maybe the ships were simply turning. Men who claimed they were certain they saw something were dismissed as unreliable because the light and shadows were so stark and weird nobody in his right mind could be sure what he saw. Some men stationed aft claimed to have seen the Japanese destroyer to starboard nosing under and transports going down with soldiers jumping off their decks. A lot of on-deck men saw at least one of Chief Boyd's torpedoes explode into the Japanese cruiser. Seaman Duvall, the torpedo mount lookout, claimed he saw both torpedoes hit the cruiser, and he said the cruiser split open right after the second torpedo exploded amidships. Duvall was considered reliable because it was his job to watch the track of the torpedoes.

Lt. Bryan took special interest in who had stayed with Lt.(jg) Fowler through the night. Officers are always touched by stories of enlisted men risking their lives to save officers. Hauck had tried to reconstruct how Fowler made it aboard *McCalla*. He interviewed everybody he could think of. Chief Paige told him how he, Sobelman, Queen, and Bilbro had lowered Fowler to the main deck. Bilbro told him how he, Sobelman, Queen, and Dunlop got Fowler into the water. Bilbro claimed he and Queen stayed with Fowler all night. Queen must have gone along with Bilbro's story. No one ever mentioned mess attendants, and Hauck never thought to question them. LCdr. Cooper could have informed the investigation since he saw the mess attendants in the water with Fowler, but nobody thought to ask him. So Hauck was left with the impression that Bilbro and Queen delivered Fowler on board.

Taylor, Bryan, and Hauck spent hours going over the information they had. They took a stab at constructing a timeline—the approach to Guadalcanal, maneuvers off the northwest coast, the turn toward Savo, the final reverse turn into battle. With all this in hand, the three senior officers went off to write their own reports.

At about 2100, *McCalla* received a TBS challenge. "This is 88," LCdr. Cooper replied. "This is 86" came the reply—*Lansdowne*. Relieved to hear LCdr. Smedberg's voice, Cooper shouted, "I have Whitey on board! I picked up Whitey!"

At about 2200, word was passed among the survivors that Lt.(jg) Fowler was dying and that if anybody wanted to go and see him now was the time. About twenty men went down. "It was a gang of us went. I remember Schimmel and Milek—a whole slew of us," DeLucca remembered. "Half a dozen of us got in the compartment. The rest were out in the passageway, all squeezing their heads in the hatch. Mr. Fowler couldn't speak, but his eyes were open. He recognized we were there. There was blood all over him. He was drugged up. I touched him. I was crying like the rest of them. When we came up from saying goodbye, somebody said, 'The good die young.' Fowler, Broccolo, Lane are all dead, and we're thinking about all them other bastards who could've went."

A lot of the men were so tired they could not sleep. Bethune went down to sickbay to get a shot of booze, but all they had were "empties."

Sobelman slept on the roof of the bridge curled up inside the canvass torpedo director cover. He was awakened by shouting—"Radar contact 3500 yards!"—and general quarters sounding. An unidentified ship was demanding *McCalla* identify herself. It was even darker than the night before. Cooper would forget and leave the mic open so the whole ship could hear his worried mutterings. Panic spread. A dark shape loomed to starboard. "I was scared," DeLucca remembered. "In a moment, she was right on top of us. I was shaking. I'm saying, 'Please, please don't make me go in that water again.' I was really scared of sharks now." A shot fired across *McCalla*'s bow. Cooper came on the TBS, "This is 88."

"This is 50," a voice came back—*Helena*. *McCalla* and *Lansdowne* fell in with *Helena* shortly before midnight.

Down in officer country, Wharton was awakened by activity across the passageway. Dr.Potter was leaning over Fowler.

"How's he doing?" Wharton asked.

"We lost that one," Potter said. "Just as well."

Potter recorded Fowler's time of death as 0200, October 13, 1942. On the death certificate, he wrote "intercranial injury" as the cause, with "intercranial hemorrhage" a contributing factor.

Wharton was surprised how peaceful Bobby looked. "He looked like he was sleeping," Wharton remembered. "His face barely had a mark, a few scratches, nothing serious." Noticing his silver ID bracelet, Wharton removed it from his wrist, promising himself that if he ever made it home he would look up Bobby's wife and return it to her.

Part IV

AFTERMATH
October 1942-November 1943

My conclusions have cost me some labor from the want of coincidence between accounts of the same occurrences by different eyewitnesses, arising sometimes from imperfect memory, sometimes from undue partiality for one side or the other.

—Thucydides

Chapter 9
THE OFFICIAL VERSION
October 13-November 28

When you write the biography of a friend, you must do it as if you were
taking revenge for him.

—Gustave Flaubert (to Ernest Feydeau)

At first light on October 13, *Helena*, *Lansdowne*, and
McCalla were steaming east toward the New Hebrides.
Lt.(jg) Fowler's canvas-wrapped body lay on *McCalla*'s deck.
Torpedoman Schimmel and others in the torpedo gang cried
when they heard he had died.

At morning quarters, Taylor addressed them. Many were still
in shock, including Taylor. All of them had thought of *Duncan*
as a living thing. Taylor said he would always think of her as
his first ship. For most of them, she *was* their first ship. When
he told them they sank a cruiser *and* a destroyer, there was only
half-hearted applause. He said that he was going to try to get a
new ship and that he hoped they would all come back out with
him for "one more lick at the Japs." There was silence. None of
them was ready to think about coming back.

Chief Paige read aloud some dispatches *McCalla* had
decoded. The first one was from R/Adm. Scott to V/Adm.
Ghormley: "ENGAGED ENEMY WEST OF SAVO ISLAND
ABOUT MIDNIGHT. AT LEAST FOUR ENEMY DDs
[destroyers] BURNING AND PROBABLY ONE CA [heavy
cruiser] HIT BADLY." The catcalls and rude noises were cut
short when Paige read the next, which was also from Scott.

"*BOISE* BURNING BADLY WHEN LAST SEEN.
FARENHOLT NOT YET LOCATED. *McCALLA* SEARCHING.
REQUEST AIR COVERAGE. AM PROCEEDING POINT
C, SPEED 20." In an aside, Paige pointed out that nobody
had yet noticed *Duncan* was missing. Then, in the very next
dispatch, Scott reported that *Boise* had turned up but that
Farenholt was still missing and so was *Duncan*. That brought an
eruption of hoots and whistles. "HAVE LOCATED *DUNCAN*,"

Cooper radioed Scott. "SHE HAS BEEN ABANDONED. AM SEARCHING FOR SURVIVORS THEN WILL ATTEMPT TO TOW *DUNCAN*." Scott must have been in an expansive mood when he radioed Ghormley: "POSSIBLE FIVE DDs SUNK OR OUT OF ACTION, ONE NACHI [*Myoko*-class heavy cruiser] SUNK, ONE OTHER CA [heavy cruiser] PROBABLY SUNK, ONE AP [transport] SUNK." Ghormley replied without apparent irony: "ONCE MORE THE ENEMY PLANS HAVE BEEN UPSET. CONGRATULATIONS." Ghormley radioed Cooper: "IF CONDITIONS DO NOT WARRANT TOWING *DUNCAN* YOU ARE AUTHORIZED TO DESTROY HER TO PREVENT HER FALLING INTO ENEMY HANDS." Cooper radioed back that *Duncan* had sunk. As *McCalla* was steaming south, Cooper radioed R/Adm. Lee on *Washington*: "HAVE ABOARD NINE OFFICERS INCLUDING CAPTAIN AND EXECUTIVE OFFICER, 183 MEN SURVIVORS DUNCAN. FOUR BADLY WOUNDED. SHIP SANK 1242/12." The last message Chief Paige read was from V/Adm. Ghormley to LCdr. Cooper: "[Y]OUR PERSEVERANCE HAS BEEN REWARDED IN SAVING SO MANY FROM THE DUNCAN. WELL DONE." The survivors' enthusiastic applause was heart-felt.

Taylor and Bryan spent much of their time aboard *McCalla* piecing together the battle. Taylor knew he needed to explain the loss of his ship. Ghormley was known to look especially unkindly on captains who lost their ships. Taylor thought his best defense was that *Duncan* had sunk a cruiser. Surely, that would be seen a good trade-off.

In writing his report, Taylor picked his words carefully. Needing all the friends he could get, he omitted any mention of friendly fire. He framed his own actions in the best possible light, of course, and he fudged as much as he dared. He raised more questions than he answered. Leaning heavily on misdirection, he wrote at length about all that he did correctly and blithely skipped over his more questionable decisions. For instance, he wrote paragraphs on the approach and then rushed through everything after the reverse turn, dispensing with *Duncan*'s five-minute torpedo run in one paragraph, failing to even mention turning into *Helena*'s fire.

In mid-morning on October 14, *Helena, Lansdowne*, and *McCalla* steamed into Pallikula Bay at Espíritu Santo. More than twenty warships were in the harbor. *Duncan* survivors crowded the lifelines to try to see the damage to the other task group ships.

Boise, Salt Lake City, and *Farenholt* had "Stateside hits," which meant they were going home. *Boise* was the most severely damaged. Hit seven times, she had buried 107 men at sea. *Salt Lake City* had three major hits. *Farenholt* was hit four times— once by *Hatsuyuki*, once by *Boise*, and three times by *San Francisco*. Altogether, 176 U.S. Navy men were killed in the action.

As *McCalla* steamed across the harbor, Capt. Moran on *Boise* signaled to LCdr. Taylor that *Boise* was going home. He offered accommodations for the *Duncan* officers and some enlisted men.

As *McCalla* was passing a cruiser at anchor, the cruiser piped "Attention To Port" and rendered honors. Men on the cruiser were cheering. The ex-*Duncan* men waved, bewildered but happy to be alive. Soon, every ship in the harbor joined in the salute.

Lt.(jg) Fowler's body was transferred to the base hospital for burial. The severely wounded[1] were transferred to hospital ship *Solace,* which was in the harbor.

The remaining men transferred to *San Francisco* and *Helena.*

On the cruisers, they were issued new uniforms. They showered. They were fed all they could eat, and there was ice cream.

Everyone was sympathetic toward the *Duncan* survivors and all they had endured, but there was surprisingly little support for *Duncan*'s actions. Naval warfare was seen as a team-against-team collective proposition. The general feeling was that Taylor and Bryan had gone off solo to make points.

Duncan's sister, *Lansdowne*, was supportive. *Lansdowne* officers and enlisted men took up a collection for the *Duncan* survivors. Lt.(jg) Tom Taylor threw in his wristwatch for his brother.

From: The Division Commander, and Captain, and Officers of the USS LANSDOWNE

To: The Captain, Officers, and men of the USS DUNCAN
Dear Ted:
The contribution of $575.00 which accompanies this letter is from our Division Commander [Cdr. Ryan] and Officers and men of the USS LANSDOWNE, who feel a great sense of personal loss. We hope this will come in handy for the small items you will all want right away. It is given from deep in our hearts to our close friends of your ship.

The friendly rivalry and keen competition between our ships was the finest I have ever seen. Our Officers and men took great pride in your fine ship, praising her qualities to all outsiders; feeling that no one but ourselves had the privilege of making disparaging remarks about our sister ship, alongside of which we were built, whose Officers and men were always ready and eager to lend us a helping hand, and in whose wake we followed many times with complete confidence.

We found your ship setting mark after mark for us to shoot at and very often having just enough of an edge on us to spur us on to additional effort to make you as proud of your sister ship as we were, and always will be, of ours.

And it will ever be a source of pride to us in this Division that you went out as you did; the way a ship should go; aggressively into the enemy with all you had and mortally wounding an enemy ship several times your size.

We had very anxious hours between announcement of your disappearance and the report of the rescue of such a good proportion of your shipmates, but that news gave a lift to every one of us and we want you and your Officers and men to know how proud we are of you and that your ship will be close to us in whatever action may be ahead. We shall feel her strong support and never-failing cooperation in every crisis.

Every Officer and man joins me in sincerest best wishes to every one of you.
Smeddy

R/Adm. Scott summoned Taylor and Bryan. Capt. Hoover and his executive officer, Cdr. Gerald Linke, were also summoned. They all rode across to *San Francisco* in *Helena*'s gig.

The task group commanders and executive officers gathered

on *San Francisco*'s quarterdeck: Capt. Tobin from his new flagship, *Aaron Ward*; LCdr. Eugene Seaward and his exec, Lt. Alcorn Beckmann, from *Farenholt*; LCdr. Cooper and Lt. Myhre from *McCalla*.

Taylor had intended to claim that *Duncan* sank a cruiser, but that idea evaporated when he realized that most of the others were planning to claim the same cruiser. Taylor had a chance to speak briefly with Capt. Tobin and was shocked when Tobin told him with a laugh that he did not even know the Japanese were there. Until that moment, Taylor had thought he was following *Farenholt* on a torpedo run. It must have dawned on him then that he could be facing serious questions. He quickly began adjusting his story. Having written in his after-action report that he ordered *Duncan* to follow *Farenholt*, he revised it to say that he ordered a torpedo run in accordance with the Admiral's order for destroyers to attack without orders as soon as an enemy ship was spotted.

On the flag bridge, Scott greeted them solemnly, as if welcoming mourners to a funeral. Everyone in SoPac was downhearted because, during the night, two Japanese battleships had bombarded Henderson Field and landed soldiers and supplies at Tassafaronga. Scott took the news personally, as a slap in the face. Their skirmish did nothing to dissuade V/Adm. Mikawa from resupplying Guadalcanal, not even for one night. He was right back the next night—with battleships.

As depressed as he was, Scott tried to buck them up. He said they had fought the first major naval surface action in two months, since the battle off Savo Island, and he declared they "won." Their mission was to turn the Japanese back, and they did that. Scott expressed regret about the dead and wounded. He told Taylor and Bryan that he was sorry about the *Duncan*. He said she would be "long remembered as the first U.S. destroyer to penetrate a major Japanese battle line."

Scott believed they had accomplished more than they were being credited for, but he was otherwise vague about the battle. After claiming "[a]t least four enemy DDs burning," he realized one was the *Duncan*. His hope was that they sank two cruisers, but Marines on scene estimated "less than a thousand" Japanese in the water. The complement of an *Aoba*-class cruiser was 622. This suggested that more than one cruiser was sunk but less than two.

They all knew they should have been able to inflict far heavier casualties on the Japanese force. They had every advantage—numerical advantage, the element of surprise, the perfect tactical position. And, incredibly, they crossed the Japanese T. Yet the battle was a wash.

Scott was gratified that they were not caught by surprise, at least, not completely like at Savo. He did not mention that was only thanks to Capt. Hoover. If *Helena* had not opened fire when she did, the Japanese ships would have plowed through the U.S. line, probably without any U.S. ship firing a shot. Scott virtually admitted as much when he said he did not think the U.S. Navy was the equal of the Imperial Navy in night tactics—not yet. "But we will learn," he vowed.

They discussed what they might have done differently. Turning off the SG radars on San *Francisco* and *Salt Lake City* was probably not such a good idea, because it meant the task group commander went into battle blind. The destroyer officers thought all the destroyers should have been in the van.

As elementary as Scott's battle plan was, his ships had failed to execute it. All that had saved them from complete destruction was that the Japanese improbably withheld fire for seven minutes, during which time *Boise* and *Helena* fired about 300 6-inch rounds at *Aoba*.

They were all painfully aware they screwed up, as a group and individually. Every cruiser captain had authorized the use of searchlights during the battle. Capt. Moran and Capt. Small had allowed searchlights once too often.

Scott had met earlier with the captains and execs of the other task group ships, so he already had a track chart roughed out. A nautical chart of Guadalcanal's northwest coast was rolled out on the navigation table. The task group's track was drawn in grease pencil on a succession of clear plastic overlays, one for every few minutes. The movements of the task group ships relative to one another were pictured almost to the minute. The stack of overlays detailed awful errors on both sides.

Scott's approach plan had worked, until 1715 when *San Francisco*'s floatplane crashed. After that, Scott felt he had lost the element of surprise, and he began thinking defensively.

Capt. Tobin made a string of bad decisions. The first (and the worst) was choosing to remain aboard *Farenholt* after her surface-search radar went out. Scott had not objected to having his destroyer commander in the van without surface-search radar. This was a reflection of both men's disdain for radar. Tobin made another bad decision when he delegated *Buchanan* to rescue the crew from *San Francisco*'s downed plane when he knew *Buchanan*'s FD radar was out. Again, Scott did not question Tobin's decision. Tobin made two more bad decisions off the north coast of Guadalcanal that Scott never learned about: *Farenholt*'s FC radar made a contact to the northwest that Tobin dismissed as a radar malfunction or Russell Island, and he did not report it; and then *Farenholt* lookouts spotted two blue lights on the beach at Tassafaronga, and Tobin did not report them because he assumed *San Francisco* lookouts would see them, but they did not.

Farenholt's TBS radio started malfunctioning after the task group turned northwest toward Savo, but nobody noticed it was malfunctioning because they were maintaining radio silence. So Capt. Tobin was essentially blind *and* deaf, but he did not know it. This explains why *Farenholt* missed the reverse turn order and led the van destroyers a mile out of position, and why, five minutes before the battle, *Farenholt* led the van destroyers on a course between the battle lines. *Farenholt* did hear *Helena*'s report of enemy ships to starboard, and Tobin had *Farenholt* slow down. Then, hearing *Boise*'s report of "bogies," Tobin had *Farenholt* head for the rear of the column. When Scott called him to make sure the van destroyers were to starboard, Tobin assured him they were, even though he was heading for the rear at full speed. He assumed *Duncan* and *Laffey* were behind him, but, when *Farenholt* came around and headed for the van again, she crossed *Duncan*'s wake. Tobin failed to report this quickly enough (before *Farenholt*'s TBS antenna was knocked out by a shell from *Boise*), so Scott never knew *Duncan* was ahead of *Farenholt* on a torpedo run.

Radar failure was the new excuse-of-choice. This was the first time in the annals of naval history that radar was used as an excuse. It would have been inconceivable just months earlier when nobody trusted radar enough to base command decisions on it.

The 2332 overlay pictured the situation moments before the reverse turn—the task group steaming northwest with Savo Island 4½ miles to starboard. Scott blamed *San Francisco*'s unexpected early turn on "a communications error." However inadvertent, the turn was exceedingly well timed to put them on course to cross the Japanese T.

Ten minutes after the turn execute, *Helena* reported the contact to the west, and the flag bridge responded, "Roger." Capt. Hoover was still angry about that. He told Scott he was not sure their contact was genuine so he delayed reporting it. Scott responded scathingly, "It's too bad you didn't report it *before* the countermarch," he said. Before the contermarch when there was no doubt where the van destroyers were, in other words. "I had no reason to think the Admiral was unaware of the situation," Hoover snapped back. Even though he doubted the contact was genuine, Hoover had rushed to report it because the van destroyers were heading into his line of fire on the lead Japanese cruiser. Scott admitted that he had assumed *Helena* and *Boise* were reporting the van destroyers because he could not imagine why Japanese warships would be bearing for Savo Island. He said it was not until he saw they were firing incendiary shells that he realized they were headed down the coast to bombard the airfield.

Capt. Tobin omitted mentioning in his report anything about *Farenholt* heading for the rear. The track chart overlays after 2346 showed *Farenholt* steaming for the new van, *Laffey* racing for the rear, and *Duncan* steaming southwest on a torpedo run. Successive overlays had *Farenholt* achieving the new van, *Laffey* falling in at the rear, and *Duncan* veering off in a series of curlicues and ending in a question mark.

When it came LCdr. Taylor's turn to explain how *Duncan* got in *Helena*'s fire, he said he came to port to try to hold their torpedo-firing angle on the Japanese van cruiser that was swinging away to starboard. He said *Duncan* got off a torpedo at the van cruiser that missed. Scott was horrified because he could see on the overlay that both *San Francisco* and *Farenholt* were just beyond the Japanese cruiser when *Duncan* fired in that direction. Scott caustically asked Taylor if he was aware that he almost sank a U.S. warship.

The loss of *Duncan* was an embarrassment to all of them because the worst damage done to her was by *Boise*. *Boise*'s main battery, pouring out a round a second, might have fired as many as a hundred shells at *Duncan*.

Capt. Moran was not present, but Scott told them Moran's explanation, which was that *Boise*'s SG radar blew a fuse at 2347. All her radarscopes were blank for 5 minutes, until 2352. Lt. Bryan snorted when he heard that. Scott asked Bryan if he doubted Moran's story. Bryan muttered that it was awfully convenient how neatly the 5-minute blackout overlapped the minute *Boise* had *Duncan* under fire, but he declined to pursue it.

Capt. Moran had made a worse mistake than destroying *Duncan*: he got his own ship destroyed by allowing *Boise* to illuminate *Farenholt*. One hundred and ten *Boise* men died as a result, and the new light cruiser would be out of the war for six months.

When six 8-inch shells from *Salt Lake City* struck into and around *Furutaka* at 2356, torpedomen on *Duncan* and *Buchanan*, who were timing their torpedoes to the same target, saw two large columns of water rising close aboard the Japanese cruiser. On both destroyers, the torpedomen thought it was their torpedoes. *Buchanan* had fired a full spread of five torpedoes in a near-perfect broadside from about 2,000 yards. LCdr. Wilson of *Buchanan* did not believe that all five could have missed. LCdr. Taylor countered that he knew precisely which of *Duncan*'s two torpedoes sank the cruiser—the second fired by Chief Boyd. In support, he offered the sworn statement of Seaman Ward Duvall, the torpedo mount lookout.

Duncan's claim had more than a few doubters among the Admiral's staff. They had all heard so many reports of torpedo failures they were instinctively skeptical of a reported success. For Chief Boyd, aiming the tubes by eye, it was a difficult shot at a target swinging away. And *both* torpedoes hit the target? And *both* exploded? Even at such close range that seemed unlikely. The consensus was it was more likely neither hit and neither exploded. There was a side debate about whether or not torpedoes could even arm in such a short distance (maybe under 800 yards for the supposedly fatal shot).

The cruiser captains all insisted that it was cumulative damage from their shells that cut *Furutaka* in half. Scott thought the cruiser splitting in two sounded more like a torpedo than shellfire, but he sidestepped making the call between *Duncan* and *Buchanan*. Among his staff, the consensus was heavily for *Buchanan* because it seemed so unlikely that all her torpedoes could have missed, whereas if both *Duncan*'s torpedoes hit *and* exploded it must have been a miracle. In the end, Taylor had to settle for a piece of the prize: he was only allowed to state in his report that the "two torpedo hits obtained [by *Duncan*] contributed to the sinking of the enemy cruiser."

All of them had a stake in the outcome of the battle not looking like dumb luck. They were all Gun Club members, and one unspoken purpose of this conference was to give them a chance to compare notes and polish their stories. For instance, Scott had suddenly remembered ordering commence firing, so he needed Tobin's support. And Tobin did not want to admit his indecision in heading for the van, so he needed Scott to forget that he had erred in reporting where the van destroyers were.

Taylor was in a weak position and could ill-afford to alienate anyone. He was relieved to see there were deals to be made. This was just the sort of backscratching he was good at.

According to Tobin's story, *Farenholt* was racing for the new van when the battle erupted. *Duncan* and *Laffey* were presumed to be following her. So Taylor needed to explain why *Duncan* was off on a solo torpedo run. He probably did not want to admit passing *Farenholt* because, if he really thought he was following her on a torpedo run, how could he suddenly *not* be following her?

This required a whole new story: *Duncan* passed *Farenholt* five minutes earlier during the confusion in the reverse turn. Tobin must have conspired with Taylor in this creative solution because Tobin omitted mentioning in his report that *Farenholt* had crossed *Duncan*'s wake, and he also did not mention that *Farenholt*'s FD radar was out nor that her TBS radio was malfunctioning. Incredibly, Tobin did not even mention leading the van destroyers a mile out of the position. For his part, Taylor did not mention following *Farenholt* northwest for four minutes after the reverse turn.

Tobin's chronic indecisiveness made all his bad decisions worse. When he realized he had led the van destroyers a mile off course, he stalled for another minute on the remote possibility that LCdr. Wilson might have led *Buchanan* and *McCalla* to the new van. When *Duncan* overtook *Farenholt* in the turn, Tobin was spurred to launch on a run to the new van. He explained away his unfortunate choice of the starboard track: "Up to this time there had been no contact of enemy forces in the vicinity, and from previously reported position of enemy forces [off Tassafaronga], it was estimated that they would be Southeast of our own forces, or on cruisers port flank." In other words, starboard was the unengaged side as far as he knew.

The sequence of *Farenholt*'s movements made Tobin seem cowardly and confused, yet in his after-action report he sounded confident that everything he did was correct and by the book. Tobin knew how to write an after-action report—sound upbeat, do not sound defensive, do not admit mistakes, and keep it short. Tobin's report is only $4^{1/2}$ pages. He made even his most disastrous mistakes sound like reasonable errors in judgment; even his confusions seem intentional and contrived. For instance, *Helena* issued the first contact report, but Tobin miscredits *San Francisco*. This may have been his way of supporting Scott's new claim that he knew all along that the enemy was to starboard. Tobin wrote that, upon first hearing of a contact, he had *Farenholt* slow down while he gave "consideration" to heading for the rear, implying that *Farenholt* never actually headed for the rear. In his purposely-confused chronology, Scott then comes on the TBS and asks him if he is taking station ahead. In fact, *Boise* came on the TBS next and re-reported her contact. Tobin miscredited *San Francisco* for the second contact report as well. He said gunfire opened up "[b]efore any action could be taken," implying that *Farenholt* was still racing for the new van. So Tobin was having it both ways: he wisely considered turning back, but heroically pressed onward.

All this left Taylor to explain *Duncan*'s port turn into *Helena*'s fire. What he apparently did not want to admit was *purposely* steering into *Helena*'s fire. His initial instinct was to lie about it. In his first rough-draft report, he stated that he ordered the torpedoes fired to port and that he never ordered the helm to port. Except this left him at a loss to explain how *Duncan* wound up in *Helena*'s line of fire. Also, Lt. Myhre stated in his report that *Duncan*'s wheel was hard to port.

Scott rejected Taylor's denial of the left turn. In fact, he rejected Taylor's entire report. He told him to rewrite it and turn in his new version to V/Adm. Ghormley in Nouméa.

After the conference, Taylor asked Scott if he would help him keep the *Duncan* crew together. They were fully trained and battle-tested, he argued. He wanted Scott to recommend to Ghormley that they all be sent home together to put another destroyer in commission. Scott agreed that they all deserved to go home, but he noted that there was a war going on and that SoPac had a severe manpower shortage, not to mention a shipping shortage. He said he thought it was unlikely that transportation would be available for so many men. When Taylor told him about Capt. Moran's offer, Scott agreed to dictate a dispatch to Ghormley:

HELENA LANSDOWNE MC CALLA ARRIVED BUTTON TEN HUNDRED FOURTEEN. SURVIVORS OF DUNCAN THREE OFFICERS ONE HUNDRED EIGHTY SIX MEN TEN HOSPITAL CASES BEING DIVIDED TEMPORARILY BETWEEN SAN FRANCISCO AND HELENA. DUNCAN

COMMANDING OFFICER URGENTLY REQUESTS AND COMTASKFORCE 64 CONCUR THAT ABOVE PERSONNEL BE KEPT AS A UNIT RETURNED TO UNITED STATES AND PLACE NEW DD IN COMMISSION. THEY FOUGHT A GOOD FIGHT. BY HAND TO COMMANDING OFFICER DUNCAN.

The *Duncan* survivors on *Helena* had been issued new uniforms, showered, and fed by the time Taylor and Bryan returned aboard. Word spread quickly that Taylor was carrying Scott's endorsement for keeping them together to put a new destroyer in commission. Everybody knew that this meant returning to the States.

Eight more *Duncan* wounded[2] were transferred to *Solace* by order of *Helena*'s doctor, who decided they were seriously injured enough to be hospitalized. *San Francisco* and *Helena* received orders: they were to depart at dusk and escort *Solace* to Nouméa. Ex-*Duncan* men were given a choice: either remain on the cruiser they were on or transfer to the *Fuller*.

All the officers and chiefs were transferring to the *Fuller*, which was rumored to be bound for Nouméa. Officers and chiefs normally received assignments in Washington directly from BuNav, so they all knew they were going home. Expecting to be home in time for Christmas, they were already celebrating. But lower-rated men were anxious about their fate. Adm. Nimitz had recently decreed that every man who survived a ship sinking had "survivor's leave" coming, but, given the manpower shortage, they suspected that was a long shot. It was rumored that there was a receiving ship at Nouméa. They were afraid if they got aboard *Fuller* they were going to wind up on the receiving ship and be fed onto some other warship in the area. Taylor's promise to try to keep them together sounded like pie in the sky, except Taylor had a reputation for getting his way in the Navy. Given a choice between remaining on a cruiser in the war zone and sticking with their captain, the prevailing wisdom was: stick with Taylor if you want to be home for Christmas.

Six hours after they boarded *Helena* and *San Francisco*, the remaining ex-*Duncan* men all transferred to the *Fuller*. Except for Seaman Elvin Scott, who was still unaccounted for, every survivor—six officers and 170 enlisted—transferred with Taylor to the *Fuller*.

Fuller was a troopship known as the "Tulagi Express." Once they were on board, Bryan ordered them all to write a letter home. "Of course, we couldn't mention sinking or anything," Torpedoman Ham remembered. "He just told us to write a letter and use *Duncan* as the return address. We were to print today's date—October 14, 1942—across the top in big letters."

Late that afternoon, Chief Paige was summoned to Taylor's cabin. Taylor handed him an envelope. It was Taylor's letter of condolence to R/Adm. Noyes upon the death of his son-in-law, Ens. Lane. Taylor told Paige it was the hardest letter he ever wrote.

All the survivors were on deck at dusk to watch *Solace* depart. Seventeen ex-*Duncan* men were among the hospital cases en route to New Zealand. *San Francisco, Helena,* and *Aaron Ward* were the escorts.

The *Fuller* was an old ocean liner with a crew of more than one hundred. Coincidentally, *Fuller*'s captain was Lt.(jg) Beebe's NROTC commander at Yale. The ex-*Duncan* men were the only passengers. The officers and chiefs grabbed all the first- class staterooms on deck. Enlisted men claimed cabins according to their rate. There were more than enough cabins to go around. They could each have had a private cabin if they had wanted, but many of them were not ready to be alone. *Fuller* was carrying meat for the troops. "We ate good," Bethune remembered. "Just lounged around and ate, meat mostly."

In the morning, Taylor and Bryan led a contingent of *Duncan* officers and enlisted men ashore to attend the burial of Lt.(jg) Fowler. Every officer who was not on duty and about twenty enlisted men went, including every man from the torpedo group and most of the fire controlmen.

The American Military Cemetery was in a coconut plantation on Segond Channel. Less than two months old, it still had a makeshift look, but there were already rows and rows of graves. The graves were on high ground near the beach. Each was marked by a crude wooden cross sloppily stenciled with only the deceased's name and branch of service. Beebe noted the location of Fowler's grave: "From the southeast corner of the Cemetery, his grave is 24th to the North on the Eastern boundary."[3]

A Navy chaplain, Lt. B.B. Brown, performed the committal service. The ceremony was well attended. A lot of *Boise* men showed up because some *Boise* dead were also being buried. DeLucca caught himself crying during the service, and he glanced around and was surprised to see others crying.

That evening, *Fuller* got underway, escorted by the three cripples—*Salt Lake City*, *Boise*, and *Farenholt*. Capt. Small on *Salt Lake City* was in overall command.

Fuller no sooner emerged from Pekoa Channel than a torpedo hit her. It was a dud. DeLucca, who was in a cabin below the waterline, heard a loud metallic bang just on the other side of the ship's steel skin.

The voyage from Espíritu Santo to New Caledonia took a day and a half. Taylor spent much of the time rewriting his report. He had identified six questionable decisions he made: allowing Bryan to be absent from his battle station in the run-up to the battle; allowing *Duncan* to get ahead of *Farenholt*; ordering a torpedo fired (at *Aoba*) when the angle offered a low probability of success and a high risk of hitting a U.S. warship; purposely steering into friendly fire; abandoning ship while half the crew remained on board; and, in addition, he now he needed to explain his initial denial of his purposeful turn into friendly fire.

Taylor's initial lie about the port turn was his most serious problem because U.S. Navy officers do not lie, certainly not in writing in an official report. They do become proficient in obfuscation. Taylor distanced himself from himself, referring to himself in the third person—as "the writer" or "the Commanding Officer" or simply "he." He employed the old magician's trick of misdirection, burying his more questionable decisions in a litany of tasks done right. The rewritten final report was ten pages single- spaced, more than twice as long as Capt. Tobin's and longer even than R/Adm. Scott's.

Taylor began his new version already on the defensive. Taking the lie head-on in the first paragraph, he explained that this new version differed in only one respect from the previous version: where he said before that he turned to starboard *out* of the crossfire, he meant that he turned to port *into* the crossfire. His explanation for this error was that "the yeoman detailed to maintain the record of the action" was killed.

Taylor explained that he had intended to "release" Lt. Bryan "when it appeared action would be imminent," but "[t]he rapidity of subsequent events prevented" Bryan from making it back to his battle station. Ironically, the regulation requiring the exec to be at after conn at GQ existed for just this situation. If Bryan had been at his battle station, he presumably would have led the salvage effort and might have succeeded in running *Duncan* onto a beach at Savo, maybe saving her to fight another day.

How *Duncan* wound up ahead of *Farenholt* took some explaining. Taylor began his explanation before the 2333 reverse turn. He did not mention following *Farenholt* for four minutes, only that "*Duncan* remained in column astern of *Farenholt* until this turn was approximately three-quarters completed." He said that, as *Duncan* was steadying "on an approximately westerly (270°) course," the surface-search radar firmed up a contact. In fact, it was the fire-control radar that firmed up the contact; the surface- search radar had been holding the contact for eight minutes. But Taylor had not reported the contact, which is probably why he did not mention it. He also did not mention idling with *Farenholt* in the turn for another minute. He said simply that "*Farenholt* appeared to be on an approximately parallel course off the port bow, and the Commanding Officer [Taylor] believed that [*Farenholt*] was heading to close these radar contacts." He implied that *Duncan* took off after the contacts and that was how she got ahead of *Farenholt*.

On the new southwest bearing, *Duncan* was quickly at 30 knots and was gaining on the 20-knot U.S. formation at a rate of about 350 yards a minute. Three minutes into the run, *Helena* reported the contact. *Duncan* was almost caught up to rear destroyer *McCalla* but was 600 yards west. A minute later, after

Boise reported the contact, *Farenholt* was headed east toward the rear of the formation. Taylor did not mention this because, among other reasons, *Farenholt* should have been astern *Duncan* for the last 8 minutes, since 2334, according to his story.

Taylor slipped it in that there was an open fire order: "Almost immediately [after Scott's 'Were we shooting at 12?' question to Tobin], the orders to 'Commence Firing' were heard over the TBS." He did not say he heard Scott give the order or even that he heard the order, but he implied that somebody ordered it and, well, if somebody ordered it, it must have been Scott because only he was authorized to order "Commence Firing."

Duncan had been on her torpedo run for more than four minutes when the cruisers' guns opened up. *Duncan*'s run would continue for another three minutes while the battle raged. Taylor disposed of the last three minutes in a few sentences. This time, he omitted the part about firing a torpedo at *Aoba*.

He said that when he heard the U.S. cruisers open fire he swung hard starboard to clear *Helena*'s line of fire. Obviously, he could not leave it at that because Lt. Myhre had said *Duncan*'s wheel was hard to port. To reconcile all this, Taylor constructed a complicated tale of maneuverings, a story apparently designed to resolve two glaring inconsistencies in his story: how *Duncan*, despite swinging hard starboard to avoid *Helena*'s fire, wound up in *Helena*'s fire; and how he, the captain, was so mistaken about the direction he turned his ship.

Taylor probably should have swung to starboard a minute into the torpedo run when Chief Lehman informed him *Duncan* was going to get caught in a pincer between the two fleets. There was time then to reset the computer and swing the torpedo tubes to port. For most of the torpedo run, they were waiting for the fire-control computer to achieve a firing solution. The computer finally achieved a port-side torpedo-firing solution on the unseen *Furutaka* at about the moment that *Helena* opened up on *Aoba*. Taylor saw *Aoba* lit by the first starshell and impulsively switched targets, from one he could not see that was at about 2,200 yards to one suddenly lit up right in front of him at more 3,000 yards. The reason *Duncan*'s first main battery salvo at

Aoba fell short by 200 yards was because their firing-solution was for *Furutaka,* which was 800 yards closer.

Under a barrage of withering fire, *Aoba* swung hard to starboard, then hard to port, then back to starboard, all while shells exploded on her bridge. As she started swinging away to starboard again, Taylor ordered hard port rudder to try to hold their torpedo setup long enough for Lt.(jg) Fowler to get the torpedoes off. Taylor did not mention any of this because Scott had ridiculed his decision to fire torpedoes at *Aoba.*

Unwilling to admit purposely steering into *Helena*'s fire, Taylor presented a convoluted story of interim maneuverings that demonstrated how hard he tried to *avoid* steering into *Helena*'s fire. He began with the false claim that, upon hearing the cruisers opening fire, he turned *Duncan* to starboard out of *Helena*'s fire. ("In order to clear the line of fire of HELENA, right standard rudder was ordered... ") He then introduced a new element:

> ... and almost immediately after the swing to starboard had started a second large warship [*Furutaka*] was reported close aboard forward of our starboard beam ... Orders were given to prepare to fire torpedoes to port.

Embellishing, he claimed that, in turning hard to starboard, *Duncan* almost overran *Laffey* ("Possible collision appeared imminent."). He implied that he ordered the wheel hard to port to keep the two destroyers from colliding. In fact, *Laffey* had turned back at opening fire three minutes earlier. But, in Taylor's valiant re-telling, he selflessly chose to sacrifice his ship by steering into *Helena*'s fire to save *Laffey.* "[A]s a result of the foregoing maneuver, *Duncan* was now abaft the beam of [*Furutaka*] and had missed the opportunity to fire torpedoes to port [at *Aoba*]." Having conjured all these maneuverings, Taylor was finally able to admit, "Orders were then given for 'Left full rudder, prepare to fire torpedoes to starboard.'" Their target now was second cruiser *Furutaka.*

Taylor's new construction of *Duncan*'s timeline for the three minutes after *Helena* opened fire contained enough truth to seem plausible, but it was all an elegant deceit designed to explain away (or at least minimize) many of Taylor's more questionable decisions. His new story showed him intending to fire torpedoes from port but, upon opening fire, swinging to starboard out of *Helena*'s fire, and then, to avoid colliding with *Laffey*, swinging back to port into *Helena*'s fire—and then getting off torpedoes that contributed to sinking a Japanese cruiser.

Taylor's story was a masterpiece of obfuscation. It explained why he fired from starboard, why he steamed into friendly fire, how he saved *Laffey*, and sank *Furutaka*. The story even dismissed his initial lie about the direction he turned as understandable confusion—because he turned *both* ways.

* * *

At dawn on October 17, *Fuller* was off Amadee Light approaching New Caledonia. The town of Nouméa was visible 11 miles to the north.

Fuller had to wait a couple of hours outside the reef while convoys of warships exited Great Roads Harbor. The *Duncan* survivors had finished breakfast and held muster before *Fuller* was finally permitted to enter the channel.

There were always a great many warships in Great Roads Harbor because V/Adm. Ghormley's flagship, submarine repair ship *Argonne,* which was SoPac Headquarters, was anchored there semi-permanently. On this particular morning, there were even more warships than usual in the harbor.

Fuller, *Boise*, *Salt Lake City*, and *Farenholt* moored in the harbor midmorning. Taylor took the first liberty boat over to *Argonne* to try to resurrect his career. His plan was to campaign to keep his crew together and put a new destroyer in commission, with himself as captain. Boarding *Argonne*, he was apprehensive because he half-expected to be greeted as a pariah for losing his ship.

He found *Argonne* in a state of disorder and confusion. All lower-level decision- making had been halted. A dozen top admirals were on board, and they were all in conferences. Nobody knew what was going on. Rumors were flying.

Taylor hoped to buttonhole an admiral. He caught a glimpse of R/Adm. Scott rushing into a meeting. Remaining aboard *Argonne* for lunch, he was able to speak briefly with Ghormley's chief of staff, R/Adm. Daniel Callaghan, who arranged meetings for him with R/Adm. Turner and R/Adm. Raymond Spruance. Both admirals told him in no uncertain terms that he would not be getting a new destroyer command and also that he had no hope of keeping his crew together.

All the ex-*Duncan* men went ashore that afternoon. Everybody wanted to see Nouméa, "the Paris of the Pacific." New Caledonia was a backwater—the French still operated a penal colony on Ile Nou—but Nouméa, the capital city, where more than half the population of the islands lived, had a genteel, colonial air. Robert Louis Stevenson passed through in 1890 and observed that the town looked like it was "built from vermouth cases." Fifty years later, it was largely unchanged.

It was a Saturday. Crowds of Allied sailors were everywhere, but the streets were relatively empty of locals because many of the inhabitants had moved out since the Americans moved in. There was always a long line outside the Pink House, a glorified whorehouse that was a renowned South Pacific landmark. Every sailor yearned to see inside before he died. The Pink House had a U.S. medical officer on staff and even a couple of white women, supposedly. It was surrounded by a high wall. Day and night, there was a crowd in front, whether the fleet was in or not. The going rate for a place in line on a Saturday night was $5. Usually, half the men in line were New Zealanders holding places they would later try to sell. Most of the people hanging around in front were just there for the music. If everybody was quiet, you could hear the piano.

The next day was Sunday. Many of the ex-*Duncan* men attended mass at St. Joseph's, the Catholic cathedral built by convict labor that was famed for its stained-glass windows. Slovenec spotted a woman at the service who he thought was the most beautiful woman he ever saw. Afterward, he went up to her, "and I said, 'You're the most beautiful lady I ever seen.' And she was, too. Y'know what she said? 'Merci.' Oh, man. I was in love. That dame's why I never married. Nobody could measure up to her."

That afternoon, a large seaplane touched down on Great Roads Harbor. A whaleboat from *Argonne* was alongside before the props stopped turning. V/Adm. William Halsey, Senior Carrier Admiral, Pacific, stepped from the plane into the whaleboat, followed by Capt. Miles Browning, his chief of staff, and Maj. Julian Brown, his staff intelligence officer. Halsey had come to take over the *Enterprise* task force. He was looking forward to being back on a carrier flag bridge.

V/Adm. Ghormley's flag lieutenant was in the whaleboat. He saluted Halsey and handed him an envelope. Halsey took it reluctantly. He knew right then that he was in for it, because what could be so important it could not wait a few minutes until he was aboard *Argonne*? With a sinking heart, he sat down and opened the envelope. Inside was another envelope that was marked "SECRET." Opening it, Halsey unfolded a sheet of paper containing orders from Adm. Nimitz:

> Immediately upon your arrival at Noumea, you will relieve Vice Admiral Robert L. Ghormley of the duties of Commander South Pacific and South Pacific Force.

"Jesus Christ and General Jackson," V/Adm. Halsey reportedly bellowed. He fell into a silent gloom, dreading what lay ahead.

Decision-making aboard *Argonne* resumed. Halsey canceled most pending operations. He let it be known he intended to put everything into the fight for Guadalcanal.

The next day, in Washington, the Navy Department released a story by USMC combat correspondent Sgt. James Hurlburt that contained the first published mention of the sinking of *Duncan*, albeit without mentioning her by name:

> GUADALCANAL, Solomon Islands, Oct. 18 (AP)--It has been quiet in this powder keg of the Pacific since dawn - but we've still got our fingers crossed. We welcome a breathing spell. The past week has been the most hectic seven days of martial activity our harassed correspondents have had to undergo - let alone cover. A

naval battle off our coast last Sunday night (Oct. 11) started this week off with a bang. For over an hour, the entire skyline was ablaze with the white light of shell- fire, punctuated by occasional dull-red flare-ups. Early Monday morning we boarded boats dispatched to the battle area to pick up more than 100 survivors from an American destroyer - the only one lost in the engagement.

Luxuriating aboard *Fuller*, ex-*Duncan* men were living slow and eating high. Almost everyone went ashore on liberty at least once every day and often again in the evening. Initially, they went for the excitement of the place, but, as the days dragged on, it was more to escape the boredom of the *Fuller*. Even after their money ran out, they aimlessly wandered the town and usually wound up standing in front of the Pink House listening to the piano.

Taylor hung around on *Argonne* day after day, hoping to get in a word with one admiral or another. He engaged in a lot of conversations about the battle. Everybody was trying to extract lessons from it because it was the U.S. Navy's first actual *planned* battle in two generations.

One lesson was that an admiral needed to know precisely and positively the location of his ships. Radar suddenly seemed like a plausible weapon. Another lesson was that radar contacts should be reported immediately and in true bearing and range. A lot of the talk was about whether simultaneous turns were a better way to countermarch in enemy territory at night. It was obvious to everybody that van destroyers should not try to regain a new van in enemy territory at night prior to battle. The sporadic starshell illumination was debated. It was widely believed that if the whole area had been better illuminated every Japanese ship could have been sunk. Everybody recognized how well surprise had worked. It was clear that searchlights should not be used in a night battle. There were loading problems in 5-inch batteries because some loaders were night- blinded by the first muzzle flashes. [The long-term solution would be enclosing gun mounts.] Gunnery officers recommended that radar be installed in every main battery gun. Many gunnery officers thought that once a target ship was set on fire gunners should shift to another target and finish off the lame ducks later.

One morning on *Argonne*, Taylor was walking along a passageway when he ran into R/Adm. Callaghan leading a contingent of admirals. Before Taylor knew it, Callaghan was introducing him to V/Adm. Halsey, "Admiral, this is Whitey Taylor."

"Sorry about your ship, Commander, and your men," Halsey said, shaking Taylor's hand.

"Thank you, sir," Taylor fumbled.

"I understand your desire to keep them together, but I'm too new here to make that decision right now." Halsey turned then and walked away, and the others hurried after him.

For a few days, SoPac command was focused on issues and concerns more pressing than what to do with Whitey Taylor and his crew. Then, one day, R/Adm. Callaghan mentioned to Taylor that it might help his cause if Capt. Moran would agree to take *all* his crew back to the States.

Taylor dreaded the thought of going to Moran hat in hand because he blamed Moran for sinking the *Duncan* and was deeply angry at him. Taylor stalled for almost a full day before flagging his request for a meeting. Moran immediately agreed to see him at Taylor's convenience.

The next day, Taylor took the liberty boat to the nickel docks where *Boise* was tied up. She was a sad sight. Her forward main battery guns were twisted and collapsed on the deck. Her worst damage was below the waterline where she had several holes. She was listing slightly. Her crew was loading nickel ore into the bilge to try to level her.

The nickel docks were a beehive of activity. New Caledonia has one of the world's richest nickel deposits, and the U.S. Navy was hauling nickel home as ballast. Wooden carts full of what looked like black rocks were being wheeled onto the dock and dumped onto cargo nets.

Taylor was escorted up to Capt. Moran's cabin. Moran was sitting at his desk. He returned Taylor's salute but did not invite him to sit. Taylor thanked him for his offer but said he could not accept because it meant leaving most of his crew behind.

He explained that he needed transport for *all* his men—seven officers and 172 enlisted.

"That'll be fine," Moran replied.

Taylor was so grateful to R/Adm. Callaghan he went straight over to the *Argonne* to thank him, but it was moving day aboard *Argonne*. Headquarters staff was moving to new offices on shore. Callaghan had been replaced by Halsey's chief of staff. His office was stripped bare. Callaghan was nowhere to be found. It was rumored he was getting a new cruiser-destroyer task group. Taylor never saw R/Adm. Callaghan again.

Taylor returned to the *Fuller* satisfied he had everything back on track, including his career. "[Taylor] had a lot of good contacts [in Personnel]," Andrews remembered, "and he thought he had it all fixed so he'd get a new destroyer and he'd get Bryan one, too."

Early that evening, *Fuller* received a flag message from COMSERVRONSOPAC: "TRANSFER ALL OFFICERS AND ENLISTED PERSONNEL OF DUNCAN TO BOISE FOR TRANSPORTATION US OCT TWENTY TWO."

The ex-*Duncan* men waited excitedly all day on the 22nd. Taylor was distressed to be leaving the war zone without saying goodbye to his best friend LCdr. Smedberg. He spent the morning writing to him.

> Dear Bill:
> I fully expected to see you all again before we separated, and therefore did not adequately express the gratitude which the Officers and men of the DUNCAN feel towards the Commodore [Cdr. Ryan], Officers and men of your ship for the exceedingly generous gift of money.
> The association between the LANSDOWNE and DUNCAN was marked by a healthy rivalry and mutual admiration. When the former got her first two subs, our envy in your success was only exceeded by our pride in our sister ship. The feeling of confidence and reassurance which we had when operating with you cannot be put in words. It was the spirit which was molding our Division into a unit, and it is the element which cannot be handed one with orders for a new command.
> Even now I cannot fully realize that my ship is gone - no more steaming out of the harbor in the wake of the LANSDOWNE

and LARDNER. At least there is the consolation that she had the chance to fight back, and the remaining three [ships of DesDiv24 - *Lansdowne*, *Lardner*, and *McCalla*] need not be ashamed of their sister ship ...

How lost I am without my ship!

... Apparently they had not realized here how complete a job was done [by Scott's task group] the night of the 11th. By request I submitted copies of my final report to the big staff and to Admiral Turner. They have pretty definitely determined we caught the same babies who played hell the night of the 8th ...

You know, Bill, how closely I will watch for news of your ship. I hope that our separation will not be too long a duration.

Best of luck to you and your ship.

Sincerely, Whitey

Late in the afternoon, when the order to transfer to *Boise* came, Taylor quickly jotted a postscript:

P.S. Have just received orders to transfer my officers and crew to BOISE. It is the first step - with many hurdles yet to jump. Have written Admiral [Louis] Denfield [at Personnel] for help in getting me a new DD. I am not gifted with the ability to extol my own virtues gracefully, but I know that I am a good destroyer officer and a better than average destroyer captain. The Commodore's fitness report won't hurt my chances if I am able to use it in time.

Most of the ex-*Duncan* men had not dared to even dream that they might be going home until they were walking up *Boise*'s gangplank. At the quarterdeck, they were in for a shock. Painted on the bulkhead just below the bridge was an elaborate artwork

THE ARTWORK ON BOISE'S BULKHEAD
CLAIMED SHE SANK SIX JAPANESE SHIPS IN THE BATTLE.

showing six Japanese flags beside six sinking ships—two heavy cruisers, one light cruiser, and three destroyers. *Boise* was claiming she sank six Japanese ships! Ex- *Duncan* men joked bitterly that one of them was the *Duncan*. They all immediately realized they were probably not going to be treated like heroes aboard *Boise*.

The reason *Boise* had space for so many passengers was that so many *Boise* men had been killed. Capt. Moran may have needed the extra men to load nickel. Some of the more conspiratorially-minded ex-*Duncan* men thought Moran just wanted to keep them all from blabbing around SoPac about how *Boise* sank them.

The lower-rated ex-*Duncan* men were surprised when they were led up to hangar deck and told to grab a mattress and pick a spot on the deck. They had all assumed they would be integrated into the *Boise* crew for the duration. "I stood a couple of watches," Bethune remembered, "but I wasn't a cruiserman so I was a little out of my line." The less disciplined destroyer lifestyle was too apparent in the ex-*Duncan* men. Moran arranged to keep his crew apart from them.

The next morning, the lower-rated ex-*Duncan* men loaded nickel with the *Boise*'s crew. Nickel rocks are heavy as cast iron. It took two men to push one small cartload.

At 0925, Halsey boarded *Boise* to preside at a medal ceremony for six ex-*Duncan* men who were being awarded the Navy and Marine Medal for their actions during the sinking of the *Wasp* a month before, which now seemed like an eternity ago. Most of the honorees had been in the small boat crews.

Halsey saluted Moran but did not shake his hand or speak to him. It was widely suspected that Moran was in the doghouse for getting so many of his crew killed and almost getting his ship sunk.

The ceremony was a sad affair. Halsey seemed uncomfortable. He fidgeted as the names were read. Each time that somebody said the honoree was dead, Halsey noticeably winced. Of the six men being honored, two were dead and one was wounded and enroute to New Zealand. Halsey pinned medals on Ens. Andrews, Seaman Tousignant, and Boatswain's Mate McIntosh.

That afternoon, *Boise* received the message from ComSoPac they were all waiting for: "BOISE HEREBY DETACHED FROM TASK FORCE 64."

Boise got underway from Great Roads Harbor at dusk, carrying 200 tons of nickel ore and 178 ex-*Duncan* men. After she cleared the barrier reef, a voice on the PA announced: "THIS SHIP IS UNDERWAY FOR PHILADELPHIA, U.S.A." Everybody was screaming.

*   *   *

At dawn on October 27, after three days at sea, *Boise* was already 1,600 miles to the east and approaching Tutuila Island in Samoa. Ships operating without escort in the war zone were to hide in safe harbors during daylight hours wherever possible.

Tutuila Island is the setting for Somerset Maugham's short story, "Miss Thompson," about the "breezy dame" and the preacher trying to save her for himself. Pago Pago Harbor is one of the finest harbors in the Pacific. It looks like a fjord but is a submerged crater that almost bisects the island. It is such a good harbor the U.S. Navy was turning the whole of Eastern Samoa into one huge naval base.

Boise tied up to the starboard side of former United Fruit Company luxury liner-fruit carrier *Talamanca*. *Boise* was scheduled to depart at dusk, so only communications officers were permitted ashore. *Boise* and *Talamanca* held a joint swimming party. The rest of the day everybody lounged on the decks and stared at the shore.

LCdr. Taylor holed up with Lt. Bryan and Chief Paige to put the finishing touches on his final accounting of the casualties and the missing. He was required to submit a final accounting to the Secretary of the Navy, as a captain's last act as commander of a warship.

Duncan ended her voyage with forty-four dead and four missing. Normally, the dead would be accounted for by bodies or at least identification tags. Taylor had only three identification tags. Lt(jg) Fowler's was the only body buried.

At dusk, *Boise* got underway to Bora Bora.

That day, Tom Yarborough, the Associated Press correspondent who was aboard *San Francisco,* was finally allowed to file his story on the battle off Cape Esperance. It was datelined, "Aboard a United States Cruiser in the Solomons Sea, Oct. 27 (Delayed)." It began: "This is the story of the United States Navy's first surface victory in a battle between heavy ships since the Spanish-American War." It was R/Adm. Scott's version—the American ships sank "three cruisers and five destroyers and lost only one destroyer." It concluded:

> The first battle of Savo Island was a stinging defeat that cost us four cruisers—the Australian CANBERRA and the United States' ASTORIA, VINCENNES, and QUINCY. The second battle of Savo Island evened the score at almost the same spot and in much the same manner—a lightning stroke in the dark that caught the enemy entirely off guard.

During the long voyage home, most of the lower-rated ex-*Duncan* men were kept busy during the day chipping paint. They seldom saw their former officers.

The ex-*Duncan* officers were living in officer country doing almost nothing. After they wrote condolence letters to the families of the dead, there was nothing for them to do. They spent a lot of time rehashing the battle down to the minutest episodes.

Capt. Moran was remarkably successful in keeping ex-*Duncan* men from fraternizing with his crew. "I think he was afraid of us comparing notes," Sobelman remembered. Sobelman tried for days to connect with a *Boise* fire controlman named Ronald Eagle who he knew from Fire Control School. When they finally did manage to get together, Eagle told Sobelman that *Boise* demasted *Farenholt* and bombarded *Duncan.*

After another three days at sea (and one repeated date upon crossing the Dateline), *Boise* was 3,000 miles to the east in the Society Islands. At dawn on October 30, she was approaching

Bora Bora.

At Bora Bora, they found at last the South Pacific of their dreams. DeLucca remembered, "The island, naked people all running around. It was the first place I saw out there that looked like the Pacific is supposed to."

Boise dropped anchor in Fanni Bay. Capt. Moran issued a dictum: no one out of uniform would be allowed ashore. The ex-*Duncan* men knew the rule was aimed at them because they were all still wearing the clothes they were issued weeks ago. Taylor went up and argued about it with Moran but got nowhere. Moran was determined that the slovenly ex-*Duncan* men not reflect poorly on his ship. A few ex-*Duncan* men managed to get ashore wearing uniforms borrowed from *Boise* friends.

Boise remained in Fanni Bay for two days. *Boise*'s crew went ashore on liberty both days. The ex-*Duncan* men could only stare longingly at the shore. On the second day, a little boat full of giggling, topless women sailed close by to check them out. The rumor was that U.S. Marines stationed there made out like bandits with all the topless women.

On November 1, *Boise* raised anchor just after noon. The Society Islands were so far from the war zone ships were no longer required to wait until dusk before departing. "Anchor aweigh, underway from anchorage to seaward," *Boise*'s log noted. Destroyer *Warrington* got underway as escort.

On November 2, Associated Press ran an interview with Capt. Ernest Small datelined Pearl Harbor, where *Salt Lake City* was in for repairs. Capt. Small described the battle off Cape Esperance as "a hell of a melee":

> It was one of those things naval officers wait for twenty years to see. We capped their 'T'... Within the first four minutes I saw our salvos going in like red boxcars on a Jap heavy cruiser, plunging right into her ... I can best describe this night action for the layman as a Fourth of July fireworks lasting 40 minutes and its conclusion like the dying set pieces burning out.

The cornerstone of the U.S. Navy's evolving public relations strategy was that the U.S. had gotten even for Savo. The article pointed out that the battle took place "just two months after the first Savo Island battle ... but the tables were turned ... with much heavier loss than they inflicted on the American cruisers last Aug. 8-9."

On November 6, Mr. and Mrs. E.B. Taylor, Sr. of 1141 Rice Avenue in Lima, Ohio, received a letter from their son about losing his ship. He reminded them not to say anything until the Navy made it official.

Four days later, on November 10, *The Lima* [Ohio] *News* carried a banner headline: "LIMA SKIPPER SAVED WHEN DESTROYER SINKS IN BIG PACIFIC BATTLE."

The story was based on an interview with Taylor's father. It described "the heaviest United States surface craft naval engagement since the battle of Santiago during the Spanish-American War. " The skipper's proud father said his son's ship put two torpedoes into a Japanese cruiser.

At 2242 on November 12, *Boise* lookouts sighted Morro Puercos Light, Republic of Panama. For the ex-*Duncan* men, it had been 90 days since they last saw Panama.

A third naval battle off Savo Island took place on November 13. That battle came to be known as the Battle of Friday the 13th. R/Adm. Callaghan and R/Adm. Scott were both killed in the first five minutes. *San Francisco* mistook *Atlanta* for Japanese and fired 8-inch shells into her. One exploded just as R/Adm. Scott was emerging from the charthouse with three of his staff. All that was recovered of R/Adm. Scott was his left arm, which was identified by his 1911 Academy class ring.

In Panama, on November 13, *Boise* transited the canal. No one out of uniform was allowed on deck. They passed battleship *Indiana* and cruiser *Columbia* and destroyers *DeHaven* and *Saufley*—all to port on the opposite course bound for the Pacific. Fresh- faced boys on their decks stared wide-eyed at the holed wreck that was the *Boise*.

Boise dropped anchor at Gatun Locks. While they were waiting in Anchorage Basin, DeLucca was summoned to the fantail for a surprise birthday party. A *Boise* cook had baked a cake.

Boise steamed into Limon Bay that evening. As a tug was nosing her into a pier at Cristóbal, the PA announced that they would be leaving for Philadelphia in the morning. They were warned not to overextend their liberty. Only men in uniform were allowed ashore. Bethune managed to get ashore in a uniform he borrowed from an old *Boise* chief. He was stopped by a shore patrol who noticed the four hash marks on his uniform and asked him how old he was. "Nineteen," Bethune replied. "Hey, we're just back from the Canal." That was enough to get him off. Another ex-*Duncan* man who got ashore, Seaman Donald Clement, was caught smuggling liquor aboard and was "made prisoner at large on order of commanding officer for introducing alcoholic beverages aboard ship."

The following afternoon, November 14, *Boise* cast off. A tug nudged her into the channel. Off the sea buoy, she was joined by destroyers *Borie* and *Champlin*. They were her escorts. *Borie* was an old flush-decker that had been on Caribbean convoy with *Duncan*. *Champlin* was a newly-minted *Livermore*. As *Boise* swung onto a northerly heading, *Champlin* took the van and *Borie* fell in astern.

Living in officer country, preoccupied with his own concerns, Taylor was cut off from the lives of his former crew. He did not even get wind that they were chipping paint until the first afternoon in the Caribbean. He was so embarrassed that it took him three weeks to find out that he overreacted, storming up to Moran's cabin. He told Moran that *Boise* had her own crew to chip and paint, that the ex-*Duncan* men were passengers. "I didn't do much of anything after that," DeLucca remembered, "except lay on the fantail and get the sun."

Taylor received a message that day informing him that Halsey was awarding him the Navy Cross. The U.S. military was undergoing an institutional awakening to the fact that now a different type of officer was needed—men who had demonstrated a willingness to fight. Suddenly, the Navy was actively seeking out and advancing these men. Taylor receiving the Navy Cross was an early reflection of this new policy change. Just weeks earlier, Ghormley might have court-martialed

VICE ADMIRAL WILLIAM HALSEY PINS THE NAVY CROSS
ON CAPTAIN ROBERT TOBIN, COMMANDER DESTROYER SQUADRON 12,
OCTOBER 7, 1943.

him. Surprisingly, Capt. Tobin was also awarded the Navy Cross. This new idea was quickly carried to its ultimate absurdity when Medals of Honor were awarded to the late rear admirals Scott and Callaghan.

On November 18, *Boise* received a message for the ex-*Duncan* officers from the Bureau of Personnel: Taylor and Bryan were getting commands of newly constructed destroyers. Taylor's new command was the *Bennett* (DD-473), a *Fletcher*-class, and Bryan's was the *Shubrick* (DD-639), one of the last of the *Livermores*. Hauck was to go with Taylor to the *Bennett* as his exec, and Andrews, Beebe, and Coley were to go with Bryan to the *Shubrick*.

Other than these few directed assignments, Taylor and Bryan were free to divvy up the remaining 171 men. They split them down the middle—eighty-six to *Bennett*, eighty-five to *Shubrick*.

On November 19, *Boise* entered Delaware Bay.

The Navy saw *Boise*'s homecoming as a public relations bonanza. Hundreds of boats, large and small, were there to celebrate her return. All the way up the Delaware River to Philadelphia, horns tooted and bands along the riverbank played

BRAVE BOISE LIMPED HOME.

martial music. As *Boise* was approaching the Navy Yard, the
cacophony of horns and music intensified. There was a big
crowd on the pier cheering and waving. *Boise* moored "starboard
side to pier 4" at 1318. Many in the crowd were weeping at the
sight of brave *Boise* limping home.

The Navy's P.R. effort was aimed at shaping the second
Savo battle as a great lopsided U.S. victory, the Navy's reply to
the first Savo battle. It was a tough sell because the only ships
that could be mentioned in telling the story were those that had
returned (or been announced as lost)—*Boise, Salt Lake City,
Farenholt* and *Duncan.* The Navy's effort focused on *Boise*
because *Boise* claimed to have sunk six Japanese warships and
she looked as if she had been in a single-handed brawl.

As soon as the gangway was down, the ex-*Duncan* men were
hurried off the ship. Adm. Ernest King was expected aboard, and
Capt. Moran did not want the Commander in Chief of the U.S.
Fleet to see all the shabby ex-*Duncan* men.

They were a sight to behold. As they stumbled down the
gangway, people on the dock assumed they were *Boise* wounded
and applauded them.

After they had shambled off down the pier far enough to be
out of sight, they were lined up in a ragged formation. It had

been 153 days since they had departed New York Harbor. It seemed so much longer.

Soon, a convoy of staff cars pulled up. Among the VIPs were Secretary of the Navy Frank Knox and Adm. King. LCdr. Taylor went right up to Adm. King and practically dragged him over to shake hands with his officers. While King was chatting with the ex- *Duncan* officers, he kept glancing over uneasily at the enlisted men. He walked over as if to have a closer look at them. Somebody shouted, "Attention," but it did not have much noticeable effect. "King says, 'Well done. Well done,'" Palmer remembered. "You know how they talk in the Navy."

The ex-*Duncan* men were "marched" off the pier and across the Yard to the Receiving Station. They looked like a mob of pirates. A lot of them carried knives, and most were holding up their pants. People stopped and stared.

ADM. ERNEST KING, COMMANDER IN CHIEF U.S. FLEET, GREETS U.S.S. DUNCAN SURVIVORS AT PHILADELPHIA NAVY YARD, NOVEMBER 19, 1942.

On *Boise*, the crew was on deck at attention when Adm. King was received aboard at 1427. He "stormed by us like he's angry," Lt.(jg) Sidney Biddle remembered. King acted toward Moran with the same transparent disgust that Halsey had exhibited. Moran took King up to his cabin, where King supposedly gave Moran hell. That was the rumor on *Boise*. Biddle heard it was for opening fire first. [Except *Helena* opened fire first, so it was probably for allowing the use of searchlights during the battle and getting the new cruiser knocked out of the war. Moran was awarded the Navy Cross for his part in the battle, but he never commanded another warship. In mid-1943, he returned to the Solomons with the temporary rank of commodore to command the motor torpedo boat squadrons.]

As soon as King and his entourage left *Boise*, a Navy press officer led Ranald MacDougall and William Robson aboard. They were, respectively, the writer and director of a weekly half-hour CBS radio drama called "The Man Behind the Gun," a series that was supposedly based on the battle experiences of real enlisted men. MacDougall and Robson were researching an episode about *Boise*'s battle.

The ex-*Duncan* men were assigned to barracks in the Yard. "We just wanted to get over to the beer hall," Sobelman remembered. "Except you had to be in uniform to get in." Bryan went to the Yard office. "It's the only time I ever liked the guy," Bethune remembered. "He says, 'Lookit, my crew's been out in the South Pacific some time. We lost our ship. Let 'em in the beer hall.' And they do. This is unheard of. Finally, somebody treats us like heroes."

They were allowed one free phone call home or, if they did not have a phone at home, one free telegram. They were warned not to say anything about *Duncan* sinking or the battle because they did not want anybody accidentally blabbing the names of the other ships. They were supposed to just say they were alive and on the way home.

Initially, the Navy had been confused about *Duncan*'s status. First, the next of kin of every man on the ship received a telegram saying *Duncan* was missing. Next, families of the dead, missing, and severely wounded received a telegram. On November 9, the Navy officially identified *Duncan* as the destroyer previously announced as sunk in the October 11-12 battle.

Some ex-*Duncan* men who got their family on the phone found that they were expecting the call. Others' families were startled to hear from them. Malcolm Bethune's Catholic mother sounded disappointed. "I thought you were in a better place," she told him.

LCdr. Taylor knew his wife Elizabeth was staying with friends in Massachusetts, so he asked his father-in-law to lure her to Philadelphia on some pretext. The next evening, Elizabeth was dining with her parents at a restaurant in Philadelphia when Whitey walked in. She jumped up, shrieking, and knocked over a chair running to him.

The Receiving Station processed ex-*Duncan* men all night. They could sign out as soon as processing was completed. They received a full issue of clothes, starting with a sea bag. "The Receiving Station stayed open all night issuing us clothes so we

U.S.S. DUNCAN SURVIVORS WITH THEIR NEWLY-ISSUED CLOTHING AT PHILADELPHIA NAVY YARD, NOVEMBER 20, 1942

could get out of there on the first train in the morning," Bethune remembered. They had thirty days "survivor leave" coming, plus two days travel time. The last thing they were issued were orders to their next ship. Men assigned to the *Bennett* were to report to Boston in one month, and men going to the *Shubrick* were to report in one month to Norfolk. By dawn on November 20, all the ex-*Duncan* men were on their way home.

All over the east coast that evening ex-*Duncan* men were arriving home. "I'd lost 35 pounds," DeLucca remembered. "I'd been starving. I just wanted sympathy. All everybody said was how great I looked."

That day in Washington, the Navy acknowledged the loss of another unnamed destroyer in the Solomons.

On November 27, a Navy press release for the first time gave a new name to the battle in which *Duncan* was sunk. Newspapers had been referring to it as the Second Battle of Savo. This Navy press release was titled "Last Battle Report of Rear Admiral Scott Tells of Battle of Cape Esperance." It extolled the late admiral's performance in the battle—"brilliant success rewarded his planning."

Simultaneous with the release of Scott's report, the Fourth Naval District announced that the *Duncan* survivors had been landed by *Boise* at Philadelphia on the 19th. This gave rise to the notion that *Boise,* in addition to single-handedly sinking six Japanese warships, also rescued the *Duncan* crew. A November 28 story on the *Duncan* sinking in *The Philadelphia Record* carried a three-column photograph of the *Duncan* survivors at the Philadelphia Navy Yard in their new-issue uniforms. The accompanying story re- enforced the growing *Boise* myth: "The *Boise* sank six Jap ships in that battle, and rescued the *Duncan*'s survivors when the firing was over." The constant focus on *Boise* was galling to ex-*Duncan* men.

Boise's battered hulk limping home alone created an instant legend. A deluge of newspaper stories on the Battle of Cape Esperance focused on *Boise*, the "one-ship fleet." A photograph of the six Japanese warships stenciled on *Boise*'s bulkhead accompanied almost every story. *Boise* was a ready-made symbol of America's indomitability and can- do spirit.

On November 28, the U.S. Navy again re-revised downward its estimate of the damage done to the Japanese force in the Battle of Cape Esperance. Now, it was three cruisers and three destroyers. [In fact, it was one cruiser and one destroyer.] An Associated Press story noted archly that "[t]oday's announcement ... [was] ... principally that of Scott ... "

In another story, Scott credited his great victory first on surprise and second on his commanders. He then launched into a telling explanation of his philosophy of command: "In a night action like that, I do not think you should give too many orders. It was largely up to each captain individually. I led them into it and then they fought their way out."

Postscript

To the memory nothing is ever really lost.

—Eudora Welty

By Christmas, 1942, my mother was back living with her parents in New York City. A Gold Star flag was displayed in a ground-floor window of the Cutlers' townhouse at 58 East 80th Street. A Blue Star in a front window spoke of a son gone off to fight. A Gold Star flag said he was not coming back.

Ben Bradlee remembered in his autobiography:

> More than fifty years later, I wonder what we were wondering about: getting married, when we knew I was going to war in a destroyer in a few months, almost surely to the Pacific where destroyers were sinking like stones, when we knew I would be gone for months, if not for good. Even as we discussed marriage, one of Jean's best friends, Pat Cutler, had married a Harvard ROTC ensign named Bob Fowler and was carrying his child when he was killed in action on a destroyer in the Pacific. We grieved, but we pushed on with innocent confidence...

A succession of ex-*Duncan* men stopped by over Christmas to pay their respects, including LCdr. Bryan. My mother was too shaken to grasp whatever they told her about the battle.

A few days before Christmas, Dick Wharton phoned and asked if he could drop by. Pat invited him to tea. Wharton remembered, "So I went by the house. She was wearing a wrapper. She looked frail. She was very pregnant but at the same time seemed to be wasting away. I worried for the baby. We had tea. She was silent so I kept talking. I told her how I was taken to New Zealand with the wounded. I could see she wasn't interested. I said I brought her Bobby's ID bracelet. I'd carried it halfway around the world. I thought she'd be pleased. She took it and put it in her pocket without hardly looking at it. I was surprised, more than surprised. I remember trying to think of something to tell her about Bobby to cheer her up. I said, 'Bobby read us all what you wrote him about the baby.' That letter was in the last batch of mail we ever got. It was on that blue Merrimade stationery. I told her how proud he was about the baby. I think she was pleased. I asked her if there was anything I could tell her. The only thing she asked me was if he was in pain. I said he wasn't. She really didn't want to talk about it beyond that."

My grandfather was waiting hopefully for news of his son's medal. In January 1943, a month after he met with Cdr. Taylor at the Biltmore, he wrote to Taylor "c/o USS BENNETT, Fleet Postmaster, New York" to stir the coals. "I am sure Bobby deserves the Cross," he wrote, "but I suppose it will take some time for your recommendation to bear fruit."

My mother checked in to Doctors' Hospital in New York City the last week of February. I was born before dawn on February 26, 1943.

The birth of "Bobby's baby" rejuvenated my grandfather. He threw himself into his campaign to get Bobby the Navy Cross, writing to anybody he thought could help. He wrote repeatedly to his son-in-law, Lt.(jg) Wylie, at the Pentagon, and to Taylor to keep a fire under him.

In mid-March, my mother received in the mail a Navy Cross and Citation. ("Lieutenant (j.g.) Fowler in firing his first torpedo, secured the initial hit on a hostile cruiser.")

On two consecutive Sunday nights in late-March, the CBS radio drama "The Man Behind the Gun" told the story of the *Boise* at the Battle of Cape Esperance in two action-packed half-hour episodes. The hero of *Boise*'s story was a nameless old gunner's mate who was stationed in a 6-inch gun. As the announcer warned, the stories were "based on fact" but were "wholly fictitious." In this heroic retelling, the old gunner's mate sinks the six Japanese warships by himself.

In June, my mother received a letter from the Secretary of the Navy:

Dear Mrs. Fowler:
The name FOWLER has recently been assigned to a Destroyer Escort vessel in honor of your husband, the late Lieutenant (j.g.) Robert Ludlow Fowler, U.S. Naval Reserve.
It gives me great pleasure to designate you as sponsor for the

USS FOWLER, which is scheduled to be launched at the Navy Yard, Philadelphia, Pa., on July 3rd, 1943.

Sincerely,

Frank Knox

On July 2, my mother took a train to Philadelphia with relatives. The next day, at the Navy Yard, two destroyer escorts were launched, the *Fowler* and the *Spangenberg*. Newspaper stories noted they were put in the water with a minimum of pomp. However, more than a thousand people were in attendance, mostly family and guests of the ships' crews. The *Fowler* was launched first, christened by the widow in black. My mother slammed a champagne bottle against *Fowler*'s bow three times before it broke.

Later that week, my mother received a form letter from the Chief of Naval Personnel informing her that her late husband was being awarded the Purple Heart, "in accordance with General Order 186 of January 21, 1943" which, the letter went on to explain, directed that anyone in the U.S. military killed in action since December 6, 1941 was to receive a Purple Heart posthumously.

PAT CHRISTENS U.S.S. FOWLER (DE-222), PHILADELPHIA NAVY YARD, JULY 2, 1943.

On the first anniversary of my father's death, October 12, 1943, he was memorialized with a headstone in the graveyard at St. Matthew's Church in Bedford.

Two months later, in December 1943, my mother tried to enlist in the Navy but was rejected because she was a widow with a child. The recruiter suggested she try the Office of Strategic Services.

The O.S.S. accepted her, and soon she was working as a coding clerk at the O.S.S. offices at 30 Rockefeller Plaza, where her first boss was future author and critic Marya Mannes. Several months later, she was transferred to Washington, D.C., for training, and she took me with her. We were in Washington for six months. In the fall of 1944, she was sent to Europe. I was left with my grandparents.

My mother was first stationed in London. She was a coding clerk at the O.S.S. offices on Ryder Street. Her boss was Norman Holmes Pearson, the head of counterespionage in Europe. Pearson had been an American literature professor at Yale. His codename was "The Last Puritan."

After a few months in London, my mother flew to Lisbon for two weeks of indoctrination. Then she travelled by train to Madrid, where she was stationed at the American Consulate.

PAT, A SPY IN SPAIN, FALL 1944.

She would spend part of the day coding and decoding, and then go out and try to "connect," which involved striking up friendships. She made friends with flamenco dancers and bullfighters. She was tailed by a Spaniard who worked for the German Consulate and who rifled her hotel room and stole her cherished book of Goya drawings.

By early 1945, with the war in Europe winding down and my second birthday approaching, my mother was anxious to get home. When Harry Fowler heard she might be returning, he wrote her: "I think you really should + I'm sure you will find it OK now."

Before my mother left London, Norman Holmes Pearson handed her a letter that he had written to me explaining why she had left me and gone off "on a mission which her generation and [his] shared:"

> It was a mission to make the world better for you to live in, or at least to save what we thought was a good world in which we lived. You will then know better than we do now whether that mission was successful. You can never know better than we that it was a task worth trying to effect. For we saw, your mother and I, the horror that faced us of a world in which all honor, all faith in each other, all human decency might be absent.
>
> This belief that the world was, and could continue to be, a place of honor and faith and decency was the belief which made it possible for your father to risk his life, and made the losing of it tolerable to those who like your mother knew and loved him as a person, or to those who like myself respect and love him as a symbol of the greatness of the human will. One day people may tell you, as I was told in my generation, of an earlier group in an earlier war, that the men of our country were conscripted and forced into war. I hope it will not fool you, as it did us, into believing that those of us who shared in the war did so because there was no other course open. That would be a lie. Your father need not have fought for his beliefs, need not have risked his life, and in this case need not have lost it, had he not been willing to do so. Because he saw and recognized his responsibility towards those just born and those whom he wished to be born - amongst whom you were - he shouldered willingly his burden for the future. We are all Puritans, we Americans, and we all know that we are our brothers' and our fathers' and our children's keepers. I hope that

you will recognize, if the necessity ever comes to you, that this
responsibility is yours also.

My mother arrived home three days before my second
birthday. My parents' war was over.

BOBBY'S GRAVE AT THE PUNCHBOWL, HONOLULU, HAWAII

Glassell Park, California
thegunclub.book@gmail.com

U.S.S. DUNCAN CREW ROSTER

Ship's company: 248
CAPS = *Duncan* plank owners, April 16, 1942
(R) = U.S. Naval Reserve
dates = time aboard *Duncan*
rating/rank = at time of the battle
last = duty and/or battle station
Bold = died as a result of the battle
~~Strikethrough~~ = not on board for the battle
+ = transported to New Zealand

Academy Officers

TAYLOR, Edmund,'25	LCdr/CO, bridge
BRYAN, Louis,'32	LCdr/XO, bridge
HAUCK, Philip,'35	Lt/Guns, main battery director
+KABAT, Herbert,'38	Lt/Engineering/#1 engineroom
~~WEATHERUP, Robert,'40, -9/16⁺~~	~~Lt(jg)/Communications~~
Andrews, Frank,'42, 5/14-	Ens/First Lieut./after conn
Lane, Arthur,'43, 6/22-	Ens/Asst. Commo/coding room

"Officer-Passengers"

Broccolo, Frank, (R) 4/29-	Lt.(jg)/Medical Corp, mess hall
BEEBE, Clifford, (R)	Lt.(jg)/Communications, bridge
+WHARTON, Richard, (R)	Lt.(jg)/Asst. Guns, I.C.
SMYTH, Jack, (R)	Lt.(jg)/Asst. Eng., forward repair
COLEY, Wade, (R)	Ens./Asst. Guns, 1.1 gun
RHODES, Theodore, (R)	Ens./Asst. Guns, machinegun director
FOWLER, Robert, (R)	Ens./Asst. Guns, torpedo director

Chiefs

BORCYCKOWSKI, Francis	CMM/after repair party
BOYD, David	CTM/torpedo mount
CHAMBERLAIN, Whitney	CSK/bridge, captain's talker
COLBECK, Thomas	CFC/I.C.
DUCKWORTH, Chapel	CGM
FILLEBROWN, Thornton	CRM/radio room
HOLT, Lester	CWT/#2 fireroom
KING, Isaac	CPhM/wardroom
LEHMAN, William	CQM/bridge
MAGEE, Lester	CMM/#1 engineroom
MORTON, Hubert	CEM/forward repair party
+MITCHELL, William	CCStd/machinegun director,talker
PAIGE, Lennon	CY/gun director, trainer
RUSCH, Anthony, (R)	CGM

SHANAHAN, John -6/16[2]
SHREIBER, Ottomar -6/22[3]
SOLOMON, Harry

CBM
CTM
CMM/#2 engineroom

Enlisted

Abernathy, Elliott, (R) 6/23-	S2c
ALBRIGHT, Sam, (R)	SM2c/signal bridge
Allan, William, (R) 4/25-	SC2c/#1 handling room
ALLEN, David, (R)	WT1c/#1 fireroom
ALLEN, George, (R)	Matt1c/fwd.clipping room
AMMON, Martin, (R)	MM2c/#2 engineroom
BACSIK, George, (R)	MM2c/#1 engineroom
Bagalo, Augustine, (R) 8/18-	F2c
Baumgardner, Frank, 6/23-7/29[4]	S2c
Beavers, Edward, 6/23-	SC3c
BENSON, Francis	SM1c/signal bridge
BERQUIST, Helmar, (R)	MoMM2c/#1 engineroom, throttleman
Berry, John, 6/23-	S2c
BETHUNE, Malcolm, (R)	MM2c/#1 engineroom
Bilbro, James, (R) 4/23-	FC3c/gun director, rangefinder
BOEHM, Roy	Cox/#2 mount, sightsetter
BOWERS, Edward, (R)	SC3c/#2 magazine
BOYLE, Romney	WT2c/after repair party
Bray, Jack, 8/19-	S2c
Brooks, Donald, 5/27-	MM2c
BUCKNER, James, (R)	MM1c
Bunkley, Emory, (R) 6/23-8/18[5]	S2c
Burnham, Floyd, 8/18-	S1c/gun director
BURNS, Leo	Cox
Butler, Hoyt, (R) 6/23-8/19[6]	S2c
Byram, Rebel, (R) 4/18-	GM2c/1.1 gun, capt.
Carlson, Robert, (R) 6/4-	S2c/20mm, ammo passer
CARROLL, Francis, (R)	S2c/steering engineroom
Case, Maxwell, (R) 6/23-	S2c/#2 gun
CASLER, Raymond, (R)	S2c
Castellano, Gaspare, (R) 4/20-	S1c
CATLOW, Raymond, (R)	S2c/#1 handling room
CECHARIO, Frank	S2c/port bridgewing, lookout
CHABINEC, Myron, (R)	S2c
Cherubina, Jack	S2c
CHISHOLM, Edward	S2c
Chism, Carlos, 4/18-6/28[7]	GM3c
CHRISTENSEN, Clarence	EM1c/I.C., electric board
CHRISTIANO, Frank, (R)	S2c
CISEK, John	S1c/20mm
Clark, William, 4/18-4/27[8]	F2c

Name	Rating/Position
Clement, Donald, (R) 6/23-	S2c
~~Coit, Willam, 6/4-6/18~~[9]	~~S2c~~
+COMBS, Carl	FC1c/I.C., computer operator
CONINX, Frank, (R)	Y2c/bridge
CONLON, Frank, (R)	EM3c
CONNELL, Thomas, (R)	S2c/after repair party
CONROY, Francis, (R)	S1c
~~CONSTANTELLO, Daniel, (R) -8/18~~[10]	~~S2c~~
COOK, James	TM3c/K-gun
CORMACK, John, (R)	S1c/20mm
CORRIGAN, George	S2c/20mm
~~COTTLE, Robert, (R) -4/27~~[11]	~~AS~~
COTTON, Charles, (R)	F3c
Coveny, Alfred, (R) 4/20-	S2c
CRAFT, Ralph, (R)	S2c
CRAIG, Warren	F2c/#1 magazine
CRANDALL, George	S2c/20mm, talker
Critchett, William, 4/20-	S2c/depth charge rack
~~CRUM, Raymond, (R) -5/13~~[12]	~~AS~~
+CRUZ, Louis	S2c/gun director, lookout
Cutler, Emery, 6/23-	S2c/#4 gun, loader
DAILEY, Norman	F1c/forward repair party
~~Davenport, Lawson, (R) 4/18-6/28~~[13]	~~S2c~~
DAVENPORT, Paul	BM2c/#1 mount, capt.
Davis, Arthur, (R) 6/16-	S2c/radio room
Davis, Arthur, 4/18-	F1c/#2 fireroom
DAVIS, George	F2c/#2 gun
DAWSON, George	WT2c/#2 fireroom
DAZEN, Russell, (R)	S1c
DEITZ, Thomas, (R)	WT2c/#1 fireroom
DELUCCA, Louis, (R)	S2c/#3 gun, loader
DeOnofrio, Dominic, 4/29-	F2c
Dernehl, Howard, 6/4-	BM1c/forward repair party
~~Derr, Aaron, 6/23-7/12~~[14]	~~S2c~~
DiFELICE, Leonard, (R)	F2c/#2 fireroom
Dignin, Robert, 5/27-	F1c/#1 engineroom
DIKKER, William, (R)	S1c
DINKINS, William	SoM3c
~~Dipzinski, Clement, (R) 6/23-8/18~~[15]	~~S2c~~
+DiRITTO, Domenic	F3c
DLUGOZIMA, Alexander, (R)	S2c/#4 gun, trainer
DOMERY, John, (R)	EM2c
DONELLE, Frederick	F3c
DOTY, John	S2c/torpedo director, talker
DRISCOLL, James, (R)	S2c
DUBIEL, Stanley, (R)	S2c/#2 mount
DUFFY, Paul, (R)	F3c

Name	Rate/Position
DUNCAN, James	S2c/#2 magazine
Dunisch, Donald, 5/27-	F1c/#1 fireroom
DUNLOP, William, (R)	S2c/gun director
+DUNN, Howard	GM1c/#2 mount, capt.
DUNN, Robert, (R) 5/27	S1c/20mm, 2nd loader
Duvall, Ward, 6/23-	S2c/torpedo mount, lookout
EDWARDS, Quinton	TM3c/torpedo director
EGGLESTON, Robert, (R)	MM2c
EHRENBERG, Arthur	S2c/#3 gun, hot shellman
Elkin, Jack, (R) 6/23-	S2c
Elrich, Harold, (R) 6/23-	S2c
EMOND, Robert, (R)	F3c
~~FAFAUL, Michael, -8/18~~	~~MM1c~~
Faford, Albert, (R) 4/20-	F3c
Fair, William, (R)	S2c
+FALLON, Joseph, (R)	S2c/2HR, 2d shellman
~~FARINA, Jospeh, (R) -8/20~~[16]	~~S2c~~
~~FEDORCHAK, Walter, (R) -8/18~~[17]	~~S2c~~
+FERREIRA, Edward, (R)	F3c/#2 handling room, shellman
Ferris, Millard, (R) 4/20-	S2c
+FIELDING, Charles, (R)	RM3c
FIFFICK, Andrew, (R)	S2c
~~FILEWICZ, Leo, (R) -8/21~~[18]	~~S2c~~
+Fischer, Arthur, 4/20-	S1c/#2 mount, pointer
FITZSIMMONS, Eddie	S2c
~~Flaherty, Charles, (R) -7/28~~[19]	~~S2c~~
FLAHERTY, James, (R)	S2c/starboard bridgewing, lookout
FLEMING, James	S2c
FLOWERS, Bruner	PhM1c
FLORCZAK, Walter	F3c
~~FLYNN, William, (R) -4/27~~[20]	~~AS~~
FOWLER, David, (R)	S2c/20mm, gunner
Freels, Tilman, (R) 6/23-	RM2c/radio room, telegrapher
Gagne, Gideon, 6/23-	S1c
Galganski, Russell, 8/18-	S2c
Ginder, George, 6/23-	S1c/#2 mount
Gist, William, 6/23-	S1c/1.1 gun, pointer
Goodman, George, (R) 4/29-	EM3c/#2 handling room, powderman
Grant, George, (R) 6/23-	S2c
GREENE, Robert	S1c/#4 gun, loader
GRIFFIN, Cyril, (R)	WT2c/#2 fireroom
GRIFFITH, Charles	F2c
GRIGG, James Arthur, (R)	SoM3c/TBS recorder
GUENTHER, Warren	RM1c/radio room
GUNTHER, Albert	MM2c/#2 fireroom
Guthery, Dewey, (R) 5/27-	SoM3c
HALBERT, Bentley	SoM3c/bridge, sound operator

HAM, Earle, (R)	TM3c/I.C., rangefinder operator
HAVEMAN, John, (R)	Y3c/bridge, War Diary recorder
HAWKINS, James	SoM3c/bridge, sound operator
HERNDAY, John	MM2c/#2 engineroom
HESS, Ernest	FC3c/I.C.
HIGGINS, William	MM1c/#2 engineroom
HOHNSBEHN, Frank	SC3c
~~Jenkins, Patrick, (R) 5/17-8/19²¹~~	~~F1c~~
Johnson, Emil, 5/27-	SC1c/galley
JOHNSON, E. Russell	QM2c/bridge, QM at the helm
JOHNSON, Newell, (R)	F1c
JOHNSON, Thomas	S1c/20mm
Jones, Samuel, 6/23-	Matt3c/fwd.clipping rm.
~~JORDAN, Edmund, -6/7²²~~	~~S2c~~
Kandravi, Francis, 4/18-	F1c/#2 fireroom
Keeble, Emmett, 6/23-8/14²³	~~AS²⁴~~
KEGEL, William	S1c
Kemp, John, 4/18-	F1c/#2 magazine
KLINE, Frank, (R)	RM2c/bridge, radar operator
~~Knight, William, (R) -6/23²⁵~~	~~Bmkr1c~~
KOEHLER, Carl	FC1c/gun director, rangefinder
LA BEAU, Donald	TM2c/torpedo mount
~~Lake, Darrell, 6/23-8/21²⁶~~	~~S1c~~
LAPPIN, Delbert	S1c/bridge, QM
Largent, Robert, 4/18-	F1c
LARSON, Harold	GM3c/20mm
LASSEIGNE, Arthur, (R)	MM2c/#2 engineroom
LeValley, Elwood, (R) 5/17-	F1c
Lyons, Phillip, 4/18-	F2c/#2 fireroom
Mahan, Glenn, 5/27-	Bmkr2c
MALLETTE, Charles, (R)	S1c
Manna, Joseph, (R) 4/24-	S2c/bridge, radio transmitter op.
MARDOS, August, (R)	MM2c/#2 engineroom
MARSHALL, Ancel	Msmth1c/after repair party
Martinelli, Paul, (R) 8/19-	F1c/#1 engineroom, talker
MARZAN, Tomas, (FR)	OC1c
McAdams, Robert, 4/20-	CM2c/forward repair party
McCleary, Gerald, 6/23-	S1c/#1 mount, pointer
McDowell, John, (R) 6/19-	S1c/I.C.
McINTOSH, George	BM2c
Meyer, Roy, (R) 6/7-	S2c/1.1 clipping room
Milek, Charles, 6/23-	BM2c/#3 mount, capt.
~~Moffat, Alfred, (R) 4/18-6/20²⁷~~	~~F2c~~
Moore, Robert, 5/19-	F1c
MOORE, William	S1c
Moreland, Matthew, (R) 6/30-	Matt2c/fwd.clipping rm.
NICOLL, David	QM3c/steering engineroom

NOLAN, James	S1c
NORMAN, LaVerne, (R)	F2c
NORTON, Robert	MM2c/#1 engineroom, throttleman
O'Brien, John, (R) 8/19-	F2c
O'Brien, Leo, (R) 4/20-	GM3c/#2 mount, spademan
+OLEK, Roman	MM1c/forward repair party
O'MARA, Edward	F2c/#1 handling room
~~Owen, Harold, 5/17-8/19~~[28]	~~F1c~~
Packwood, William, 5/29-	FC2c/gun director, pointer
PALLANSCH, Edward, (R)	FC3c/I.C.
PALMER, George	S1c/#1 gun
PAPACODA, Anthony	TM1c/torpedo director, setter
Pastore, Samuel, (R) 4/29-	F1c/#2 fireroom
PETET, Frank	F2c
PORTERFIELD, George	F2c
PURGETT, Robert	SM3c/signal bridge
PUZINES, John, (R)	WT2c/forward repair party
Queen, James, 8/18-	S1c/gun director, talker
QUINN, Francis, (R)	MM2c/steering engineroom, talker
Rasch, Joseph, (R) 4/24-	RM3c
RIZZI, Rosalio	S1c/#2 handling room, shellman
Roberts, Edgar, 5/27-	F1c/#1 fireroom
~~Ronan, Carl, 4/18-8/19~~[29]	~~F2c~~
~~Root, Harold, (R) 6/7-8/4~~[30]	~~S2c~~
Rosenfelt, James, 5/27-	F1c
ROSHTO, Burton	GM2c
SARGENT, Jacob	Cox
Schaefer, John, (R) 5/27-	F1c
SCHIMMEL, George	TM3c/torpedo mount
Scott, Dan, 8/19-	S2c/torpedo mount
Scott, Elvin, 5/29-	S2c/forward repair party
Shurney, William, 4/18-	Matt1c/#2 mount, shellman
+SIFERS, George	SF3c/forward repair party
Skwarla, Metro, 5/27-	F1c
SLOVINEC, Andrew	F3c/#2 engineroom
Smith, Archibald, (R) 8/20-	WT2c/#1 fireroom
~~SMITH, Jesse, -6/16~~[31]	~~SC2c~~
SNYDER, Robert	F1c
Sobelman, Jack, 4/20-	FC1c/gun director, pointer
+STANFILL, Kelly	S1c/gun director, lookout
STIVERS, Everett	F1c
Taylor, Robert, 8/19-	GM2c/20mm
TOUSIGNANT, Roger	S1c
TRIPP, Ted	S2c/1FR
TUCKER, Earl	S1c/4gun, pointer
VANDONKELAAR, John	BM2c, after repair party
VanDyke, Amos, 8/18-	S1c

+VANEK, Joseph — S1c
Veitch, Henry, 6/23- — S2c/#1 handling room
VIERING, Albert, (R) — FC2c/#1 mount, talker
~~WAGNER, Bennett, -6/20~~[32] — ~~S2c~~
WALTERS, Lucious — OS3c
~~WARREN, Charles, (R) -6/20~~[33] — ~~Matt3c~~
WATERBURY, William, (R) — EM2c
WATSON, Frank, (R) — TM3c/torpedo mount
WELHOUSE, Joseph — EM3c/20mm
Wheet, Kimball, 5/29- — S2c
+WHELAN, Raymond — GM2c/#1 gun
WHITTEN, Duane — GM3c
WICKSTROM, Clarence — SF1c/after repair party
~~WIEMER, Bruce, -6/23~~[34] — ~~S1c~~
WILLIAMS, Leo — MM2c
WIZENRITH, Willam, (R) — WT1c/#1 fireroom
+WOOD, Clovis — S1c
~~WOODBURN, Reese, -8/19~~[35] — ~~S1c~~
Wright, Edward, 6/4- — EM3c
Young, Irvine, 8/20- — S2c/#1 handling room
ZDRADZINSKI, Anthony, (R) — EM2c
ZIEGLER, Gerald, (R) — GM3c

SELECTIONS FROM AFTER ACTION REPORTS AND STATEMENTS

Lieutenant Commander Edmund Taylor's After Action Report:

... 4. The tactical maneuver of the DUNCAN as reported in the following differs only in one respect from that as reported [in Preliminary Report made to R/Adm. Scott on October 14, 1942]. In preparing the latter, the Commanding Officer was under the impression that the turn of the DUNCAN from an easterly to a northwesterly course to uncover the torpedo battery to starboard was made to the right. The Executive Officer positively states, confirmed by the helmsman, that upon clearing one of our destroyers, the Commanding Officer gave the order "Left full rudder, prepare to fire torpedoes to starboard" and that the DUNCAN actually swung left towards the Japanese cruiser in gaining the torpedo firing course instead of right as previously reported.

Lieutenant Louis Bryan's After Action Report:

... As executive officer, my regular battle station was at secondary conn, but due to the recent transfer of the communications officer [Lt.(jg) Robert Weatherup], there was no sufficiently trained officer available to assist in conning the ship. On verbal orders from the Commanding Officer, I was directed to remain on the bridge until released just prior to action, to assist in conning. At about 2315, the *Duncan* was following the *Farenholt* in column and attempting to gain the van of the cruisers after force had reversed course to 230oT. when action commenced. It was at this moment that I sighted a Jap cruiser [*Furutaka*] close aboard our starboard bow, silhouetted in the searchlight beams of our own cruisers to port, who were engaging another Jap cruiser [*Aoba*] and several destroyers further ahead. I called the attention of our Commanding Officer to the target, and he immediately directed that the torpedo battery fire on it. He further turned away, to port, to uncover the torpedo tube. [Note that he stresses only a turn to port.] At this stage, the last cruiser in our own line [*Helena*], opened fire, catching the *Duncan* in crossfire. *Duncan* was hit many times from both sides forward of #1 stack. The ship burst into flames immediately and all control from the bridge was lost. I started aft but was blocked by flames from the fireroom and radio shack area. It was impossible to get either forward or aft, since Gun #2 was burning furiously and ammunition from our ready boxes was exploding continuously both forward and aft of the bridge area. Since the bridge ladder was blocked off, I directed that the forestays, which had been carried away, and signal halyards be hung over the starboard wing of the bridge for use in lowering men into the water. Since it was impossible to get away from this area, and it appeared that to remain longer would unnecessarily endanger life, the Commanding Officer directed the personnel that had gathered there to abandon ship. The Commanding Officer and I made one last tour of the area and attempted to use the various means of communications once more, but without success.

Lieutenant Philip Hauck's After Action Report:

The main battery opened fire on a cruiser [*Aoba*] on our port bow, range about 3,300 yards, radar ranges. Guns and director in automatic, fire control solution good. First shots landed short of the target waterline. A spot up of 200 was applied, and all remaining salvos were observed to pass into the superstructure area. After about eight salvos were fired, the target was observed to 'blow up,' and fire was shifted to a destroyer [he thought cruiser *Furutaka* was a destroyer] to the right of the cruiser, range 2,250 yards, without waiting for a computer solution, using radar ranges.

Two salvos, both hitting, were fired before *Duncan* was hit in the bridge area and director. Operations, radar, and all communications went out. I directed the director crew to remain within the director shield while I went below to take control of the forward battery at Gun #2. Upon observing Gun #2 and the superstructure below the bridge to be on fire, I passed word up to the director for the crew to lay down on the bridge. I left the ship when directed by the Executive Officer.

When the gun director and communications went, guns #1, #3, and #4 went to local control. Gun #1 fired one shot at the destroyer but further firing was impractical due to the rapid swing of the ship. Gun #2 was entirely out of commission due to an explosion in the upper handling room.

Lieutenant (junior grade) Frank Andrews's statement:

... Duncan was steaming in company with force when order came through and was passed over entire battle circuit for information, 'We are turning 180o.' After the turn, [main battery] control reported radar contact bearing 025 [astern to starboard]. I noticed [from my station at after conn that] Gun #3 and #4 trained on that bearing. At approximately one minute later, a Jap destroyer [*Hatsuyuki*] passed abeam parallel to our course at what seemed about 1,000 yards. Not more that 15 seconds [later], a Jap cruiser [*Aoba*] relative bearing 025, distance about 2,500 yards, was suddenly illuminated by our force, and about ten salvos from other ships seemed to hit this cruiser. Control [Lt. Hauck] instantly gave commence firing, and our guns opened fire. We fired approximately four salvos from #3 and #4 [at *Hatsuyuki*] of which most seemed to hit. The Jap cruiser looked all red, and almost instantly broke at the foremast and started down. [Now, he is talking about cruiser *Furutaka*.] *Duncan* was going what seemed like about 25 or 30 knots and closing the enemy. Suddenly after our fourth salvo we got hit, and the soot, steam, and smoke prevented me from seeing anything more.

I went aft where a crowd had started to gather. It was clear there, and I could see nothing around us. I went to secondary conn [after conn], and the aft engines and steering aft were the only ones on line. Steering aft straightened the rudder out, and then I gave hard right rudder to try to beach the *Duncan* on what I later found out was Savo Island. But there was considerable firing in that direction, so I gave hard left rudder. We cleared that spot and I gave hard right again, but about that time aft engineroom [was] secured because there was no steam left. Mr. Kabat, Mr. Coley had been trying to get more steam, but were unable. The gang back aft abandoned ship later at Mr. Kabat's orders. Mr. Coley and myself and a group stayed aboard. Mr. Coley, [CMM] Borcykowski and [CWT] Holt were working below in aft boiler [#2 fireroom] trying to pump salt water for purposes of making steam in boilers. But the pump could not build up enough pressure. We attempted to put the fires out but to no avail. I later abandoned the ship with the remainder of the crew.

Lieutenant (junior grade) Wade Coley's statement:

Enemy had been reported on our starboard bow. Direction of opening fire from ships on our port bow was such that I believed them to be the enemy. Control did not designate target - did not give orders for 1.1" to open fire. Received hits [in forward] fireroom, and flame and smoke made visibility impossible.

Gave orders to 1.1" crew to fight fires, flood 1.1" and 20mm. magazine and dump gasoline and kerosene. Believed bridge had control.

Went down to main decks, helped fight fire, run hoses, etc. After conn reported an officer was needed to conn the ship. Reported to Mr. Kabat [that the] bridge did not have control. Mr. Kabat was directing men fighting fire which was spreading aft.

Had reports from after engineroom and fireroom that they were O.K. Told [CMM] Borcykowski to get the ship going astern to aid in fighting fire and to enable us to see where we were going. Had men try to call main radio [room], via radio. After fireroom reported loss of feed water and no steam; no pressure on fire mains [main water lines]. Word was passed to abandon ship. Volunteers stayed aboard. Got steam secured in after engineroom in hope that remaining steam pressure in boiler would run fire and bilge pump long enough to get salt water in the boiler. Steam pressure was not great enough.

Received word forward magazine had not been flooded. Again passed word to abandon ship. Volunteers stayed aboard.

Manned the hand fuel oil pump in after fireroom to bring up steam pressure for fire and bilge pump. There was not enough water left in the boiler.

Connected up gasoline pump [handybilly] to feed water to the boiler. The cold water flashed into steam. The resulting pressure forced water and steam back out of the pump. Again abandon ship. Volunteers stayed aboard.

Set up gasoline pump on starboard side to fight fires; it would not start. Gathered up all CO2 extinguishers and all buckets to fight fire on starboard side.

Ammunition was exploding intermittently since fire started. Increasing explosions and flying debris made fire fighting impractical. Ordered men to abandon ship. Had one raft and made another of 4"X4" shoring. We were the last to leave, 0136, 12 October 1942.

I saw no action that would be a discredit to the men. All the men were calmly doing their jobs. No man abandoned ship until word was given. In particular, men from the after part of the ship who remained on board deserve credit. There was no risk or sacrifice they would not have made to save the ship.

Chief Torpedoman David Boyd's statement:

At the time of commence firing, [TM3c Frank] Watson and [S2c Dan] Scott were on the tubes. Star shells had been fired and I saw two targets, what I believed was a Jap destroyer and light cruiser. Control [torpedo director] set up the problem and fired the center barrel with the tube trained on about 55o train [at *Aoba*]. A few seconds after we were hit forward on starboard side and then I believe a second time before an order of fire two was given. Then we lost communications with control. We were next hit on #1 stack. The flames, sparks and smoke were coming aft heavily and visibility was poor. We then saw the forward stack starting to fall so we all went aft. After the stack, which fell outboard, was down, I went forward and saw flames blazing up around the forward torpedo tubes. My first thought was to get rid of the torpedoes before the warheads exploded. I climbed up on the tubes and was about to jettison the torpedoes when I saw a cruiser on the starboard side at about 3,500 yards. [Probably, Boyd was confusing two targets - *Aoba* at 3,500 yards and *Furutaka* at 1,200 yards.] It was too good a shot to waste so I led her with about 23° sight angle and fired. Target angle was about 270° and I estimated her speed at 25 knots and fired. I waited to see the results of that shot, which hit the cruiser amidships. Then before I could get another shot out, we started turning hard to port and I didn't have time to fire second shot. [?]

I looked then for a place to fire the remaining three torpedoes, and, as it looked clear to our starboard, which was then facing the Island [Guadalcanal], I fired the other three torpedoes. However, the right barrel had not fired, though I didn't know it at the time. I then went back to after conn and started to help get fire hose led out to put out the fires and was so engaged when someone said that there wasn't anyone at after conn. So I went up to after conn at about the same time that Ens. Andrews got there, and stayed with him.

It appeared that we had turned to port into the crossfire of a running fight so continued to turn to get away from it. We then headed down what we thought was the northwest side of Guadalcanal, but before we got very far we lost boiler pressure and stopped. We then went to the assistance of the fire fighting party but gave that up as there was no pressure on the fire mains.

Shortly after this, five star shells were dropped on our port quarter and it looked as though someone were trying to get a range on us so Lt. Kabat passed the word to abandon ship.

Chief Storekeeper Whitney Chamberlain's statement

[edits are his]: We were steaming second in column, *USS Farenholt* leading on course 070 or 080 true, when we received a voice message over TBS in color code to change course to 230 true. As we commenced the turn to port, another message over TBS announcing "Four bogies" and giving bearing and distance was heard. Then another message announcing "Five bogies" came immediately. Word was passed to the control officer {Lt. Hauck}, who immediately reported four excellent pips on FD radar on same bearing and range. We had completed the turn to were changing course to 230 true. Word was passed to stand by for action.

The *Farenholt* appeared to turn left and our cruisers on our port bow opened up with starshells and service ammunition. Then a ship or ships aft [*Helena*] on our port side opened up, and the firing was across our bow and stern. Firing went on for what I estimate as one minute and then ceased. We did not open fire because of the following:

When firing first started, control reported on target.

When illumination lit up the area, ships lay on both sides and ahead of us, and it was hard to determine which was which. Captain asked if we were on an enemy or on one of our own ships. Control reported that they were not positive, so we held our fire.

After a lull of an estimated twenty seconds, illumination and firing commenced again. We were turning to port towards our own forces starboard when a Japanese vessel appeared on our starboard bow, at about 1,200 yards. The Captain and Executive Officer both saw her at the same time and exclaimed that it was a perfect setup for torpedoes. I issued order to torpedo director to fire one torpedo. Seconds afterwards, our ships were firing at her, including our own battery opening up for the first time. Whether our torpedo hit her, I do not know. She burst into flames, appeared to break up, and sank within seconds.

Then a Japanese ship, what I think to be a cruiser, appeared on our starboard side, just forward of the beam, coming through the smoke at a target angle to us of about 285°. We opened fire on her and, later, I found out that [CTM Boyd] fired two torpedoes at her, scoring hits with both.

Then the Japanese got their guns firing for the first time. We took a salvo on our starboard side - most of the hits forward, and evidently two in #2 handling room. The concussion knocked me against the bulkhead and the flash blinded me momentarily. During the few moments that I was blinded, I felt numerous shells hit the *Duncan*. After regaining vision, I could see we were in a crossfire, apparently almost midway between both forces, and we were getting hit from both sides. After taking hits from both sides and realizing our forces were firing on us also, the Captain ordered the battle lights (recognition reply) turned on. Lights functioned only a few seconds, when they went out, probably as a result of the hit in the I.C. room, or the hit on the director platform. I was told about that hit later.

No one in the pilothouse was hurt, but the pilothouse was filled with smoke and debris. Complete order was observed at all times, and all hands that I saw and heard kept cool heads.

Ports were opened in an effort to drive out the smoke but to no avail. Communications was lost after we took the first salvo and was not regained except for a weak signal from plotting room [I.C.]. CFC Colbeck informed me that they had sustained a hit in the I.C. room, that the place was flooding, a fire had started in that area, and asked for orders. He also said all power was out, the switchboard panels were shot away and the computer was inoperative.

The Captain was busy so I took it upon myself to order him [CFC Colbeck] to get his men together, rescue the pay accounts if possible, and stand by for further instructions, and to be ready to abandon ship if necessary.

Communications was then entirely lost and all phone circuits and public address systems inoperative. Also, we lost steering control and could not raise secondary conn [after conn] or steering aft [the after steering engineroom] to shift control.

There were wounded or dead men, number unknown, on the starboard wing of the bridge by the searchlight platform and SM1c Sam Albright was sitting on the starboard pelorus platform, doubled over, covered with blood and moaning. I figured that he had been wounded in the stomach.

The fire, smoke and showers of sparks and debris were rising to the bridge from #2 handling room while the ammunition there was exploding. The Captain said, in effect, 'Get the kapok lifejackets, boys, and you'd better leave while you have time. Good luck to all of you.'

I secured three kapok jackets and gave two of them to persons I couldn't identify. The third I put on and we lined up to go over the side. The first three or four men went down the side or jumped, and then a light manila line was rigged to the voice tube. I was about the fifth one over. The line reached only a little over halfway to the fo'csle deck, and, when I reached the end, someone above fell on me, [and] I dropped to the deck and bounced over the side.

In the water, I met Lt. Hauck and CY Paige. We tied ourselves together with manila lanyards and I gave a pneumatic lifebelt that I had to Paige as he did not have kapok [vest]. We swam all night, trying to make an island to starboard of the action [Guadalcanal], and during the morning, the *USS McCalla* showed up. We made our way to her and were later taken on board.

All hands on the bridge appeared cool and calm, and showed an exceptionally high degree of courage. In the heat and excitement of battle, I was not able to observe any outstanding action on the part of any one particular person, my attentions being directed solely on the Captain for orders, and for occasional glimpses of the Japanese vessels.

I wish to say that all Japanese ships seemed to burst into flames after sustaining about six hits, and that they all sank quickly except for one or two in a running fight to the westward.

Chief Motor Machinist's Mate Lester Magee's statement:

On or about 2344, I heard first gun salvo. About 2350, enemy salvo hit #1 fireroom. Fireroom telephone talker reported #1 fireroom badly shot up. Ordered #1 fireroom to secure. #1 fireroom secured, but [fireroom crew] refused to leave station until the fireroom was straightened out. About three minutes later, contact with #1 fireroom failed.

Upon ordering #1 fireroom to secure, we closed the bulkhead stops going to #1 and #2 boilers and the auxiliary steam stop. We opened our auxiliary steam stop coming from aft in order to keep our generator and pumps running.

One shell hit port side about frame 99 just about the waterline. Shrapnel hit the generator board, port side, cutting out power and tripping generator. Cut in emergency electrical power from #2 generator coming down the starboard side. Secured #1 generator.

Enemy shells hit machine shop, setting it ablaze. Secured intake and exhaust blowers because flames and smoke was coming down the blowers. Steam supply from the after fireroom failed. Fire main pressure from #1 flushing pump dropped from 120 to 5 lbs. All our communication went dead and could not contact any other stations.

Tried to send messenger to after stations for information but was unable to leave the engineroom due to both the escape hatches being enveloped in flame.

Heat, smoke and gasses forced me to order my men to secure the engineroom and go out through the escape hatch on the starboard side, which was made possible by the after repair party putting out the fire around the hatch. We abandoned the forward engineroom about 2400.

All men carried out their duties promptly and remained at their stations calmly until the word to secure was given. Then they left in an orderly fashion.

Chief Motor Machinist's Mate Harry Solomon's statement:

Action started at 2344. The first indication that we had been hit was when smoke and fumes came down the vent blowers [into #2 engineroom]. I secured the blowers as the after engineroom was filling with smoke. After repair party asked for extra hose, as we were running hose up to them through the escape hatch. Another explosion occurred and we lost contact with #1 fireroom and had a faint contact with #1 engineroom and #2 fireroom, and we lost our feed water. I had the vacuum drag line opened and had after fireroom start #2 emergency feed pump, and they were unable to get any feed water. #2 fireroom had to secure #3 and #4 boilers. Received word to secure #2 engine room from Chief Engineer [CMM Magee]. Few minutes later, received word to secure engineroom and abandon ship. Secured all steam valves, ordered all personnel to leave engineroom, and we secured hatches.

After getting on the topside, the fireroom force went back to the fireroom to try to feed the after boilers with salt water. I asked for men to go back to #2 engineroom to light off again ... #2 fireroom was unable to feed the after boilers with salt water, and we abandoned the engineroom again, stayed on the topside until word to abandon ship was passed.

All personnel in #2 engineroom carried out their duties calmly and only left their stations when I ordered them to.

Chief Fire Controlman Thomas Colbeck's statement:

Received order to commence firing at 2330, checked fire 2333, commenced firing on new target on new target. Stable element started to vibrate. I stepped over to adjust, received shell in I.C. room. Shell entered overhead at doorway and exploded. I.C. electrician, EM1c Christensen, received full effect of explosion.

This is what saved the rest of compluter crew. FC3c Hess notified the bridge I.C. room was hit. [I] tried to contact all stations. Received weak voice over line. All stations dead. Power failure bell was ringing. FC1c Combs cut ship's gyro to battery, running O.K. Checked and found all fire control circuits dead. D.C. power lights on I.C. panel were still on. I.C. room flooded with about 4" water. Ordered FC3c Pallansh, FC3c Hess, S1c Ham, and S1c McDowell to carry EM1c Christensen to the mess hall.

They placed him on a table. Heard somebody ask for a hand from top of ladder. Found doctor Broccolo attempting to drag CPhM King down to the mess. Lent a hand and placed King on mess table. Went back up ladder and found galley passageway blocked with debris. Went towards wardroom, found it was on fire. Asked to have fire hose passed up. Received fire hose, but no water pressure. Attempted to put fire out with CO2 tank. Stopped fire for a few moments and then returned to mess hall. Asked the Doctor if he needed any help. He said he didn't have any medical supplies, so he couldn't do anything.

He pronounced Christensen as being dead, and said he was going forward through CPO quarters and out. Just then, we received two hits in the mess hall. The first hit started a fire. McDowell put it out, and the four of us - McDowell, Combs, Pallansh, and myself - went up the ladder over the debris in the galley passageway and got to the starboard door and found a hole in the door. When looking through, saw a wall of flame and heard the hiss of steam, so turned back and tried to go out port door, but found it blocked. Turned back to starboard door, opened it, and dropped on deck to escape any possible steam. McDowell went through the door and over the side, followed by Pallansh, and then Combs and myself. After hitting the water, made my way to Combs, and he suggested going aboard aft. So we made our way over to the ship, and they dropped us a telephone cable and then passed us a line which I tied around Combs.

They hoisted him aboard, and then I tied the line around myself and came aboard. After this Combs and I worked with Ens. Andrews, Lt. Kabat and Lt.(jg) Coley aft.

Chief Gunner's Mate Chapel Duckworth's statement:

I was temporarily blinded when the first salvo hit the starboard, probably from sand in the 40mm foundation. I cleared my eyes and noticed that #4 [machine] gun had ceased firing. I climbed inside and found that the control system was out. After shifting to local control, I started forward and found I could not reach #1 and #2 [machine] guns.

I then went to #3 [machine] gun handling room and found that it had been flooded. At this point, I was called to the 20mm clipping room and ordered to set all depth charges on the starboard side on safe by the Chief Engineer (CMM Holt).

After setting the starboard depth charges on safe, I checked all the others and then found that the fire main [line] was out throughout the ship. I assisted in relaying word from secondary conn to steering aft before and after the engines stopped. I found that most of the ship's company had abandoned ship, so I went to #4 handling room and broke out a number of powder tanks for the men that called for them, giving one to [CMM Holt]. I checked with the pharmacist's mate [Flowers] in regards to taking the wounded and found that they had already gone.

Fire Controlman Second Class William Packwood's statement:

The first indication of actual presence of enemy I had was when there appeared on our FD radar screen in the [main battery] director several pips, indicating ships off our starboard bow. The radar operator picked out the closest target, and, by continuously sending ranges to plot, a problem was set up on the computer. The last range sent to plot was 2,250 [yards]. About that time, starshells appeared in the air and simultaneously the firing from our ships began. Almost immediately the enemy began firing in return. From previous reports, we had learned that there were two enemy cruisers and six destroyers. We purposefully maneuvered into the crossfire as much as necessary to protect our cruiser force and in so doing, torpedoed one enemy cruiser, completely destroying same. We then opened fire with our main battery on the other enemy cruiser. The first salvo hit the target [Aoba] but was slightly low.

The rangefinder operator ordered a 200 yard up spot in range which I applied before our next salvo was fired. The second salvo hit just aft of the bridge at about the waterline and the third and fouth salvos appeared to hit in approximately the same place. By that time the target was no longer visible because of the fire and smoke from it. After the fourth salvo, we were hit, and the [main battery] director was put entirely out of commission as were all means of communication. When the gunnery officer saw that the director could be of no more use, he told is in the director that he was going down to the [machine gun] director platform and take charge of the machine gun battery and that we could follow if we liked, which we all did, as there was much flame both forward and aft of us and the director was an uncomfortable position.

On the way down, FC1c Sobelman found the torpedo officer [Lt.(jg) Fowler] very gravely wounded and asking for help. Sobelman took off his own lifejacket, strapped it around Mr. Fowler and by sheer strength and determination managed to get him over the side and, with the assistance of several others began towing him toward the nearest island. When I reached the bridge after leaving the director, someone told the Captain that gun #2's magazine was going off any time, so the Captain gave the order to abandon ship.

We were all on the starboard side and the Executive Officer told some of us to go over to the port side and break out the life net. We tried to but were unable to reach it. A cable and a line were secured at the bridge and the other end thrown over for escape lines. Before I left, I noted large fires at #2 gun and below where #1 stack was.

Watertender Second Class Cyril Griffin's statement:

The men in #2 fireroom carried out their orders and stayed at their posts until we were completely out of water. Everything was done to keep power on our ship ... We had to switch to emergency feed water as our main feed pressure was so low we could not feed two boilers properly. We had to shift back and forth till out. Feed water was completely exhausted.

Seaman Second Class Ward Duvall's statement:

I observed two torpedoes in succession leave the *Duncan*. The first one struck the bow of the Japanese cruiser [Furutaka] on our starboard bow. The second struck the cruiser's port quarter.

Lieutenant Commander William Cooper's (*McCalla*) report about the Japanese prisoners:

1. At 1430, 12 October, 1942, following the rescue of the survivors of the U.S.S. DUNCAN, this vessel, while in position: 9-03 south; 159-40 east, sighted numerous men floating in the sea. Upon approach it was noted that these were survivors from enemy ships sunk during the previous night's engagement. McCALLA attempted to pick up several of these survivors by maneuvering the ship and throwing them lines, but all refused to take the lines. A boat was lowered and three of the survivors were captured. No attempt was made to capture any additional ones because of the already crowded condition of the ship and the limited facilities for keeping them confined. A message was sent to the Commanding General, Guadalcanal Island, requesting that he rescue those remaining in the water.

The three prisoners were placed in custody of the marine guard ashore at Espiritu Santo Island ...

The Japanese survivors were in the water closely adjacent to the scene of the action of the previous night. When this vessel got underway after hoisting her boat, a definite indication was seen on the ship's magnetic radar detector. There were no other indications of the presence of a submarine, and it appears entirely logical to deduce that McCALLA passed directly over one of the enemy ships sunk during the engagement. This circumstance is mentioned to show the dispatch with which at least one of the enemy was sent to the bottom.

COMMENDATIONS

Commendations by Lieutenant Louis Bryan:

Bryan singled out thirty-two men - four officers, seven chiefs, and twenty-one other enlisted men - "deserving of special praise for their exemplary conduct under the most trying conditions": - Lt.(jg) Fowler, for "coolly setting up the torpedo fire control problem and firing one torpedo before being knocked out." - Lt. Hauck, "for efficiently controlling his battery under the most adverse conditions and obtaining hits on both targets - a cruiser and a destroyer." - Lt.(jg) Coley, "for coolly taking charge of the after fireroom and attempting to regain steam and keep power on the ship." - Ens. Andrews, "for taking charge of the ship from secondary conn, attempting to steer clear of the subsequent action, and putting out the fires."

Chiefs singled out were: - CSK Chamberlain (captain's talker), "for cool resourcefulness and initiative in giving correct instructions to the plotting room crew." - CTM Boyd (torpedo mount captain), "for efficiently taking charge of his mount after the torpedo officer was knocked out, and firing torpedoes with local control and obtaining an additional hit on the Jap cruiser" (i.e., in addition to any of *Buchanan*'s torpedoes that might have hit *Furutaka*). - CMM Solomon, "for efficiently handling his engine room under the most adverse conditions." - CFC Colbeck, "for efficiently handling serious casualties in the plotting room [and] for abandoning ship with [FC1c] Combs to get around the fires amidships and returning aboard aft." - CMM Borcykowski, "for exhausting efforts to put out the fires in the forward part of the ship." - CWT Holt, "for superhuman efforts to put out fires forward and keep up steam aft." -CGM Duckworth, "for devotion to duty under hazardous circumstances."

Seven men stationed in #1 fireroom - WT1c D. Allen, WT1c Winzenrith, WT2c Dietz, WT2c A. Smith, F1c Dunisch, F1c Roberts, and F1c Tripp - were commended for refusing to leave their stations after the first hit, "until they straightened out the damages - subsequently being killed by the second shell hit." GM2c Taylor and S1c Cormack, who were killed in the forward 20mms, for sticking "to their posts despite heavy shells bursting all around them." Also, S1c Rizzi, "for remaining at his station [in #2 handling room] though severely wounded and continuing to serve his gun." MM2c Guenther (#2 engine room), "for devotion to duty;" WT2c Griffin (#2 fireroom), for being "an inspiration to all near him;" SC2c Allan (#1 handling room), "for efficiently taking charge of the men in handling room under most trying conditions when his men were panicky;" MM1c Olek, a survivor of the forward repair party, "for efforts beyond the call of duty" in fighting the fires despite his injuries; and WT2c Boyle "for devotion to duty." He also commended S1c Duvall, battle lookout on the torpedo mount, for nothing more apparently than stating in writing that he saw two *Duncan* torpedoes explode into *Furutaka*. PhM1c Flowers was commended "for efficient and untiring efforts to administer first aid both during and after the battle." Finally, Lt. Bryan commended no less than five men "for efforts to save [Lt.(jg)] Fowler and successfully bringing him through the night" - CY Paige, FC1c Sobelman, FC2c Packwood, FC3c Bilbro, and S1c Queen. [No mention of the three mess stewards.]

Commendations by Lieutenant Philip Hauck:

Ens. Fowler was lying on deck alongside the torpedo director with a severe neck and head wound. As CY Paige passed him enroute from the gun director to the bridge, he administered morphine. Upon leaving the gun director, FC2c Sobelman and FC3c Bilbro joined S1c Queen in administering first aid to Mr. Fowler. The three above named men then assisted Mr. Fowler down to the bridge, then to the fo'csle deck. A line formed of individual lanyards was then made and Mr. Fowler was passed into the water. While in the water, Mr. Fowler was placed on a mattress. Shortly thereafter, the mattress sank and Mr. Fowler, having lost his lifebelt, was without support. Sobelman removed his belt, placed it on Mr. Fowler, and joined Queen and Bilbro for support.

Commendations by Lieutnant (junior grade) Wade Coley:

The following list of officers and men is by no means complete. It includes only the ones I saw and was with most of the time. Their action, resourcefulness and leadership was particularly meritorious: Lt. Kabat, Ens. Andrews, CWT Holt, CMM Borcykowski, CFC Colbeck, CTM Boyd, [WT1c] Dawson, [WT2c] Boyle, [MM2c] Bacsik, [MM1c] Higgins.

Again, the list is not complete, the last group of men to leave the ship, about 15 or 20 men, should all be included.

Commendation by Chief Torpedoman David Boyd:

I would like to state that all the men who were aft, however a little bewildered, did a good job all around.

Commendations by Chief Motor Machinist's Mate Lester Magee:

I would like to commend the men in #1 fireroom who gave their lives in order to secure their fireroom in such a manner as not to endanger the rest of the ship.

Commendation by Chief Motor Machinist's Mate Francis Borcykowski:

Stationed at the forward repair party, despite his wounds, Olek went to the after part of the ship on account of the fire on the forward part of the ship. He lent all possible assistance to the fighting of the fire and when he abandoned ship, he towed F2c DeOnofrio clear of the ship, never once mentioning his wounds to DeOnofrio or anyone else.

Commendation by Chief Watertender Lester Holt:

I wish to commend WT2c Boyle for his actions during the night of 11 October 1942. Boyle's battle station was with the after repair party. When the forward fireroom area was hit and enveloped in escaping steam, fire and smoke, Boyle repeatedly ventured as near as possible to the fireroom hatch with a firehose, in attempts to help put out the fires. Throughout the entire action, from time of receiving first damage until abandoning ship, he was constantly on hand and many times endangered his own life to fight fires and help keep the ship afloat.

Commendations by Watertender Second Class Cyril Griffin:

I want to remark on the performance of MM2c Gunther, who helped with my job, as well as his own.

Also, WT1c Dawson, who kept a cool head[, and,] even though he was overcome by gas and smoke several times[, h]e kept his watch steady.

Commendation by Seaman Second Class Roy Boehm:

S1c Rizzi, while badly wounded by shrapnel and burns, continued to send powder up to the mount. The powder tins were so hot that they blew up in the handling room.

Commendation by Seaman First Class Clovis Wood:

S1c Cormack stuck to his trunion station on Machine Gun #1 with shells bursting all around.

MEDALS/LETTERS OF COMMENDATION

Medal of Honor:

R/Adm. Norman Scott

Navy Cross:

Capt. Gilbert Hoover (*Helena*)	10/11/42 & 11/12/-13/42
Capt. Robert Tobin (ComDesRon 12)	10/11-12/42
LCdr. Edmund Taylor	10/11/42
Lt.(jg) Robert Fowler	10/11/42
CTM David Boyd	10/11/42
LCdr. William Cooper (*McCalla*)	10/12/42

Silver Star:

Lt. Louis Bryan	10/11/42
Lt. Philip Hauck	10/11/42
Lt.(jg) Frank Broccolo	10/11/42
PhM1c Bruner Flowers	10/11/42
WT1c Romney Boyle	10/11/42
MM1c Roman Olek	9/15/42
Ens. George Weems (*McCalla*)	10/11/42

Navy and Marine Corps Medal:

Ens. Jack Smyth	9/15/42
MM2c Roman Olek	10/11/42

Letter of Commendation Ribbon:

LCdr. Edmund Taylor	9/15/42
CFC Thomas Colbeck	10/11/42
PhM1c Bruner Flowers	9/15/42
FC1c Carl Combs	10/11/42
MM2c John Hernday	10/11/42

CITATIONS

Rear Admiral Norman Scott's Medal of Honor:

For extraordinary heroism and conspicuous intrepidity above and beyond the call of duty during action against enemy Japanese forces during the Battle of Cape Esperance on the night of October 11-12, 1942, and again during the Battle of Guadalcanal on the night of November 12-13, 1942. In the earlier action, intercepting a Japanese task force intent upon storming our island positions and landing reinforcements at Guadalcanal, Rear Admiral Scott, with courageous skill and superb coordination of the units under his command, destroyed eight hostile vessels and put the others to flight. Again challenged, a month later, by the return of a stubborn and persistent foe, he led his force into a desperate battle against tremendous odds, directing close-range operations against the invading enemy until he himself was killed in the furious bombardment by their superior fire-power. On each of these occasions his dauntless initiative, inspiring leadership and judicious foresight in a crisis of grave responsibility contributed decisively to the rout of a powerful invasion fleet and to the consequent frustration of a formable Japanese offensive. He gallantly gave up his life in the service of his country.

Captain Gilbert Hoover's Navy Cross:

For extraordinary heroism in the line of his profession during action with enemy forces on the night of November 12-13, 1942, on which occasion the forces to which he was attached engaged at close quarters and defeated a superior enemy force. His daring and determination contributed materially to the victory which prevented the enemy from accomplishing their purposes.

Captain Gilbert Hoover's Gold Star in Lieu of Third Navy Cross:

For extraordinary heroism as Commanding Officer of the *USS Helena* during the night action against an enemy Japanese force of cruisers and destroyers, October 11-12, 1942. Maintaining the security of the rear in the battle column, Captain Hoover fought his ship valiantly despite the difficulties of night combat and succeeded in sinking a Japanese destroyer on the disengaged side. The determined and effective gunfire of his ship under his skillful command was largely responsible for holding to a minimum the damage to our destroyers to the rear.

Captain Robert Tobin's Navy Cross:

For extraordinary heroism as Commanding Officer of a Destroyer Squadron during the night action against an enemy Japanese force of cruisers and destroyers off Savo Island, October 11-12, 1942. Maintaining a screen ahead of the cruisers during the entire approach through dangerous waters, Captain Tobin skillfully extricated his division from their precarious position at the opening of the engagement and brought them all into effective action. His efficient performance of duty and his outstanding leadership characterize him as an expert and distinguished seaman, in keeping with the highest traditions of the United States Naval Service.

Lieutenant Commander Edmund Taylor's Navy Cross:

For extraordinary heroism ... during action against enemy Japanese naval forces off Savo Island on October 11, 1942. Although his ship had sustained heavy damage under hostile bombardment, Lieutenant Commander Taylor, by skillful maneuvering, successfully launched torpedoes which contributed to the destruction of a Japanese cruiser. Maintaining the guns of the *Duncan* in effective fire throughout the battle, he, when the vessel was finally put out of action, persistently employed to the fullest extent all possible measures to extinguish raging fires and control severe damage...

Lieutenant Commander Edmund Taylor's Letter of Commendation:

For meritorious action and distinguished service ... during the rescue operations subsequent to the loss of the *USS Wasp*. His fine judgement in seamanship made possible the successful rescue of many officers and men in an area where enemy submarines were actively present ...

Lieutenant Louis Bryan's Silver Star:

For conspicuous gallantry and intrepidity aboard the *USS Duncan* during action against enemy Japanese off Savo Island on the night of October 11, 1942. While his ship was under tremendous hostile bombardment, Lt. Bryan, despite severe wounds and repeated shell hits in the vicinity of his station, supervised evacuation of other injured personnel and survivors trapped by fire on the starboard wing of the bridge. By his grim determination and sturdy endurance, maintained at great risk in the face of grave danger, he undoubtedly saved the lives of many men who otherwise might have perished.

Lieutenant Philip Hauck's Silver Star:

... Hauck most ably and efficiently controlled the fire of the main battery of his ship. He secured hits on an enemy cruiser in nine out of ten salvos fired at it. When he observed this target to break up, on his own initiative he shifted fire to an enemy destroyer, securing hits on this ship in at least four salvos ...

Lieutenant (junior grade) Robert Fowler's Navy Cross:

For extraordinary heroism as Torpedo Officer aboard the *U.S.S. Duncan* during an engagement with enemy Japanese naval forces off Savo Island on the night of October 12, 1942. Lieutenant (j.g.) Fowler in the firing of his first torpedo, secured the initial hit on a hostile cruiser. Before he could fire the remaining torpedoes, he was fatally wounded by a shell which burst in the vicinity of his station. His conscientious devotion to duty and intrepid conduct under fire were in keeping with the highest traditions of the United States Naval Service. He gallantly gave up his life in the defense of his country.

Ensign Jack Smyth's Navy and Marine Corps Medal:

... [Smyth, as a small boat officer during the *Wasp* sinking,] repeatedly took his boat through waters covered with burning gasoline to drag survivors clear of burning areas...

Ensign George Weems's (*McCalla*) Silver Star:

... As the salvage party approached the burning vessel, Weems swam to a point alongside and positively identified her. Later, he boarded *Duncan* and contributed materially to the salvage operations.

Chief Torpedoman David Boyd's Navy Cross:

... After the torpedo officer was mortally wounded and director lost control after the launching of one torpedo, Boyd mounted the torpedo tube and, in spite of fire, succeeded in launching remaining torpedoes, with one of which he succeeded in making a second positive hit in the side of enemy cruiser...

Chief Fire Controlman Thomas Colbeck's Letter of Commendation:

... Colbeck efficiently handled the major casualties in the plotting room of his ship, a destroyer, and determinedly fought the serious fires in his part of the ship ...

Watertender Second Class Romney Boyle's Silver Star:

... Boyle repeatedly attempted to prevent fires from spreading in the area around #1 fireroom. By determined effort, he succeeded in clearing the flames away from #1 engineroom escape hatch long enough to permit the engineroom crew to escape ...

Pharmacist's Mate First Class Bruner Flowers's Silver Star:

... During and after the battle, Flowers administered effective first aid to the wounded. When he was rescued, after spending about ten hours in the water, he continued his first aid work for a period of thirty- six hours without rest ...

Pharmacist's Mate First Class Bruner Flowers's Letter of Commendation:

... Lt.(jg) Broccolo, CPhM King, and [PhM1c] Flowers constituted the medical department of the *Duncan*. All three worked continuously for a period of over thirty hours, treating and caring for the wounded. Lt. Broccolo, assisted by King, personally treated all the more serious cases. Flowers handled the one or two serious cases quartered in the after part of the ship and supervised the treatment of the many less seriously injured personnel quartered aft.

Fire Controlman First Class Carl Combs's Letter of Commendation:

... Combs efficiently handled the major casualties in the plotting room of his ship, a destroyer, and determinedly fought the serious fires in his part of the ship. When it became necessary to abandon the forward part of the ship, he dove overboard and swam aft. He then returned aboard and assisted in ship control and fire fighting...

Motor Machinist's Mate First Class Roman Olek's Navy and Marine Corps Medal:

... Upon their own initiative Olek and [BM2c George] McIntosh, both strong swimmers, stripped off all shoes and clothing and dove into the water to assist those too weak to help themselves ... Some time later, [a boat] found Olek and McIntosh cheering and encouraging other men in the water, while swimming themselves without aid of life preservers.

Motor Machinist's Mate First Class Roman Olek's Silver Star:

... Though seriously wounded by the shell which wiped out the rest of his repair party, Olek succeeded in getting aft before fire completely segregated the forward part of the ship and gallantly joined the after fire fighting parties...

Motor Machinist's Mate Second Class John Hernday's Letter of Commendation:

... While in charge of the forward magazine group, Hernday directed the removal of ammunition to afford escape for part of the lower handling room crew who were trapped by fires above their escape hatch...

ACKNOWLEDGEMENTS

This book is largely based on *Duncan*'s log, except ships' logs never say much about what is really going on. All the detail and color is from interviews with the following former members of *Duncan's* crew:

Frank Andrews

George Bacsik

Clifford Beebe

John Berry

Roy Boehm

Malcolm Bethune

Frank Carroll

Raymond Catlow

Warren Craig

Louis Cruz

Louis DeLucca

Quinton Edwards

Arthur Ehrenberg

Arthur Fischer

James Flaherty

William Gist

Earle Hamilton

Russell Johnson

Roy Meyer

David Nicoll

Roman Olek

Edward O'Mara

Lennon Paige

George Palmer

Anthony Papacoda

Frank Quinn

George Sifers

Andrew Slovenec

Jack Sobelman

Kelly Stanfill

Earl Tucker

John Vandonkelaar

Albert Viering

Robert Weatherup

Richard Wharton

Clarence Wickstrom

SOURCE NOTES

INTRODUCTION

All the family stories are either from my own memory or interviews with my mother, Patricia Cutler Fowler Warner, and aunts, Angela Fowler Wylie and Pamela Fowler Furse, and uncle, Harry Fowler, and Helen Collins, my grandparents' cook for fifty years who lived the stories and remembered everything. The letters and papers were saved by my grandfather, Robert Fowler, Jr., and are in the possession of the author.

p.10 – **Robert Fowler, who was killed at the age of 23**: Alumni Horae, April, 1943, St. Paul's School

CHAPTER 1

This chapter is based on crew interviews and, after April 16, the *Duncan*'s log. Bobby's letters are in the author's possession.

p.30 – **Andrews hailed the twin-launchings**: R/Adm. Adolphus Andrews's letter is quoted in The [Washington, D.C.] Evening Star, "U.S. Could Launch 3 Warships a Day, Andrews Declares," February 22, 1942

p.36 – **Officers from the Navy Board of Inspection and Survey**: information on the inspection, including the JAG mailgram to Federal, is in the DD-486 file at the National Archives

p.38 – R/Adm. Marquardt's remarks are in The New York Journal-American, "Asks for 'Cold Fury' for Victory," April 16, 1942

p. 49 – **Cdr. Ryan transferred his flag**: Ryan was transferred to *Lansdowne* by order of Cominch Letter FF1/A3-1, serial 0912 of May 22, 1942 and "[i]n accordance with BuNav orders 56850-127 Nav 31-CFB of March 13" (*Lansdowne* War Diary)

CHAPTER 2

p.69 - **A subchaser that arrived on the scene**: Roscoe, p.80

p.69 - **Over the next ten hours**: *Lansdowne* War Diary

p.70 - **One of the freighters had been converted to a transport**: *Aldis Lamp*

p.74 - **Supply officer Ens. Rhodes**: *Aldis Lamp*

p.80 - "**Men, the *Duncan* has received orders**: Boehm, p. 40

CHAPTER 3

This chapter is based almost entirely on the *Duncan*'s log and crew interviews. I relied on Eric Hammel's article, "The Death of the Wasp" for the timing of what was happening on board the carrier during her final hours.

p.106 – **Both swam among the survivors**: Olek's and McIntosh's Navy & Marine Corps Medal citations

CHAPTER 4

R/Adm. Scott's conferences with the commanders of TF.64 were reconstructed from the memory of Lennon Paige, who was told about them in detail by Lt. Bryan.

p.115 - **Nimitz added a tactical suggestion**: Nimitz letter, October 31, 1942

p.115 - **Ships needed more medicine**: Class of 1940 Archive Assignment #7" by RobertWeatherup (USNA Library)

p.119 - **What occasioned Ghormley's wholesale raid**: CinCPac 0035 September 22, 1942 to ComSoPac (CinCPac War Diary)

p.121 - **"Funafuti occupation completed**: ComSoPac 041206 to CTF.64 (et al.)

p.121 - **Thirty-seven U.S. warships**: *Buchanan* log F

CHAPTER 6

Ships' logs were turned in at the end of each month, so, although the *Duncan*'s log was lost in the battle, it was only the last twelve days of her voyage that needed to be reconstructed. This was accomplished through references to the *Duncan* in the logs of other ships.

Charles Cook's The Battle of Cape Esperance is the seminal book on the battle, and I depended on it for what was happening on other ships during the battle.

CHAPTER 7

p.188 - **On San Francisco's bridge, everybody was watching** *Fubuki*: Cook, p.73

CHAPTER 8

George Weems's letter to his parents is reprinted in "Solomons Battle Log" by George Weems, with additional text by Frank Andrews (*Proceedings*, August 1962)

CHAPTER 9

p.250 & 270-271 LCdr. Smedberg's letter to Taylor and a copy of Taylor's letter to Smedburg are in Taylor's personal album.

p.267 – **That afternoon, a large seaplane**: Potter, p.177-179

p.250-259 This account of the conference reflects a third-hand report by former Chief Yeoman Lennon Paige, who was on Duncan's bridge that night when Lt. Bryan recounted what had occurred at the conference, and Paige remembered it all 50 years later. When the author questioned Paige's memory, he explained the had served with Bryan until the end of both their careers -- Bryan retired a rear admiral in 1971 -- and that in the intervening years they had discussed the conference often.

AFTERWORD

All the newspaper stories are in Taylor's album.

BIBLIOGRAPHY

United States Destroyers Operations in World War II (United States Naval Institute)

Becton, F. Julian, The Ship That Would Not Die (New York: Prentice-Hall, 1980

Bell, Frederick J., Condition Red (Destroyer Action in the South Pacific) (New York: Longmans, Green and Co., 1944)

Boehm, Roy and Sasser, Charles W., First Seal (New York: Simon & Schuster/Pocket Books, 1997)

Bradlee, Ben, A Good Life (New York: Simon & Schuster, 1995)

Braynard, Frank O., By Their Works Ye Shall Know Them (The Life and Ships of William Francis Gibbs, 1886-1967) (privately printed by Gibbs & Cox: 1968)

Buderi, Robert, The Invention That Changed the World (Touchstone, 1997)

Clary, Jack, Navy Football (Annapolis: Naval Institute Press, 1997)

Cook, Charles, The Battle of Cape Esperance (New York: Thomas Y. Crowell Company, 1968)

Coombe, Jack D., Derailing the Tokyo Express (Harrisburg, PA: Stackpole Books, 1991)

Crenshaw, Russell Sydnor, South Pacific Destroyer (Annapolis: Naval Institute Press, 1998)
Dull, Paul S., Battle History of the Japanese Imperial Navy (1941-1945) (Annapolis: United States Naval Institute, 1978)

Feuer, A.B (ed.), Coast Watching in the Solomon Islands (The Bougainville Reports, December 1941-July 1943) (New York: Praeger, 1992)

Friedman, Norman, U.S. Destroyers (An Illustrated Design History) (Annapolis: United States Naval Institute, 1982)
Frank, Richard B., Guadalcanal (New York: Random House, 1990)

Goodrich, Marcus, Delilah (Southern Illinois Press, 1941)

Horne, Alistair, The Land Is Bright (London: Max Parrish, 1958)

Horne, Alistair, A Bundle from Britain (London: Macmillan London Limited, 1993)

Jernigan, E.J., Tin Can Man (Arlington, VA.: Vandamere Press, 1993)

Lott, Arnold S., Brave Ship/Brave Men (Annapolis: Naval Institute Press, 1964)

Lundstrom, John B. The First Team (Annapolis: United States Naval Institute Press, 1984)

Lundstrom, John B., The First Team and the Guadalcanal Campaign (Annapolis: United States Naval Institute Press, 1994)

Miller, John, Jr., Guadalcanal: The First Offensive (Washington: The Center of Military History, U.S. Army, 1949)

Morison, Samuel Eliot, History of United States Naval Operations in World War II, vol.1 (Boston: Little, Brown and Company, 1948)

Morris, C.G. w/ Hugh B. Cave, The Fightin'est Ship: The Story of the Cruiser Helena (New York: Dodd, Mead & Company, 1944)

Morris, Frank D., Pick out the Biggest: Mike Moran and the Men of the Boise (Boston: Houghton Mifflin Company, 1943)

Noel, John V., Jr. & Beach, Edward L., Naval Terms Dictionary (5th. ed.) (Annapolis: United States Naval Institute, 1988)

Parkin, Robert Sinclair, Blood on the Sea: American Destroyers Lost in World War II

Prados, John, Combined Fleet Decoded (New York: Random House, 1995)

Regan, Stephan D., In Bitter Tempest (Ames: Iowa State University Press, 1994)

Stanton, Shelby L., World War II Order of Battle (New York: Galahad/LDAP, Inc., 1991)

Whitley, M.J., Destroyers of World War Two (Annapolis: Naval Institute Press, 1988)

Winton, John, Ultra in the Pacific (Annapolis: Naval Institute Press, 1993)

Wouk, Herman, The Caine Mutiny (New York: Little, Brown and Company, 1951)

Logs & War Diaries:

CinCPac War Diary, SoPac War Diary, ComDesRon 12 War Diary
Duncan, Lansdowne, Farenholt, Lardner, Buchanan, Laffey, McCalla, Juneau,
San Francisco, Salt Lake City, Boise, Helena, Minneapolis, South Dakota

Personal Albums & Letters:

Robert Fowler, Jr.
Edmund Taylor
Patricia Cutler Fowler Warner

Magazine & Newspaper Articles, Newsletters, etc:

Alumni Horae (St. Paul's School alumni magazine), April, 1943

Aldis Lamp (*Duncan-O'Brien-Bennett* newsletter written by Robert Carlson and printed privately)

"Class of 1940 Archive Assignment #7" by Robert Weatherup (U.S. Naval Academy Library)

True, "Over the Side" by James A. Bilbro, "Fire controlman 2/c, U.S. Navy", as told to Will Oursler, "*True*'s correspondent in the Pacific," February 1944

Saturday Evening Post, "Back from Hell ...", Burris Jenkins, Jr.

Saturday Evening Post, November 11, 1944, "Bare Fists Against a Shark," Lt.Com. H.R. Kabat, USN, as told to Elise Stearns Hahn

Boston Evening American, January 7, 1944 (article about Lt.(jg) Richard Wharton, illus.)

World War II, "Turning Point in the Pacific" by David H. Lippman, November 1997

Sea Classics, "The Death of the *Wasp*" by Eric Hammel, February 1991

Proceedings, "A September Afternoon: The Sinking of the *Wasp*, 15 September 1942" by William Smedberg, September, 1978

Proceedings, "Solomons Battle Log" by George Weems, August 1962

Additional interviews:

Faye Taylor Butler
Adelaide Chatfield-Taylor
Helen Collins
Anthony Duke
Harry Fowler
Pamela Fowler Furse
Chris Herter
Walter Sullivan

George Thompson
Colton Wagner
Patricia Cutler Fowler Warner
Charles Warner
Sandy Whitman
Angela Fowler Wylie
Craig Wylie

Thanks to:

J. Winthrop Aldrich
Alan, Zohreh, Payam Ayazi, and Rami Garcia
David Bindon
Bethany Brown
Constance Buchanan
William Buell
Fifi Holbrook
Alistair Horne
Lillian Kabat
David Lasseigne
William Lovering

Kathleen Lloyd
Timothy Rizzuto
Kirk Scott
Sherry Sonnett
John Stolting
Michael Stolting
Susan Strange
David Streit
Tom Wharton
Andrew Wilde
Ed Zajkowski

FOOTNOTES

Chapter 1:

1.) The *Duncan* was laid down as *Benson/Livermore*-class of 1938-1941, but BuShips later recognized a new *Gleaves/Livermore* sub-class aborning with the *Laffey* (DD-459). Between March and May 1942, twelve Gleaves/*Livermores* were commissioned. BuNav grouped these as Destroyer Squadron 12 (DesRon12). The six constructed at Federal (DD-483-488) - *Aaron Ward, Buchanan, Duncan, Lansdowne, Lardner,* and *McCalla* - were designated Destroyer Division 24 (DesDiv 24), and the others - *Laffey* (DD-459), *Woodworth* (DD-460), *Farenholt* (DD-491), *Bailey* (DD-492), *Bancroft* (DD-598), and *Barton* (DD-599) - were Destroyer Division 23 (DesDiv 23).

Chapter 4:

1.) Task Group 62 consisted of a transportation unit, a landing unit, and a screen. The transports - *Crescent City, Heywood,* and *Libra* - were TU.62.6.1 (transportation unit). TU.62.6.2 (landing unit) was carrying the 5th Defense Battalion units from Nouméa with their artillery and five tanks, plus the two Marine companies from Samoa. TU.62.6.3 (screen) was cruisers *Minneapolis* and *Chester*, and destroyers *Farenholt, Lansdowne, Duncan, Lardner, Laffey,* and *Buchanan*.

Chapter 9:

1.) Lt. Kabat (multiple shark bites), FC1c Combs (multiple shrapnel wounds), GM1c Whelan (compound fracture of the tibia and shark bites), SF3c Sifers (compound fracture left forearm), S1c Fischer (multiple shrapnel wounds), S2c Cruz (multiple shrapnel wounds), S2c Fallon (1st and 2nd degree burns), and Ferreira (1st and 2nd degree burns).

2) Lt.(jg) Wharton (compound fracture 5th metacarpal left hand), CCStd. Mitchell (multiple shrapnel wounds), MM1c Olek (multiple shrapnel wounds), RM3c Fielding (multiple shrapnel wounds, fractured right elbow), S1c Stanfill (multiple shrapnel wounds, shark bite), S1c Vanek (compression fracture to vertebrae), S1c Wood (multiple shrapnel wounds), and F3c DiRitto (shrapnel wound).

3) In 1949, Fowler's body would be re-interred in Honolulu at the National Memorial Cemetery of the Pacific.

CREW ROSTER FOOTNOTES:

1) Weatherup was detached on September 16 to FARENHOLT as communications officer on DesRon12 staff.

2) Shanahan was transferred to U.S. Naval Hospital, Brooklyn, for "treatment.

3) Shreiber made chief April 16, and was transferred to USS STRONG May 22.

4) Baumgardner was AOL 7/16 at Cristobal, C.Z., missed ship, returned in custody 7/29, delivered "to C.O. Submarine Base, Coco Solo "for confinement for safekeeping."

5) Bunkley was transferred to Naval Supply Depot, Balboa, C.Z. due to seasickness.

6) Butler was transferred to CO, Inshore Patrol, Balboa, C.Z.

7) Chism was transferred to U.S. Naval Hospital, Guantánamo "for treatment."

8) Clark went AWOL and never returned.

9) Coit was transferred to Brooklyn Naval Hospital for treatment.

10) Constantello was transferred to Naval Supply Depot, Balboa, C.Z.

11) Cottle went AWOL and never returned.

12) Crum was transferred to Atlantic Fleet School, Norfolk.

13) Davenport was transferred to U.S. Naval Hospital, Guantánamo, Cuba.

14) Derr was transferred to British Naval Hospital, Portland Bight, Jamaica.

15) Dipzinski was transferred to Naval Supply Depot, Balboa, C.Z.

16) Farina was delivered to CO, 15th Naval District.

17) Fedorchak was transferred to Naval Supply Depot, Balboa, C.Z. due to seasickness.

18) Filewitz was transferred to CO, 15th Naval District, Balboa, C.Z.

19) Flaherty was transferred to Naval Dispensary, Submarine Base, Coco Solo, C.Z. "for treatment for epilepsy."

20) Flynn was transferred to Brooklyn Naval Hospital - "Diagnosis: Unknown." Declared deserter, June 20.

21) Jenkins was transferred to CO, Inshore Patrol, Balboa, C.Z.

22) Jordan was delivered as prisoner-at-large to C.O., Receiving Ship, N.Y.

23) Keeble was AOL, August 11, and AWOL while prisoner at large, August 13. Received Bad Conduct Discharge by Summary Courts-Martial, August 14, and was delivered under guard to CO, 15th Naval District, Balboa.

24) Keeble's promotion to S2c was terminated by mast, August 14.

25) Knight was transferred to Norfolk Naval Hospital.

26) Lake was delivered to CO, 15th Naval District, Balboa, C.Z.

27) Moffat was a deserter.

28) Owen was transferred to CO, Inshore Patrol, Balboa, C.Z.

29) Ronan was transferred to CO, Inshore Patrol, Balboa, C.Z.

30) Root was transferred to U.S. Naval Dispensary, Guantánamo.

31) Smith was transferred to Brooklyn Naval Hospital for "treatment".

32) Wagner was a deserter.

33) Warren was a deserter.

34) Wiemer was dropped from roll after missing ship from N.Y.

35) Woodburn was transferred to duty CO, Inshore Patrol, Balboa, C.Z.

INDEX

A

B

C

D

E

G

H

L

M

N

O

P

Q

R

S

T

U

V

W

Y

Z

Made in the USA
Columbia, SC
02 December 2018